TOP 10
OF EVERYTHING
2013

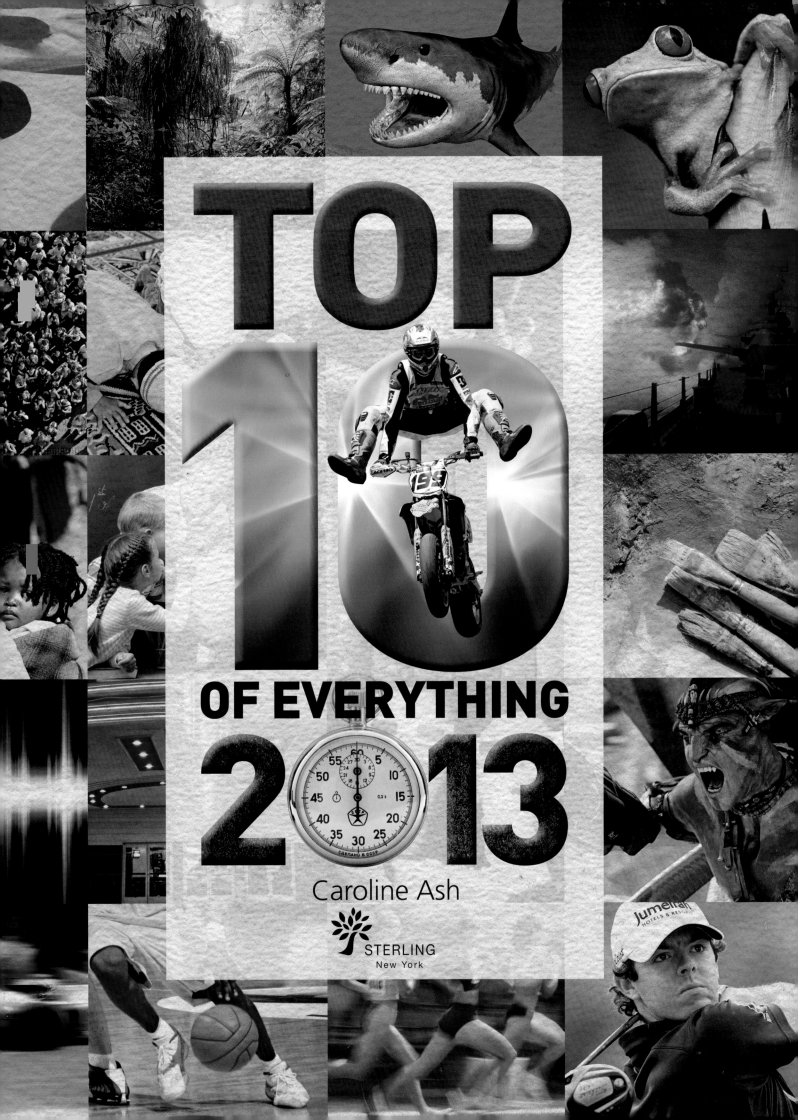

TOP 10

OF EVERYTHING

2013

Caroline Ash

STERLING
New York

CONTENTS

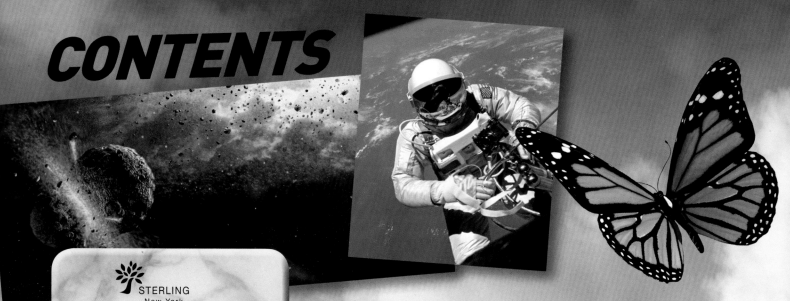

STERLING
New York

An Imprint of Sterling Publishing
387 Park Avenue South
New York, NY 10016

STERLING and the distinctive Sterling
logo are registered trademarks of Sterling
Publishing Co., Inc.

© 2012 Octopus Publishing Group Ltd

Publishing director: Colin Webb
Art director: Bernard Higton
Managing editor: Sonya Newland
Project editor: Emily Bailey
Picture researcher: Emma O'Neill

ISBN 978-1-4549-0517-2

Selected music lists courtesy of

**1 Official
Charts Company**

Distributed in Canada by Sterling Publishing
c/o Canadian Manda Group,
165 Dufferin Street
Toronto, Ontario, Canada M6K 3H6

For information about custom editions,
special sales, and premium and corporate
purchases, please contact Sterling
Special Sales at 800-805-5489 or
specialsales@sterlingpublishing.com.

Manufactured in China

10 9 8 7 6 5 4 3 2 1

www.sterlingpublishing.com

Russell Ash (1946–2010) was the originator
of *Top 10 of Everything*, and his passion
for facts, eye for detail, and pursuit of the
curious fascinated and entertained millions
of readers. His invaluable database has
continued to inform this edition.

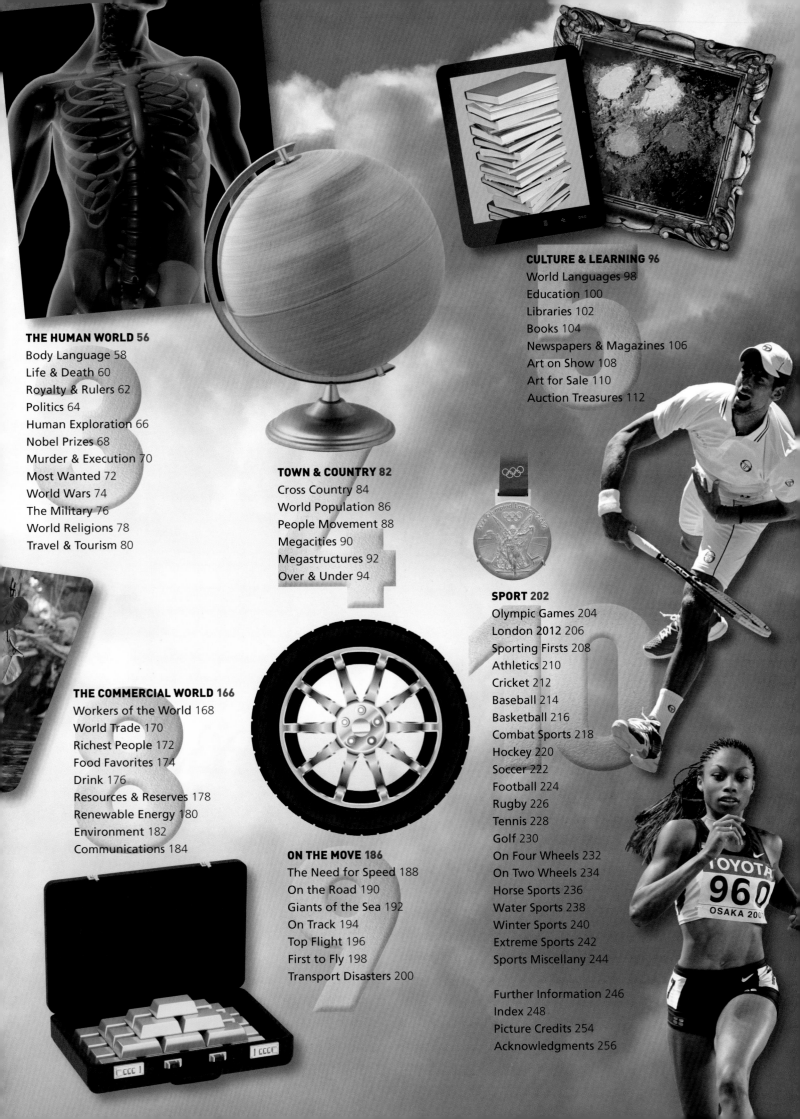

INTRODUCTION

24th Edition

24 is highly composite and is the largest number that is evenly divisible by all numbers no larger than its square root. It is the atomic number of chromium (Cr)—a shiny, hard metal with a high melting point that is added to steel to create stainless steel. In Christian literature, 24 represents the whole church, encompassing the 12 tribes of Israel and the 12 apostles. There are 24 major and minor keys in music; pure gold is 24 carat; the Greek alphabet which begins with alpha and ends with omega has 24 letters; the human body has 24 ribs. There are 24 hours in a day, and we live in a 24-hour culture, demanding an increasing number of goods and services to be available to us all the time. And this is the 24th edition of *Top 10 of Everything*.

Checklists

We are constantly bombarded with lists. The press and television shows present rankings based on market research and polls, and ranked lists have become a way of managing what might otherwise be a daunting mass of facts and figures, putting our world into a perspective that we can readily grasp. *Top 10 of Everything* provides a unique collection of lists in a diverse array of categories that are, we hope, informative, educational, and entertaining.

All Change

The majority of lists change from year to year—even "fixed" lists such as those of the highest mountains or deepest oceans are revised as more sophisticated measuring techniques are used. The minimum entry requirements for Top 10 lists are in a constant state of flux as, for example, rich people get increasingly richer and build ever-bigger yachts, and movies with bigger and bigger budgets are released and achieve higher-earning opening weekends.

It's a Fact

Top 10 lists provide a shorthand glimpse of what is happening with the world economy, global warming, deforestation, communication, and other issues that concern us all. At the same time, they convey a fascinating and entertaining overview of the amazing diversity of our planet and its people, with lists on such subjects as the largest meteorites,

the highest waterfalls, heaviest dinosaurs, longest snakes, longest-serving presidents, countries with the highest life expectancy, biggest tourist attractions, most-borrowed library books, longest bridges, highest-grossing movies, the countries producing the most oil, cities with most billionaires, the most valuable global brands, the cities with the cleanest air, the latest land speed record holders, most-followed people on Twitter, most widely spoken languages, and the bestselling albums and singles of all time.

More Than Just the No. 1

All these lists follow a rule that has been true since the first edition of *Top 10 of Everything*, which is that every list has to be quantifiable—measurable in some way or other: the biggest, smallest, first, last, tallest, deepest, sunniest, dullest, or chronologically the first or last. All the lists thus offer more than just the No. 1, and allow a comparison of the subjects of the list. There are no "bests," other than bestsellers, and "worsts" are of disasters, military losses and murders, where they are measured by numbers of victims. Unless otherwise stated, movie lists are based on cumulative global earnings, irrespective of production or marketing budgets, and—as is standard in the film industry—inflation is not taken into

account, which means that recent releases tend to feature disproportionately prominently. Countries are independent countries, not dependencies or overseas territories. All the lists are all-time and global unless a specific year or territory is noted.

Credits and Acknowledgements

Sources encompass international organizations, commercial companies and research bodies, specialized publications, and a network of experts around the world who have generously shared their knowledge. As always, their important contribution is acknowledged (see page 256 for a full list of credits), along with that of everyone who has been involved with the book at all stages of its development on this and the previous 23 annual editions.

Over To You...

We hope you enjoy the book. Your comments, corrections, and suggestions for new lists are always welcome. Please contact us via the publishers or visit the *Top 10 of Everything* website http://www.octopusbooks.co.uk/top10.

The Top 10 Team

1

THE UNIVERSE & THE EARTH

Main picture: Hurricane Katrina heads for the Gulf Coast, 2005.
Inset: Devastating floods hit Pakistan in 2010.

CLIMATE REFUGEES

Environmental factors have a huge impact on global migration, as people are forced to leave areas with harsh and difficult conditions if survival there becomes unsustainable, if they are unable to grow enough food or to live safely in an area. There are currently between 25 and 30 million climate refugees throughout the world, and it is estimated that this number will rise to a hefty 200 million by 2050. Accelerated climate change increases the frequency of extreme weather conditions such as tropical storms, floods, and heat waves, and means that more people will be affected by a gradual deterioration in environmental conditions, which include desertification, deforestation, a reduction in soil fertility, coastal erosion, a rise in sea level, and drought.

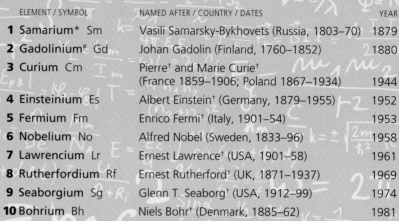

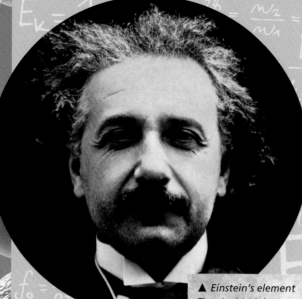

▲ **Einstein's element**
The physicist is best known for developing the theory of relativity.

THE 10 FIRST ELEMENTS TO BE NAMED AFTER REAL PEOPLE

ELEMENT / SYMBOL		NAMED AFTER / COUNTRY / DATES	YEAR
1	Samarium* Sm	Vasili Samarsky-Bykhovets (Russia, 1803–70)	1879
2	Gadolinium# Gd	Johan Gadolin (Finland, 1760–1852)	1880
3	Curium Cm	Pierre[†] and Marie Curie[†] (France 1859–1906; Poland 1867–1934)	1944
4	Einsteinium Es	Albert Einstein[†] (Germany, 1879–1955)	1952
5	Fermium Fm	Enrico Fermi[†] (Italy, 1901–54)	1953
6	Nobelium No	Alfred Nobel (Sweden, 1833–96)	1958
7	Lawrencium Lr	Ernest Lawrence[†] (USA, 1901–58)	1961
8	Rutherfordium Rf	Ernest Rutherford[†] (UK, 1871–1937)	1969
9	Seaborgium Sg	Glenn T. Seaborg[†] (USA, 1912–99)	1974
10	Bohrium Bh	Niels Bohr[†] (Denmark, 1885–62)	1981

* Named after mineral samarskite, which was named after Samarsky-Bykhovets
\# Named after mineral gadolinite, which was named after Gadolin
† Awarded Nobel Prize

TOP 10 LIGHTEST ELEMENTS*

	ELEMENT	DISCOVERER / COUNTRY	YEAR DISCOVERED	DENSITY#
1	Lithium	Johan August Arfvedson, Sweden	1817	0.53
2	Potassium	Sir Humphry Davy, UK	1807	0.86
3	Sodium	Sir Humphry Davy	1807	0.97
4	Rubidium	Robert Wilhelm Bunsen/ Gustav Kirchoff, Germany	1861	1.53
5	Calcium	Sir Humphry Davy	1808	1.55
6	Magnesium	Sir Humphry Davy	1808[†]	1.74
7	Phosphorus	Hennig Brandt, Germany	1669	1.83
8	Beryllium	Friedrich Wöhler, Germany/ Antoine-Alexandré Brutus Bussy, France	1828[§]	1.84
9	Caesium	Robert Wilhelm Bunsen/ Gustav Kirchoff	1860	1.90
10	Sulfur	–	Prehistoric	2.07

* Solids only # Grams per sq cm at 20°C
† Recognized by Joseph Black in 1755, but not isolated § Recognized by Nicholas Vauquelin in 1797, but not isolated

THE 10 MOST COMMON ELEMENTS IN THE OCEANS

	ELEMENT	SYMBOL	AMOUNT (TONS PER SQ MILE)
1	Oxygen*	O	2,442,450,000
2	Hydrogen*	H	307,230,000
3	Chlorine	Cl	56,629,500
4	Sodium	Na	31,492,500
5	Magnesium	Mg	3,779,100
6	Sulfur	S	2,644,800
7	Calcium	Ca	1,202,700
8	Potassium	K	1,185,600
9	Bromine	Br	191,805
10	Carbon	C	79,800

* Combined as water

◄ **Lithium hybrid**
Lithium-ion batteries are used increasingly to power hybrid cars.

THE 10 **MOST COMMON ELEMENTS IN THE UNIVERSE**

ELEMENT / SYMBOL / PARTS PER MILLION*

1 Hydrogen H
750,000

2 Helium He
230,000

3 Oxygen O
10,000

4 Carbon C
5,000

5 Neon Ne
1,300

6 Iron Fe
1,100

7 Nitrogen N
1,000

8 Silicon Si
700

9 Magnesium Mg
600

10 Sulfur S
500

* Mg per kg

▲ *Plutonium power*
Over a third of the energy produced in most nuclear plants comes from plutonium.

TOP 10 **HEAVIEST ELEMENTS**

	ELEMENT	SYMBOL	DENSITY*
1	Osmium	Os	22.59
2	Iridium	Ir	22.56
3	Platinum	Pt	21.45
4	Rhenium	Re	21.02
5	Neptunium	Np	20.45
6	Plutonium	Pu	19.82
7	Gold	Au	19.29
8	Tungsten	W	19.25
9	Uranium	U	19.05
10	Tantalum	Ta	16.67

* Grams per sq cm at 20°C

▼ *Light show*
Colliding particles in the atmosphere cause the aurora borealis.

THE 10 **MOST COMMON ELEMENTS IN THE EARTH'S CRUST**

ELEMENT / SYMBOL / PARTS PER MILLION*

1 Oxygen O
461,000

2 Silicon Si
282,000

3 Aluminum Al
82,300

4 Iron Fe
56,300

5 Calcium Ca
41,500

6 Sodium Na
23,600

7 Magnesium Mg
23,300

8 Potassium K
20,900

9 Titanium Ti
5,650

10 Hydrogen H
1,400

* Mg per kg, based on average percentages of elements in igneous rock

▼ *Birth of the Solar System*
Four and a half billion years ago, our Solar System was formed out of a huge cloud of dust and gas.

TOP 10 LARGEST BODIES IN THE SOLAR SYSTEM

BODY	MAX. DIAMETER MILES	KM	SIZE COMPARED WITH EARTH
1 Sun	865,036	1,392,140	109.136
2 Jupiter	88,846	142,984	11.209
3 Saturn	74,898	120,536	9.449
4 Uranus	31,763	51,118	4.007
5 Neptune	30,775	49,528	3.883
6 Earth	7,926	12,756	1.000
7 Venus	7,521	12,104	0.949
8 Mars	4,228	6,805	0.533
9 Ganymede	3,270	5,262	0.413
10 Titan	3,200	5,150	0.404

Most of the planets have been observed since ancient times. The exceptions are Uranus, discovered on March 13, 1781 by the British astronomer Sir William Herschel; Neptune, found by German astronomer Johann Galle on September 23, 1846; and, outside the Top 10, former planet Pluto.

TOP 10 LONGEST YEARS IN THE SOLAR SYSTEM

BODY*	LENGTH OF YEAR# YEARS	DAYS
1 Eris	561	135
2 Makemake	305	124
3 Haumea	281	340
4 Pluto	247	336
5 Neptune	164	289
6 Uranus	84	6
7 Saturn	29	163
8 Jupiter	11	315
9 Ceres	4	219
10 Mars	1	322

* Planets and dwarf planets, excluding satellites
# Period of orbit round the Sun, in Earth years/days

TOP 10 LONGEST DAYS IN THE SOLAR SYSTEM

BODY*	DAYS	LENGTH OF DAY# HRS	MINS	SECS
1 Venus	243	0	26	60
2 Mercury	58	15	30	14
3 Sun	25†			
4 Pluto	6	9	17	17
5 Eris	1	1	53	46
6 Mars		24	37	26
7 Earth		23	56	41
8 Makemake		22	29	17
9 Uranus		17	13	55
10 Neptune		16	6	14

* Excluding satellites
# Period of rotation, based on Earth day
† Variable

ON VENUS, A DAY IS LONGER THAN A YEAR!

▼ *Giant dwarf*
Eris is a massive dwarf planet and the 9th largest body to orbit the Sun.

Venus and Mercury are the only planets in the Solar System with years of shorter duration than Earth-years— 225 and 88 days respectively.

TOP 10 **LARGEST PLANETARY MOONS**

MOON / PLANET / DIAMETER (MILES / KM)

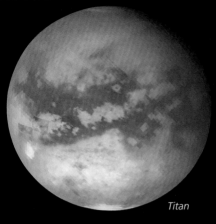

Titan

Callisto

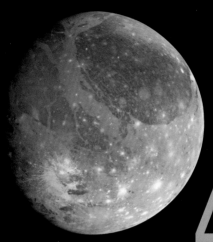
Ganymede

**1 Ganymede / Jupiter
3,269.9 / 5,262.4**
Discovered by Galileo on January 11, 1610, Ganymede is thought to have a surface of ice about 60 miles (97 km) thick. Launched in 1989, NASA's Galileo probe reached Ganymede in June 1996.

**2 Titan / Saturn
3,200.1 / 5,150.0**
Titan is larger than Mercury and Pluto. We have no idea what its surface looks like because it has such a dense atmosphere, but radio telescope observations suggest that it may have ethane "oceans" and "continents" of ice or other solid matter.

**3 Callisto / Jupiter
2,995.4 / 4,820.6**
Possessing a similar composition to Ganymede, Callisto is heavily pitted with craters, perhaps more so than any other body in the Solar System.

**4 Io / Jupiter
2,263.4 / 3,642.6**
Io has a crust of solid sulfur with massive volcanic eruptions in progress, hurling sulfurous material 186 miles (300 km) into space.

**5 Moon / Earth
2,160.0 / 3,476.2**
Our own satellite is a quarter of the size of Earth, the 5th largest in the Solar System and, to date, the only one to have been explored by humans.

**6 Europa / Jupiter
1,939.7 / 3,121.6**
Although Europa's ice-covered surface is apparently smooth and crater-free, it is covered with mysterious black lines, some of them 40 miles (64 km) wide and resembling canals.

**7 Triton / Neptune
1,681.9 / 2,706.8**
Triton is getting progressively closer to Neptune, and it is believed that in several million years the force of the planet's gravity may pull it apart, scattering it into a form like the rings of Saturn.

**8 Titania / Uranus
980.4 / 1,577.8**
The largest of Uranus's 27 moons, Titania was discovered by William Herschel on January 11, 1787. It has a snowball-like surface of ice. Its size estimate was revised by data from Voyager 2.

**9 Rhea / Saturn
947.6 / 1,528.0**
Saturn's 2nd-largest moon was discovered on December 23, 1672, by Jean-Dominique Cassini. Voyager 1 confirmed that its icy surface is pitted with craters, one of them 140 miles (225 km) in diameter.

**10 Oberon / Uranus
946.2 / 1,522.8**
Oberon was discovered by Herschel at the same time as Titania, and given the name of the fairy king husband of Queen Titania. Data from Voyager 2 relegated Oberon from 9th to 10th place in this list.

Io

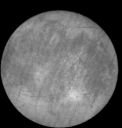
Earth's Moon

Europa

Oberon

Rhea

Titania

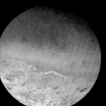
Triton

HEAVENLY BODIES

▼ **Asteroid belt**
Millions of asteroids
are found in the
"belt" between Mars
and Jupiter.

TOP 10 ASTEROIDS DUE TO COME CLOSEST TO EARTH

	NAME / DESIGNATION	DUE DATE*	DISTANCE MILES	KM
1	2012 DA14	Feb 15, 2013	35,000	21,000
2	Apophis	Apr 13, 2029	22,114	35,589
3	= 2001 WN5	Jun 26, 2028	154,585	248,781
	= 2007 YV56	Jan 2, 2101	154,585	248,781
5	1998 OX4	Jan 22, 2148	186,283	299,794
6	2005 WY55	May 28, 2065	209,151	336,596
7	1999 AN10	Aug 7, 2027	246,705	397,033
8	1997 XF11	Oct 28, 2136	256,744	413,190
9	2001 GQ2	Apr 27, 2100	316,236	508,932
10	2004 FU4	Oct 26, 2166	326,461	525,388

* Closest point to Earth

TOP 10 LARGEST STARS

STAR NAME / SOLAR DIAMETER*

1 VY Canis Majoris
1,800–2,100

2 VV Cephei A
1,600–1,900

3 Mu Cephei
1,650

4 V838 Monocerotis
1,570±400

5 WOH G64
1,540

6 V354 Cephei
1,520

7 KW Sagittarii
1,460

8 KY Cygni
1,420–2,850

9 RW Cephei
1,260–1,610

10 Betelgeuse
(Alpha Orionis)
1,180

* Compared with the Sun = 1 (864,950 miles / 1,392,000 km)

▼ **Bright star**
The 5th-brightest star
in the night sky, Vega
is about 25 light years
from Earth.

TOP 10 BRIGHTEST STARS*

	STAR	CONSTELLATION	DISTANCE#	APPARENT MAGNITUDE
1	Sirius	Canis Major	8.61	-1.46
2	Canopus	Carina	312.73	-0.72
3	Arcturus	Boötes	36.39	-0.04†
4	Rigil Kentaurus	Centaurus	4.40	-0.01
5	Vega	Lyra	25.31	+0.03
6	Rigel	Orion	772.91	+0.12
7	Procyon	Canis Minor	11.42	+0.34
8	Betelgeuse	Orion	640.0	+0.42†
9	Achernar	Eridanus	143.81	+0.50
10	Beta Centauri	Centaurus	525.22	+0.61

* Excluding the Sun
\# From the Earth in light years
† Variable

THE 10 MOST RECENT OBSERVATIONS OF HALLEY'S COMET

1 1986
The Japanese *Suisei* probe passed within 93,827 miles (151,000 km) of its 9-mile (15-km) nucleus on March 8, 1986, revealing a whirling nucleus within a hydrogen cloud emitting 22–55 tons of water per second.

2 1910
Predictions of disaster were widely published, with many people convinced that the world would come to an end. American author Mark Twain, who had been born at the time of the 1835 appearance and believed that his fate was linked to that of the comet, died when it reappeared this year.

3 1835
Widely observed, but noticeably dimmer than in 1759.

4 1759
The comet's first return, as predicted by Halley, and thus proving his calculations correct.

5 1682
Observed in Africa and China, and extensively in Europe, where it was viewed from September 5–19 by Edmond Halley, who predicted its return.

6 1607
Seen extensively in China, Japan, Korea, and Europe, and described by German astronomer Johannes Kepler, its position

▲ **Comet in close-up**
The European Space Agency's probe Giotto passed Halley's Comet as close as 370 miles (596 km).

was accurately measured by amateur Welsh astronomer Thomas Harriot.

7 1531
Observed in China, Japan, and Korea, and in Europe on August 13–23 by Peter Appian, a German geographer and astronomer who noted that comets' tails point away from the Sun.

8 1456
Observed in China, Japan, and Korea, and by the Turkish army that was threatening to invade Europe. When the Turks were defeated by papal forces, it was seen as a portent of victory.

9 1378
Observed in China, Japan, Korea, and Europe.

10 1301
Seen in Iceland, parts of Europe, China, Japan, and Korea.

◄ **Halley's Comet**
Its return predicted by Edmond Halley, the comet is visible every 75 years.

THE LARGEST METEORITES EVER FOUND

The Hoba meteorite, the largest in the world, was found on a farm in 1920. A 9 × 8 ft (2.73 × 2.43 m) slab, it consists of 82% iron and 16% nickel. "The Tent," now known by its original Inuit name, Ahnighito, was used as a source of metals for harpoons and other tools. Along with two other large fragments, it was discovered in 1894, taken to the USA in 1897 by the American Arctic explorer Admiral Robert Peary, and is now in the Hayden Planetarium at the New York Museum of Natural History. It is the largest meteorite in the world on exhibition. Canyon Diabolo in Arizona (pictured) is the crater of the 4th-largest meteorite.

EXPLORING THE UNIVERSE

THE 10 **FIRST PLANETARY MOONS TO BE DISCOVERED**

	MOON	PLANET	DISCOVERER / NATIONALITY	YEAR
1	Moon	Earth	–	Ancient
2	Io	Jupiter	Galileo Galilei (Italian)	1610
3	Europa	Jupiter	Galileo Galilei	1610
4	Ganymede	Jupiter	Galileo Galilei	1610
5	Callisto	Jupiter	Galileo Galilei	1610
6	Titan	Saturn	Christian Huygens (Dutch)	1655
7	Iapetus	Saturn	Giovanni Cassini (Italian/French)	1671
8	Rhea	Saturn	Giovanni Cassini	1672
9	Tethys	Saturn	Giovanni Cassini	1684
10	Dione	Saturn	Giovanni Cassini	1684

◀ *Galileo explains*
Galileo developed his own telescopes and made many astronomical discoveries.

FIRST ANIMALS IN SPACE

Laika, the first dog in space, went up in *Sputnik 2* on November 3, 1957, with no hope of coming down alive. Two monkeys, Able and Baker, launched in a *Jupiter* missile on May 28, 1959, were the first animals to be recovered (although Able died a few days later). On November 29, 1961 Enos, a male chimpanzee, successfully completed two orbits and survived.

▶ Vostok 1
Yuri Gagarin was the only crew member on Vostok 1 during the first manned flight into space.

THE 10 **FIRST MEN TO ORBIT EARTH**

	NAME	AGE	ORBITS	DURATION DAYS:HRS:MINS	SPACECRAFT / COUNTRY	DATE
1	Yuri A. Gagarin	27	1	0:1:48	Vostok 1, USSR	Apr 12, 1961
2	Gherman S. Titov	25	17	1:1:18	Vostok 2, USSR	Aug 6–7, 1961
3	John H. Glenn	40	3	0:4:55	Friendship 7, USA	Feb 20, 1962
4	Malcolm S. Carpenter	37	3	0:4:56	Aurora 7, USA	May 24, 1962
5	Andrian G. Nikolayev	32	64	3:22:22	Vostok 3, USSR	Aug 11–15, 1962
6	Pavel R. Popovich	31	48	2:22:56	Vostok 4, USSR	Aug 12–15, 1962
7	Walter M. Schirra	39	6	0:9:13	Sigma 7, USA	Oct 3, 1962
8	Leroy G. Cooper	36	22	1:10:19	Faith 7, USA	May 15–16, 1963
9	Valeri F. Bykovsky	28	81	4:23:7	Vostok V, USSR	Jun 14–19, 1963
10 =	Konstantin P. Feoktistov	38	16	1:0:17	Voskhod 1, USSR	Oct 12–13, 1964
=	Vladimir M. Komarov	37	16	1:0:17	Voskhod 1, USSR	Oct 12–13, 1964
=	Boris B. Yegorov	26	16	1:0:17	Voskhod 1, USSR	Oct 12–13, 1964

FIRST WOMAN TO ORBIT EARTH

Valentina Tereshkova was the first woman to orbit Earth. She was in space June 16–19,1963, for a two-day, 22-hour, 50-minute mission. Tereshkova was also the first mother in space and the first to be married to another space traveler—cosmonaut Andrian Nikolayev.

▶ *Probing Venus*
Probes have to be sturdily built to withstand Venus's dense atmosphere.

THE 10 **FIRST PLANETARY PROBES**

	PROBE*	PLANET	ARRIVAL#
1	Venera 4	Venus	Oct 18, 1967
2	Venera 5	Venus	May 16, 1969
3	Venera 6	Venus	May 17, 1969
4	Venera 7	Venus	Dec 15, 1970
5	Mariner 9 (USA)	Mars	Nov 13, 1971
6	Mars 2	Mars	Nov 27, 1971
7	Mars 3	Mars	Dec 2, 1971
8	Venera 8	Venus	Jul 22, 1972
9	Venera 9	Venus	Oct 22, 1975
10	Venera 10	Venus	Oct 25, 1975

* USSR unless otherwise stated
\# Successfully entered orbit or landed

This list excludes "flybys"—probes that passed by but did not land on the surface of another planet. *Pioneer 10*, for example, launched on March 2, 1972, flew past Jupiter on December 3, 1973, but did not land. *Venera 4* was the first unmanned probe to land on a planet, and *Venera 9* the first to transmit pictures from a planet's surface.

THE 10 **FIRST SPACEWALKERS**

	ASTRONAUT*	SPACECRAFT	EVA# HRS:MINS	EVA DATE
1	Alexei A. Leonov	Voskhod 2	0.12	Mar 18, 1965
2	Edward H. White	Gemini 4	0:20	Jun 3, 1965
3	Eugene A. Cernan	Gemini 9	2:07	Jun 3, 1966
4	Michael Collins	Gemini 10	0:50	Jul 19, 1966
5	Richard F. Gordon	Gemini 11	0:33	Sep 13, 1966
6	Edwin E. 'Buzz' Aldrin	Gemini 12	2:29	Nov 12, 1966
7	= Alexei S. Yeliseyev	Soyuz 5	0:37	Jan 16, 1969
	= Yevgeny V. Khrunov	Soyuz 5	0:37	Jan 16, 1969
9	= Russell L. Schweickart	Apollo 9	1:17	Mar 6, 1969
	= David R. Scott	Apollo 9	1:17	Mar 6, 1969

* Excluding repeat spacewalks on the same mission
\# Extra-Vehicular Activity

Leonov's first spacewalk almost ended in disaster when his spacesuit "ballooned." He was unable to return through the airlock into the *Voskhod 2* capsule until he reduced the pressure in his suit to a dangerously low level. Edward H. White, the first American to walk in space, was killed in the *Apollo* spacecraft fire of January 27, 1967.

▶ *Edward H. White*
White was killed in 1967 when a fire broke out during a launch-pad test.

BODIES OF WATER

TOP 10 LARGEST OCEANS AND SEAS

NAME / APPROX. AREA* (SQ MILES / SQ KM)

Pacific Ocean
60,060,900 / 155,557,000

> THE PACIFIC OCEAN IS LARGER THAN ALL THE WORLD'S CONTINENTS PUT TOGETHER!

Atlantic Ocean
29,637,977 / 76,762,000

Indian Ocean
26,469,622 / 68,556,000

Southern Ocean[#]
7,848,299 / 20,327,000

Arctic Ocean
5,427,053 / 14,056,000

South China Sea
1,423,000 / 3,685,000

Caribbean Sea
1,049,503 / 2,718,200

Mediterranean Sea
969,117 / 2,510,000

Bering Sea
884,908 / 2,291,900

Gulf of Mexico
614,984 / 1,592,800

* Excluding tributary seas
\# As defined by the International Hydrographic Organization

▲ **Ocean paradise**
The vast Indian Ocean accounts for nearly 20% of all surface water on the planet.

OCEANS WITH THE GREATEST VOLUME

The Pacific and Atlantic oceans have the greatest volume of water, measuring 163,044,711 cu miles and 75,188,659 cu miles respectively. The total volume of the world's oceans is between 311,886,586 and 359,869,138 cu miles.

THE 10 SHALLOWEST OCEANS AND SEAS*

	SEA / OCEAN	AVERAGE DEPTH FT	M
1	Sea of Azov, Atlantic Ocean	42.7	12.99
2	Bohai Sea	65.6	20.00
3	Arabian (Persian) Sea	78.7	23.99
4	Seto Inland Sea	122.4	37.30
5	Yellow Sea	144.4	44.01
6	Java Sea	150.9	45.99
7	= East Siberian Sea, Arctic Ocean	164.0	49.98
	= Chukchi Sea, Arctic Ocean	164.0	49.98
9	Baltic Sea, Atlantic Ocean	180.4	54.98
10	Irish Sea	196.9	60.01

* Excludes landlocked seas

▼ **Seto separation**
The Seto Sea lies between the three main islands of Japan.

THE 10 DEEPEST OCEANS AND SEAS

OCEAN/SEA / AVERAGE DEPTH (FT / M)

1 Southern Ocean
14,750 / 4,496

2 Pacific Ocean
13,215 / 4,028

3 Indian Ocean
13,002 / 3,963

4 Atlantic Ocean
12,999 / 3,926

5 Caribbean Sea
8,684 / 2,647

6 South China Sea
5,420 / 1,652

7 Bering Sea
5,075 / 1,547

8 Gulf of Mexico
4,875 / 1,486

9 Mediterranean Sea
4,688 / 1,429

10 Japan Sea
4,429 / 1,350

World ocean average
12,237 / 3,730

▶ *Pacific deep*
The fangtooth of the ocean depths looks menacing, but is only 6 in (15 cm) long.

THE 10 DEEPEST DEEP-SEA TRENCHES

TRENCH* / DEEPEST POINT (FT / M)

1 Marianas
35,798 / 10,911

2 Tonga[#]
35,702 / 10,882

3 Kuril-Kamchatka
34,587 / 10,542

4 Philippine
34,578 / 10,539

5 Kermadec[#]
32,962 / 10,047

6 Bonin[†]
32,789 / 9,994

7 New Britain
32,612 / 9,940

8 Izu[†]
32,087 / 9,780

9 Puerto Rico
28,232 / 8,605

10 Yap
27,976 / 8,527

* With the exception of the Puerto Rico (Atlantic), all the trenches are in the Pacific
# Some authorities consider these parts of the same feature
† Some authorities consider these parts of the same feature

FLOWING WATER

TOP 10 LONGEST RIVERS

RIVER	LOCATION	APPROX. LENGTH MILES	KM
1 Amazon	Bolivia, Brazil, Colombia, Ecuador, Peru, Venezuela	4,250	6,800
2 Nile	Burundi, Dem. Rep. of Congo, Egypt, Eritrea, Ethiopia, Kenya, Rwanda, Sudan, Tanzania, Uganda	4,160	6,695
3 Chang Jiang	China	3,915	6,300
4 Mississippi-Missouri	USA	3,899	6,275
5 Yenisei-Angara-Selenga	Mongolia, Russia	3,441	5,539
6 Huang He	China	3,395	5,464
7 Ob-Irtysh	China, Kazakhstan, Russia	3,362	5,410
8 Congo-Chambeshi	Angola, Burundi, Cameroon, Dem. Rep. of Congo, Rep. of Congo, Central African Republic, Rwanda, Tanzania, Zambia	2,920	4,700
9 Amur-Argun	China, Mongolia, Russia	2,761	4,444
10 Lena	Russia	2,734	4,400

◄ **Great rivers**
Between them, the Amazon (top) and the Nile (bottom) stretch 8,410 miles (13,495 km) —more than a third of the Earth's circumference.

TOP 10 LONGEST GLACIERS

GLACIER	LOCATION	LENGTH MILES	KM
1 Lambert	Antarctica	249	400
2 Bering	Alaska, USA	118	190
3 Beardmore	Antarctica	99	160
4 Byrd	Antarctica	85	136
5 Nimrod	Antarctica	84	135
6 Amundsen	Antarctica	80	128
7 Hubbard	Alaska, USA	76	122
8 Slessor	Antarctica	75	120
9 Denman	Antarctica	70	112
10 Recovery	Antarctica	62	100

▼ **Melting glacier**
The size of the Bering Glacier has reduced by several hundred feet due to global warming.

TOP 10 LONGEST RIVERS IN THE USA

RIVER	LENGTH MILES	KM
1 Missouri-Red Rock	2,540	4,088
2 Mississippi	2,348	3,779
3 Missouri	2,315	3,726
4 Yukon	1,979	3,185
5 Rio Grande	1,760	2,832
6 Arkansas	1,459	2,348
7 Colorado	1,450	2,334
8 Ohio-Allegheny	1,306	2,102
9 Red	1,290	2,076
10 Columbia	1,243	2,000

The Mississippi, Missouri, and Red Rock are often combined, making it the 4th longest river in the world.

TOP 10 HIGHEST WATERFALLS

WATERFALL / WATERCOURSE / COUNTRY /
GREATEST DROP (FT / M)

1 **Angel,**
Carrao, Venezuela
2,648 / 807

2 **Wailhilau,**
Waihilau, Hawaii, USA
2,600 / 792

3 **Mongefossen,**
Monge, Norway
2,535 / 773

4 **Ølmäfossen,**
Ølmäa, Norway
2,362 / 720

5 **Mana'wai'nui,**
Mana'wai'nui, Hawaii, USA
2,360 / 719

6 **Kjeragfossen,**
Unnamed, Norway
2,345 / 715

7 **Alfred Creek Falls,**
Alfred Creek, Canada
2,296 / 700

8 **Kukenaam,**
Kukenaam, Venezuela
2,211 / 674

9 **Langfoss,**
Åkrafjorden, Norway
2,000 / 612

10 **Ramnefjellsfossen,**
Utigardselva, Norway
1,968 / 600

This list is based on the height of the greatest single drop.

TOP 10 WIDEST WATERFALLS*

WATERFALL / WATERCOURSE / COUNTRY /
WIDTH (FT / M)

1 **Khône,**
Mekong River, Laos
35,376 / 10,783

2 **Pará,**
Rio Caura, Venezuela
18,400 / 5,608

3 **Kongou,**
Ivindo River, Gabon
10,500 / 3,200

4 **Iguaçu,**
Rio Iguaçu, Argentina/Brazil
8,858 / 2,700

5 **Patos e Maribondo,**
Rio Grande, Brazil
6,600 / 2,012

6 **Vermilion Falls,**
Peace River, Canada
6,000 / 1,829

7 **Celilo,**
Columbia River, USA
5,800 / 1,768

8 **Victoria,**
Zambezi River, Zimbabwe/
Zambia 5,700 / 1,737

9 **Wagenia,**
Lualaba River, Dem. Rep.
of Congo 4,500 / 1,372

10 **Niagara,**
Niagara River, USA/Canada
3,948 / 1,203

* For which confirmed data exists

▲ *Free fall*
Angel Falls are named after Jimmie Angel, the first person to fly a plane over them.

▶ *Iguaco Falls*
Iguaco is the result of a volcanic eruption that left a large crack in the Earth.

LAKES & ISLANDS

TOP 10 LARGEST ISLANDS

ISLAND / LOCATION	AREA* SQ MILES	SQ KM
1 Greenland (Kalaatdlit Nunaat)	840,004	2,175,600
2 New Guinea, Papua New Guinea/ Indonesia	303,381	785,753
3 Borneo, Indonesia/Malaysia/Brunei	288,869	748,168
4 Madagascar	226,917	587,713
5 Baffin Island, Canada	194,574	503,944
6 Sumatra, Indonesia	171,068	443,065
7 Honshu, Japan	87,805	227,413
8 Great Britain	84,200	218,077
9 Victoria Island, Canada	83,897	217,292
10 Ellesmere Island, Canada	75,767	196,236

* Mainlands, including areas of inland water, but excluding offshore islands

▲ **Island native**
The hot, humid, damp, and rainy island of New Guinea is home to 7.5 million people.

TOP 10 LARGEST LAKE ISLANDS

ISLAND	LAKE / LOCATION	AREA SQ MILES	SQ KM
1 Manitoulin	Huron, Ontario, Canada	1,068	2,766
2 René-Lavasseur	Manicouagan Reservoir, Quebec, Canada	780	2,020
3 Sääminginsalo	Saimaa, Finland	413	1,069
4 Olkhon	Baikal, Russia	282	730
5 Samosir	Toba, Sumatra, Indonesia	243	630
6 Isle Royale	Superior, Michigan, USA	207	535
7 Ukerewe	Victoria, Tanzania	205	530
8 St. Joseph	Huron, Ontario, Canada	141	365
9 Drummond	Huron, Michigan, USA	134	347
10 Idjwi	Kivu, Dem. Rep. of Congo	110	285

THE 10 DEEPEST LAKES

LAKE / LOCATION	GREATEST DEPTH FT	M
1 Baikal Russia	5,712	1,741
2 Tanganyika Burundi/Tanzania/Dem. Rep. of Congo/Zambia	4,825	1,471
3 Caspian Sea Azerbaijan/Iran/Kazakhstan/ Russia/Turkmenistan	3,363	1,025
4 Malawi Malawi/Mozambique/ Tanzania	2,316	706
5 Issyk-kul Kyrgyzstan	2,191	668
6 Great Slave Canada	2,015	614
7 Matana Sulawesi, Indonesia	1,936	590
8 Crater Oregon, USA	1,932	589
9 Toba Sumatra, Indonesia	1,736	529
10 Hornindals Norway	1,686	514

LAKE BAIKAL IS 4.5 TIMES DEEPER THAN THE HEIGHT OF THE EMPIRE STATE BUILDING!

▶ **Olkhon**
Itself a lake island, Olkhon is large enough to have its own lakes and a small desert.

TOP 10 **MOST ISOLATED ISLANDS**

ISLAND / LOCATION / ISOLATION INDEX

1 Easter Island
South Pacific
149

2 Rapa Iti
Tubuai Islands, South Pacific
130

3 Kiritimati
Line Islands, Central Pacific
129

4 Jarvis Island
Central Pacific
128

5 = Kosrae
Micronesia, Pacific
126

= Malden
Line Islands, Central Pacific
126

= Starbuck
Line Islands, Central Pacific
126

= Vostok
Line Islands, Central Pacific
126

9 = Bouvet Island
South Atlantic
125

= Gough Island
South Atlantic
125

= Palmyra Island
Central Pacific
125

Source: United Nations

The United Nations' isolation index is calculated by adding together the square roots of the distances to the nearest island, group of islands, and continent. The higher the number, the more remote the island.

TOP 10 **LARGEST MANMADE LAKES BY SURFACE AREA**

	LAKE	LOCATION	AREA SQ MILES	AREA SQ KM
1	Volta	Ghana	3,286	8,502
2	Kujbyshevskoe	Russia	2,278	5,900
3	Smallwood	Canada	2,166	5,610
4	Kariba	Zimbabwe/Zambia	2,154	5,580
5	Bukhtarma	Kazakhstan	2,120	5,490
6	Nasser	Egypt/Sudan	2,026	5,248
7	Rybinsk	Russia	1,768	4,580
8	Bratskoye	Russia	1,728	4,476
9	Caniapiscau	Canada	1,667	4,318
10	Guri	Venezuela	1,641	4,250

▲ *Great lake*
With a mean depth of 95 ft (29 m), Kariba is 137 miles (220 km) long and 25 miles (40 km) wide.

▼ *Easter Island*
This remote Polynesian island is renowned for its Moai statues, carved from solidified volcanic ash.

MOUNTAINS OF THE WORLD

▲ **Mont Blanc**
The 7.2-mile Mont Blanc tunnel runs beneath the mountain, linking France to Italy.

▲ **Kibo**
Kibo (or KIlimanjaro) is the world's tallest freestanding mountain.

TOP 10 HIGHEST MOUNTAINS IN AUSTRALIA

	MOUNTAIN	HEIGHT FT	M
1	Mount Kosciuszko	7,309	2,228
2	Mount Townsend	7,249	2,209
3	Mount Twynham	7,203	2,195
4	Ramshead North	7,185	2,190
5	Unnamed peak Etheridge Ridge	7,152	2,180
6	Rams Head North	7,142	2,177
7	Alice Rawson Peak	7,086	2,160
8	Unnamed peak southwest of Abbott Peak	7,083	2,159
9 =	Abbott Peak	7,039	2,145
=	Carruthers Peak	7,039	2,145

TOP 10 HIGHEST MOUNTAINS IN EUROPE

	MOUNTAIN / COUNTRY	HEIGHT* FT	M
1	Mont Blanc France/Italy	15,771	4,807
2	Monte Rosa Switzerland	15,203	4,634
3	Zumsteinspitze Italy/Switzerland	14,970	4,564
4	Signalkuppe Italy/Switzerland	14,941	4,555
5	Dom Switzerland	14,911	4,545
6	Liskamm Italy/Switzerland	14,853	4,527
7	Weisshorn Switzerland	14,780	4,505
8	Täschorn Switzerland	14,733	4,491
9	Matterhorn Italy/Switzerland	14,688	4,477
10	Mont Maudit France/Italy	14,649	4,466

* Height of principal peak; lower peaks of the same mountain are excluded

TOP 10 HIGHEST MOUNTAINS IN AFRICA

	MOUNTAIN / COUNTRY	HEIGHT FT	M
1	Kibo (Kilimanjaro) Tanzania	19,341	5,895
2	Batian (Kenya) Kenya	17,057	5,199
3	Ngaliema (Stanley) Uganda/Dem. Rep. of Congo	16,763	5,109
4	Duwoni (Speke) Uganda	16,043	4,890
5	Baker Uganda	15,892	4,844
6	Emin Uganda/Dem. Rep. of Congo	15,741	4,798
7	Gessi Uganda	15,469	4,715
8	Luigi di Savoia Uganda	15,180	4,627
9	Meru Tanzania	14,980	4,566
10	Ras Dashen Ethiopia	14,928	4,550

HOW THE WORLD'S MOUNTAINS COMPARE

The world's highest mountain, Everest, is four times the height of Australia's Mount Kosciuszko and nearly twice that of Mont Blanc.

Africa
Kibo (Kilimanjaro)
19,341 / 5,895

Europe
Mont Blanc
15,771 / 4,807

Australia
Mount Kosciuszko
7,309 / 2,228

▲ **Mount McKinley**
Hudson Stuck led a party that reached the main summit of McKinley in 1913.

▲ **Cerro Aconcagua**
The 1.6-mile high south face climb is one of the most difficult in the world.

TOP 10 **HIGHEST MOUNTAINS IN NORTH AMERICA**

MOUNTAIN / COUNTRY	HEIGHT* FT	M
1 McKinley Alaska, USA	20,320	6,194
2 Logan Canada	19,545	5,959
3 Citlaltépetl (Orizaba) Mexico	18,409	5,611
4 St. Elias Alaska, USA/Canada	18,008	5,489
5 Popocatépetl Mexico	17,887	5,452
6 Foraker Alaska, USA	17,400	5,304
7 Ixtaccíhuatl Mexico	17,159	5,230
8 Lucania Canada	17,147	5,226
9 King Canada	16,971	5,173
10 Steele Canada	16,644	5,073

* Height of principal peak; lower peaks of the same mountain are excluded

TOP 10 **HIGHEST MOUNTAINS IN SOUTH AMERICA**

MOUNTAIN / COUNTRY	HEIGHT FT	M
1 Cerro Aconcagua Argentina	22,841	6,959
2 Ojos del Salado Argentina/Chile	22,615	6,893
3 Monte Pissis Argentina/Chile	22,244	6,795
4 Cerro Bonete Argentina	22,175	6,759
5 Huascarán Peru	22,133	6,746
6 Llullaillaco Argentina/Chile	22,109	6,739
7 = Cerro Mercadario Argentina/Chile	22,047	6,720
= El Libertador Argentina	22,047	6,720
9 Tres Cruces Argentina/Chile	21,748	6,629
10 Incahuasi Argentina/Chile	21,722	6,621

TOP 10 **HIGHEST MOUNTAINS IN ASIA**

MOUNTAIN / COUNTRY	HEIGHT FT	M
1 Everest Nepal	29,035	8,850
2 K2 Pakistan	28,251	8,611
3 Kangchenjunga Nepal	28,169	8,586
4 Lhotse Nepal	27,940	8,516
5 Makalu Nepal	27,838	8,485
6 Cho Oyu Nepal	26,906	8,201
7 Dhaulagiri Nepal	26,794	8,167
8 Manaslu Nepal	26,758	8,156
9 Nanga Parbat Pakistan	26,658	8,125
10 Annapurna 1 Nepal	26,545	8,091

Asia Everest 29,035 / 8,850

South America Cerro Aconcagua 22,841 / 6,959

North America McKinley 20,320 / 6,194

30,000 ft
20,000 ft
10,000 ft

TOP 10 HIGHEST VOLCANOES

▲ **Dormant danger**
The most recent large eruption from Ojos del Salado was 1,300 years ago.

VOLCANO / LOCATION	HEIGHT	
	FT	M
1 Ojos del Salado Chile	22,595	6,887
2 Llullaillaco Chile	22,110	6,739
3 Tipas Argentina	21,850	6,660
4 Nevado de Incahuasi Chile	21,722	6,621
5 Cerro el Cóndor Argentina	21,430	6,532
6 Coropuna Peru	20,922	6,377
7 Parinacota Chile	20,827	6,348
8 Chimborazo Ecuador	20,702	6,310
9 Pular Chile	20,449	6,233
10 El Solo Chile	20,308	6,190

Source: Smithsonian Institution

TOP 10 LARGEST DESERTS

DESERT / LOCATION / APPROX. AREA (SQ MILES / SQ KM)

1 Sahara
Northern Africa
3,500,000 / 9,100,000

2 Arabian
Southwest Asia
900,000 / 2,330,000

3 Gobi
central Asia
500,000 / 1,295,000

4 Kalahari
sub-Saharan Africa
360,000 / 900,000

5 Patagonian
Argentina/Chile
260,000 / 673,000

6 Great Victoria
Australia
250,000 / 647,000

7 Syrian
Middle East
200,000 / 520,000

8 Great Basin
USA
190,000 / 492,000

9 Chihuahuan
Mexico/USA
175,000 / 450,000

10 Great Sandy
Australia
150,000 / 400,000

LARGEST CANYONS

According to how it is defined, there are various candidates for the title of "largest" canyon or gorge. Based on the greatest difference between the height of the adjacent mountains and the river valley, the Kali Gandaki Gorge in Nepal, at 18,044–22,231 ft (5,500–6,800 m), is the deepest. The Yarlung Zangbo Grand Canyon in China is 308 miles (496 km) long and 17,657 ft (5,382 m) at its deepest. The Grand Canyon, Arizona, is less deep, but is as much as 18 miles (29 km) wide and 277 miles (446 km) long, while the Copper Canyon, Mexico, is a series of six canyons that together are longer and deeper than the Grand Canyon.

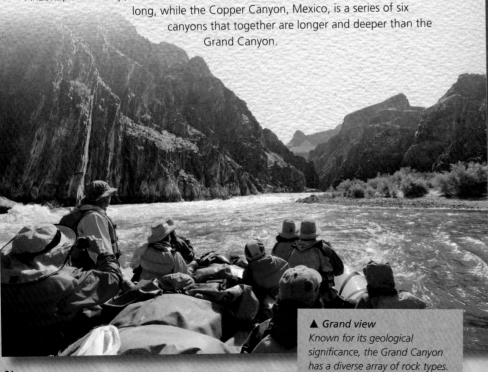

▲ **Grand view**
Known for its geological significance, the Grand Canyon has a diverse array of rock types.

This Top 10 presents the approximate areas and ranking of the world's great deserts, which are often broken down into smaller desert regions or merged. According to some authorities Australia's Gibson, Great Sandy, Great Victoria, and Simpson comprise the Australian Desert.

THE 10 **DEEPEST DEPRESSIONS**

DEPRESSION / LOCATION	MAX. DEPTH BELOW SEA LEVEL	
	FT	M
1 Dead Sea, Israel/Jordan	1,355	413
2 Sea of Galilee, Israel	686	209
3 Lake Assal, Djibouti	509	155
4 Turfan Depression, China	505	154
5 Qattâra Depression, Egypt	436	133
6 Mangyshlak Peninsula, Kazakhstan	433	132
7 Danakil (Afar) Depression, Ethiopia	410	125
8 Laguna del Carbón, Argentina	344	105
9 Death Valley, California, USA	282	86
10 Akdzhakaya Depression, Turkmenistan	266	81

The shore of the Dead Sea (right) is the lowest exposed ground below sea level, but the bed of the sea actually reaches 2,388 ft (728 m) below sea level, and that of Lake Baikal, in Russia, attains 4,872 ft (1,485 m) below sea level. Much of Antarctica is below sea level, but the land there is covered by an ice cap that averages 6,890 ft (2,100 m) in depth.

THE WORLD'S DEEPEST CAVE

The deepest known cave in the world is the Krubera in Georgia, which is 7,188 ft (2,191 m) deep. It was discovered comparatively recently, in January 2001, by a group of Ukrainian cave explorers.

TOP 10 **LONGEST CAVES**

CAVE / LOCATION / TOTAL KNOWN LENGTH (MILES / KM)

	MILES	KM
1 Mammoth Cave System, Kentucky, USA	390.0	627.6
2 Jewel Cave, South Dakota, USA	150.0	241.4
3 Optimisticeskaja, Ukraine	144.0	231.7
4 Wind Cave, South Dakota, USA	136.0	218.8
5 Sistema Sac Actun, Mexico*	135.0	217.2
6 Lechuguilla Cave, New Mexico, USA	130.0	209.2
7 Hölloch, Switzerland	122.0	196.3
8 Clear Water System, Malaysia	117.0	188.2
9 Fisher Ridge System, Kentucky, USA	114.0	183.4
10 Sistema Ox Bel Ha, Mexico#	113.0	181.8

* Majority of cave under water
\# Underwater cave

▲ *Mammoth Cave*
The world's longest cave system has vast chambers and complex labyrinths of tunnels.

CHANGES IN THE WEATHER

AVERAGE GLOBAL TEMPERATURES IN THE PAST 10 DECADES*

YEAR / °F / °C

2010
58.33° / 14.63°

2000
57.79° / 14.33°

1990
57.85° / 14.36°

1980
57.54° / 14.19°

1970
57.25° / 14.03°

1960
57.18° / 13.99°

1950
56.91° / 13.84°

1940
57.27° / 14.04°

1930
57.06° / 13.92°

1920
56.86° / 13.81°

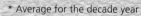

* Average for the decade year

GREENHOUSE-GAS EMISSIONS

Greenhouse-gas emissions have risen by nearly 50% since the turn of the century, greatly contributing to climate change and global warming, which has produced extremes of weather. On the one hand, warmer air is able to hold more moisture and this increase in the level of vapor contributes to the generation of heavier storms. On the other hand, hotter temperatures mean we experience prolonged and severe droughts with increasing frequency.

◄ *On thin ice*
Polar bears sinking into Arctic seas due to melting ice caps graphically illustrates the devastating effect of global warming.

ARCTIC WARMING

The temperature in the Arctic has risen by more than 3°C in the past 50 years. Arctic sea ice is at its lowest level ever and is reducing at an alarming rate. In 1980 there were 2.8 million sq miles (7.2 million sq km) of sea ice, but this has reduced to less than 2.1 million sq miles (5.5 million sq km) in the past 30 years. The Arctic is heating up at double the rate of the rest of the planet, and this is likely to increase due to the albedo effect—as the sea ice melts, darker ocean water becomes exposed. The darker water absorbs more light than its lighter counterpart, and this additional energy retention results in even greater ice melt.

THE 5 HOTTEST PLACES ON EARTH

LOCATION*	AVERAGE TEMPERATURE °F	°C
1 Dalol, Ethiopia	94.3	34.6
2 Assab, Eritrea	86.8	30.4
3 Néma, Mauritania	86.5	30.3
4 Berbera, Somalia	86.2	30.1
5 Hombori, Mali	86.1	30.1

▲ Dalol
In the 1960s, Dalol averaged 94°F (34°C), the highest temperature for an inhabited location.

THE COLDEST PLACE ON EARTH

Oymyakon in Siberia is the coldest inhabited place on Earth. In January 1962, the temperature fell to -96.2°F (-71.2°C), the lowest temperature ever recorded anywhere on the planet. Residents of Oymyakon endure an average winter temperature of -49°F (-45°C).

EXTREME WEATHER

The past decade was the hottest 10 years the world has ever experienced, with 2010 producing an average global temperature of 58.33°F (14.63°C). A hotter climate means an increase in extreme weather events, and in the recent past extreme weather throughout the world has included an excessive heat wave in Russia, dramatic fires in Israel, severe flooding in Pakistan and Australia, landslides in China, record snowfall in the USA, and severe drought in the Horn of Africa.

▲ Pakistan floods
In July 2010 Pakistan endured the worst floods in its history, affecting about 18 million people.

► Landslide in China
Heavy rain in China in September 2011 resulted in terrible floods and landslides, killing at least 57 people.

NATURE'S FURY

▲ *Tsunami devastation*
The earthquake and tsunami in Japan in 2011 were among the most massive experienced in recent times.

▼ *Tangshan*
A museum to commemorate the 1976 earthquake features over 400 exhibits and photographs depicting the disaster.

Tsunamis are powerful waves caused by undersea disturbances such as earthquakes or volcanic eruptions. Tsunamis can be so intense that they frequently cross entire oceans, devastating islands and coastal regions in their paths.

THE 10 **WORST AVALANCHES AND LANDSLIDES***

	LOCATION	INCIDENT	DATE	ESTIMATED. NO. KILLED
1	Alps, Italy	Avalanche	Oct 218 BC	18,000
2	Yungay, Peru	Landslide	May 31, 1970	17,500
3	Alps, Italy	Avalanche	Dec 13, 1916	10,000
4	Huarás, Peru	Avalanche	Dec 13, 1941	5,000
5	Nevada Huascaran, Peru	Avalanche	Jan 10, 1962	3,500
6	Chiavenna, Italy	Landslide	Sep 4, 1618	2,427
7	Plurs, Switzerland	Avalanche	Sep 4, 1618	1,496
8	Goldau Valley, Switzerland	Landslide	Sep 2, 1806	800
9	Medellin, Colombia	Landslide	Sep 27, 1987	683
10	Chungar, Peru	Avalanche	Mar 19, 1971	600

* Excluding those where most deaths resulted from flooding, earthquakes, volcanoes, etc., associated with landslides

THE 10 **WORST FOREST FIRES, 1900–2011**

	LOCATION	OUTBREAK	ESTIMATED NO. KILLED
1	Cloquet, Minnesota, USA	Oct 1918	1,000
2	Sumatra and Kalimantan, Indonesia	Aug 1997	240
3	Heilongjiang Province, China	May 1987	191
4	Victoria, Australia	Feb 2009	180
5	Cleveland, USA	Oct 1944	121
6	Landes, France	Aug 1949	80
7	Victoria, Australia	Feb 1983	75
8	Ontario, Canada	Jul 1911	73
9	Victoria, Australia	Jan 1939	71
10	Peloponnese, Greece	Aug 2007	67

This list is headed by the catastrophe that befell Carthaginian troops under Hannibal as they descended the Alps, probably in the region of the Col de la Traversette, a pass between France and Italy, when 18,000 men, 2,000 horses, and a number of elephants fell victim to a series of avalanches on a single day.

▼ *Australian inferno*
Exceptionally high temperatures, excessive winds, and minimal rainfall created conditions that produced massive firestorms.

THE 10 **WORST FLOODS**

LOCATION / DATE / ESTIMATED NO. KILLED

1 Huang He, China
Aug 1931
3,700,000

2 Huang He, China
Spring 1887
1,500,000

3 Holland
Nov 1, 1530
400,000

4 Kaifong, China
1642
300,000

5 Henan, China
Sep–Nov 1939
>200,000

6 Bengal, India
1876
200,000

7 Chang Jiang, China
Aug–Sep 1931
140,000

8 Holland
1646
110,000

9 North Vietnam
Aug 30, 1971
>100,000

10 = Friesland, Holland
1228
100,000

= Dort, Holland
Apr 16, 1421
100,000

= Canton, China
Jun 12, 1915
100,000

= Chang Jiang, China
Sep 1911
100,000

Records of floods caused by China's Huang He, or Yellow River, date back to 2297 BC. Since then, it has flooded at least 1,500 times, resulting in millions of deaths and giving it the nickname "China's Sorrow." In modern times, an extensive program of damming and dyke-building has reduced the danger of flooding.

2

LIFE ON EARTH

TIGERS IN CRISIS

In the 1900s there were at least 100,000 tigers in the wild, but the population has declined at an alarming rate, and there are now no more than 5,000 left. Poaching is a huge threat to these beautiful beasts, and the number of animals poached continues to escalate as the market for tiger skins and body parts is very lucrative. Body parts, including tiger bone, are especially prized and are used extensively in traditional Chinese medicines. Deforestation and climate change are also bringing tiger habitats increasingly under threat—tigers are solitary creatures that scent-mark their territory in order to ward off rivals, and each tiger needs a substantial area in which to roam. Russian president Vladimir Putin hosted the International Tiger Forum last year, and initiated a global campaign to try and double the number of tigers in the wild by 2022.

TOP 10 HEAVIEST DINOSAURS EVER DISCOVERED

NAME	ESTIMATED WEIGHT (TONS)

1 Bruhathkayosaurus   139
Fossil remains of this dinosaur were found in southern India. Some authorities have estimated it as having weighed as much as 240 tons, more than a blue whale, but such claims have been questioned.

2 Amphicoelias   134
Its massive size, with a length of some 82 ft (25 m) has been extrapolated from vertebrae fragments discovered in Colorado in 1877, but since lost.

3 Puertasaurus   88–110
Its huge size has been estimated from partial remains found in Patagonia in 2001.

4 Argentinosaurus   66–97
An Argentinean farmer discovered a 6-ft (1.8-m) bone in 1988. It was found to be the shinbone of a previously unknown dinosaur, which was given the name *Argentinosaurus*.

5 Argyrosaurus   88
This South American dinosaur's name means "silver lizard."

6 Sauroposeidon   55–66
Known only from vertebrae discovered in Oklahoma in 1994, its name means "Earthquake lizard-god."

7 Paralititan   65
Remains discovered in 2001 in the Sahara Desert in Egypt suggest that this was a giant plant-eater.

8 Antarctosaurus   50–55
The creature's thigh bone alone measures 7.5 ft (2.3 m) and a total length of 60 ft (18 m) has been estimated. Some authorities have put its weight as high as 88 tons.

9 Turiasaurus   44–53
The largest dinosaur yet discovered in Europe, remains of *Turiasaurus* were unearthed in Spain in 2003.

10 Supersaurus   39–44
Fragments of *Supersaurus* were unearthed in Colorado in 1972. Another more complete specimen, known as "Jimbo," has been discovered in Wyoming and is undergoing examination.

FIRST DINOSAURS TO BE NAMED

A number of dinosaurs had been named before the word "dinosaur" itself had been coined. *Dinosauria*—"fearfully great lizards"—was proposed as a name for the group by Richard Owen in 1842. The Reverend William Buckland was the first to name a dinosaur, in 1824. He called it *Megalosaurus*, meaning "great lizard."

TOP 10 COUNTRIES WITH MOST DINOSAURS

COUNTRY / NO. OF DINOSAURS*

1	USA	89
2	China	60
3	Mongolia	48
4	Canada	37
5	Argentina	29
6	UK	26
7	France	13
8	Germany	10
9	=Spain	9
	=Tanzania	9

* By genus

▶ **Argentinosaurus**
Weighing up to 97 tons—equivalent to approximately 12 London buses—this enormous creature was up to 115 ft in length.

▲ Compsognathus
About the size of a large chicken, it fed on small animals such as lizards.

THE 10 SMALLEST DINOSAURS

DINOSAUR / MAX. SIZE (IN / CM)

1	Micropachycephalosaurus	20 / 50
2	Saltopus	23 / 59
3 =	Compsognathus	24 / 60
=	Fruitadens	24 / 60
=	Microceratops	24 / 60
=	Yandangornis	24 / 60
7	Bambiraptor	27 / 69
8	Microraptor	33 / 83
9	Lesothosaurus	35 / 90
10 =	Sinosauropteryx	39 / 99
=	Wannanosaurus	39 / 99

Micropachycephalosaurus is ironically the longest name for the smallest dinosaur. Discovered in Argentina, Mussaurus (meaning "mouse lizard") is the smallest complete dinosaur skeleton found.

▲ Liopleurodon

◄ Dunkleosteus

LIOPLEURODON WAS MORE THAN FOUR TIMES THE SIZE OF A GREAT WHITE SHARK!

5 BEASTS OF THE PREHISTORIC DEEP

Dinosaurs may have been the lords of the land, but they weren't the only giants of the prehistoric world. The ancient oceans were also inhabited by beasts of nightmare proportions.

Liopleurodon
This savage marine reptile of the late Jurassic era grew to around 82 ft (25 m), and preyed on prehistoric crocodiles and other marine reptiles such as *Ichthyosaurs*.

Basilosaurus
The erroneously named *Basilosaurus* ("king lizard") was not actually a reptile, but a deadly ancestor of the whale. Its long body—up to 85 ft (26 m)—gave it an appearance more like a sea snake than a modern cetacean.

Dunkleosteus
This massive (26–33 ft/8–10 m) fish had an armor-plated head and two long blades instead of teeth, which it used to crush any prehistoric prey it could find—including sharks.

Megalodon shark
These fearsome fish may have grown to lengths of 50 ft (16 m) and had the most powerful bite of any creature known to have existed on Earth.

Giant sea scorpion
The discovery of a huge fossilized claw in 2007 revealed that giant sea scorpions of coastal swamps may have measured up to 8.2 ft (2.5 m).

ENDANGERED ANIMALS

TOP 10 COUNTRIES WITH THE MOST CRITICALLY ENDANGERED BIRD SPECIES

COUNTRY / SPECIES ENDANGERED

1	Brazil	25
2	USA	17
3	Indonesia	16
4	=India	13
	=Philippines	13
6	Colombia	11
7	Mexico	10
8	=New Zealand	9
	=Thailand	9
10	China	8

◀ At risk
The illegal capture and trade of wild cockatoos has threatened some Indonesian species.

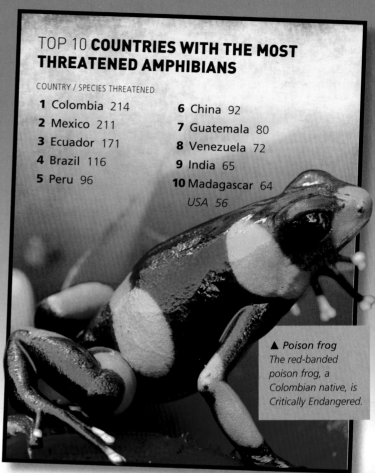

TOP 10 COUNTRIES WITH THE MOST THREATENED AMPHIBIANS

COUNTRY / SPECIES THREATENED

1	Colombia	214	6	China	92
2	Mexico	211	7	Guatemala	80
3	Ecuador	171	8	Venezuela	72
4	Brazil	116	9	India	65
5	Peru	96	10	Madagascar	64
				USA	56

▲ Poison frog
The red-banded poison frog, a Colombian native, is Critically Endangered.

TOP 10 ORGANISMS MOST RAPIDLY BECOMING ENDANGERED*

ORGANISM ENDANGERED# / SPECIES BECOMING ENDANGERED / % OF SPECIES

1 Amphibians
1,764 / 28.2%

1,764

632

3 Mollusks
632 / 1.8%

368

4 Reptiles
368 / 7.1%

2 Fish
1,259 / 6.3%

1,259

5 Corals
234 / 10.8%

234

* In the past 10 years
# Identified by the IUCN as Critically Endangered, Endangered, or Vulnerable

Source: IUCN, *Red List of Threatened Species*

TOP 10 COUNTRIES WITH THE LARGEST PROTECTED AREAS

COUNTRY	% OF TOTAL AREA	DESIGNATED AREA SQ MILES	SQ KM
1 Brazil	26.28	865,782	2,242,365
2 China	16.64	601,327	1,557,431
3 Russia	9.07	591,351	1,531,593
4 USA	12.38	446,162	1,155,553
5 Greenland	40.55	337,193	873,325
6 Australia	10.55	314,557	814,699
7 Canada	7.51	285,944	740,592
8 Saudi Arabia	31.26	233,434	604,590
9 Venezuela	53.75	190,390	493,109
10 Indonesia	14.15	104,160	269,774

The International Union for the Conservation of Nature (IUCN) has defined a national park as a relatively large area which is not altered by human exploitation and occupation. However, since there are also tracts of land that are worthy of protection, but which already have human habitation, the broader definition has evolved of "protected area," which encompasses national parks, nature reserves, natural monuments, and other sites.

▲ **Rare icefield**
Kenai Fjords National Park in the USA encompasses the Harding Icefield, one of only four remaining icefields in the USA.

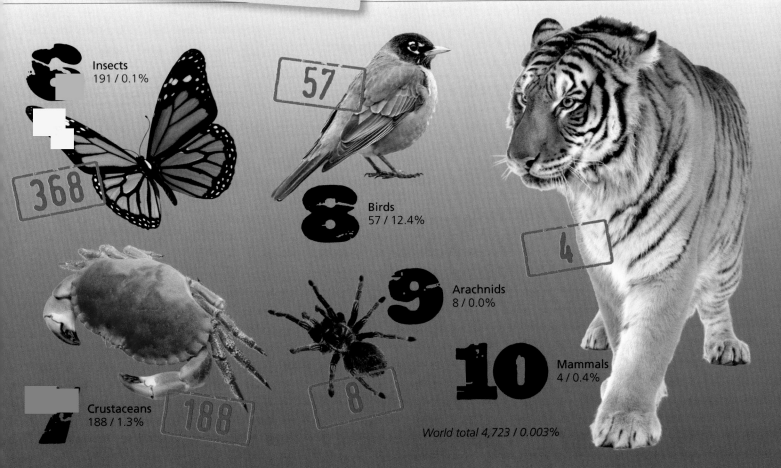

Insects
191 / 0.1%

368

57

Birds
57 / 12.4%

Arachnids
8 / 0.0%

Mammals
4 / 0.4%

Crustaceans
188 / 1.3%

World total 4,723 / 0.003%

LAND ANIMALS

◄ **Pygmy primate**
The endangered pygmy mouse lemur weighs less than a golf ball and measures just 2.4 in (6.2 cm).

THE 10 SMALLEST PRIMATES

PRIMATE* / SCIENTIFIC NAME	WEIGHT#	
	OZ	G
1 Pygmy mouse lemur (Microcebus myoxinus)	1.0	30
2 Hairy-eared dwarf lemur (Allocebus trichotis)	2.4–3.5	70–100
3 Pygmy tarsier (Tarsius pumilus)	2.8–5.8	80–165
4 Lesser bush baby (Galago moholi)	4.9–8.1	140–230
5 Greater dwarf lemur (Cheirogaleus major)	6.2–21.1	177–600
6 Buffy-headed marmoset (Callithrix flaviceps)	8.1–15.9	230–453
7 Cotton-top tamarin (Saguinus oedipus)	9.1–13.4	260–380
8 Golden potto (Arctocebus calabarensis)	9.3–16.4	266–465
9 Golden-rumped lion tamarin (Leontopithecus chrysopygus)	10.5–24.6	300–700
10 Callimico goeldii	13.8–30.3	393–860

* Lightest species per genus
# Weights range across male and female; ranked by lightest

TOP 10 HEAVIEST LAND MAMMALS

MAMMAL* / SCIENTIFIC NAME	LENGTH		WEIGHT	
	FT	M	LB	KG
1 African elephant (Loxodonta africana)	24.6	7.5	14,000	6,350
2 Hippopotamus (Hippopotamus amphibius)	14.0	4.2	8,000	3,629
3 White rhinoceros (Ceratotherium simum)	13.7	4.1	7,920	3,592
4 Giraffe (Giraffa camelopardalis)	19.0	6.0	2,800	1,270
5 American buffalo (Bison bison)	11.5	3.5	2,205	1,000
6 Moose (Alces alces)	10.1	3.1	1,820	825
7 Arabian camel (dromedary) (Camelus dromedarius)	11.5	3.5	1,600	726
8 Grizzly bear (Ursus arctos)	8.0	2.5	800	363
9 Siberian tiger (Panthera tigris altaica)	10.8	3.3	660	300
10 Gorilla (Gorilla gorilla gorilla)	6.5	2.0	485	220

* Heaviest species per genus; maximum weight, exclusively terrestrial, excluding seals, etc.

▶ **Heavyweights**
Elephants and hippos are among the world's most aggressive animals.

TOP 10 LAND ANIMALS WITH THE HEAVIEST BRAINS

ANIMAL SPECIES*	AVERAGE BRAIN WEIGHT		
	LB	OZ	G
1 Elephant	10	10	4,783
2 Adult human	3	0	1,350
3 Camel	1	11	762
4 Giraffe	1	8	680
5 Hippopotamus	1	4	582
6 Horse	1	3	532
7 Gorilla	1	2	503
8 Polar bear	1	2	498
9 Cow	1	0	442
10 Chimpanzee	0	15	420

* Heaviest species of each genus

TOP 10 **COUNTRIES WITH THE MOST MAMMAL SPECIES**

COUNTRY / MAMMAL SPECIES

1 Indonesia
667

2 Brazil
578

3 Mexico
544

4 China
502

5 USA
468

6 Colombia
467

7 Peru
441

8 Dem. Rep. of Congo
430

9 India
422

10 Kenya
407

Source: EarthTrends/World Conservation Monitoring Centre of the United Nations Environment Programme (UNEP-WCMC)

THE CHEETAH CAN SPRINT MORE THAN 2.5 TIMES FASTER THAN THE WORLD'S FASTEST MAN, USAIN BOLT!

▲ *Fast cat*
Cheetahs can accelerate from 0 to over 60 mph (97 km/h) in three seconds.

▼ *Sleeping lions*
Lions tend to do most of their hunting at night, sleeping and resting during the day.

TOP 10 **FASTEST MAMMALS**

MAMMAL / SCIENTIFIC NAME	MAX. RECORDED SPEED*	
	MPH	KM/H
1 Cheetah (*Acinonyx jubatus*)	62	110
2 Pronghorn antelope (*Antilocapra americana*)	53	86
3 Grant's gazelle (*Gazella granti*)	51	82
4 = Blue wildebeest (brindled gnu) (*Connochaetes taurinus*)	50	80
= Lion (*Panthera leo*)	50	80
= Springbok (*Antidorcas marsupialis*)	50	80
7 Red fox (*Vulpes vulpes*)	48	77
8 Thomson's gazelle (*Gazella thomsonii*)	47	76
9 = Brown hare (*Lepus capensis*)	45	72
= Horse (*Equus caballus*)	45	72

* Of those species for which data available

TOP 10 **SLEEPIEST MAMMALS**

ANIMAL / SCIENTIFIC NAME	AVERAGE HOURS SLEEP PER DAY
1 = Lion (*Panthera leo*)	20
= Three-toed sloth (*Bradypus variegatus*)	20
3 Little brown bat (*Myotis lucifugus*)	19.9
4 Big brown bat (*Eptesicus fuscus*)	19.7
5 = Opossum (*Didelphis virginiana*)	19.4
= Water opossum (Yapok) (*Chironectes minimus*)	19.4
7 Giant armadillo (*Priodontes maximus*)	18.1
8 Koala (*Phascolarctos cinereus*)	<18
9 Nine-banded armadillo (*Dasypus novemcinctus*)	17.4
10 Southern owl monkey (*Aotus azarai*)	17.0

This list excludes periods of hibernation, which can last for several months among creatures such as the ground squirrel, marmot, and brown bear.

SEA LIFE

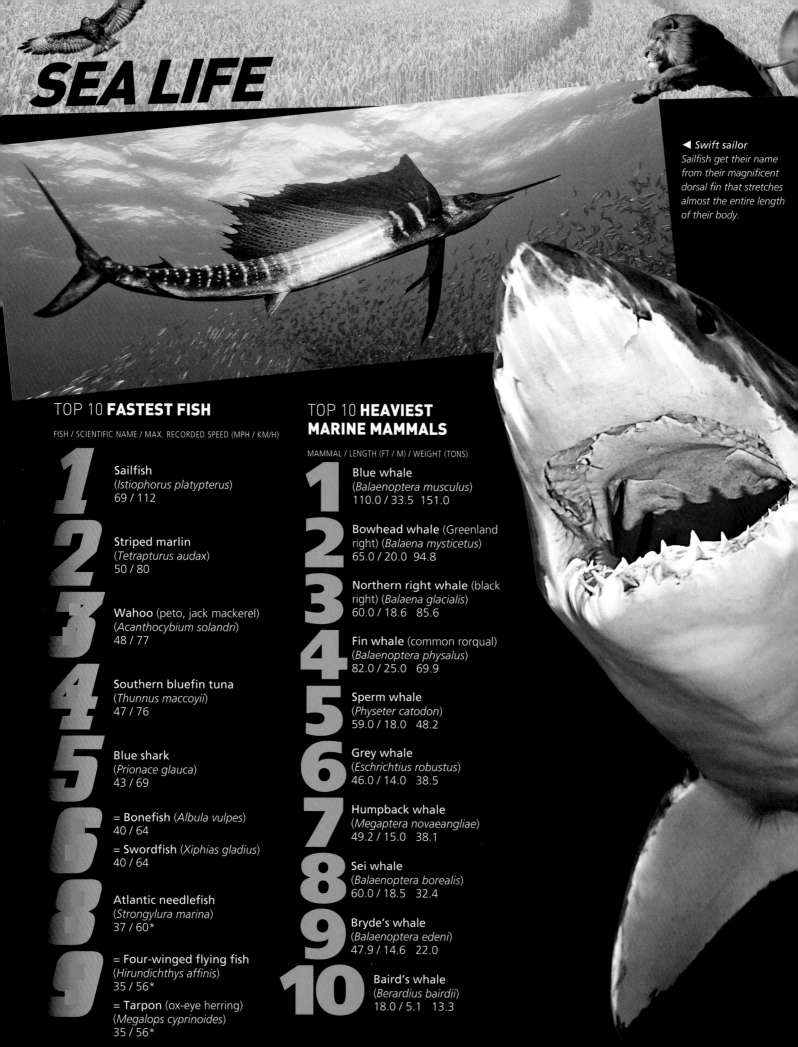

◄ **Swift sailor**
Sailfish get their name from their magnificent dorsal fin that stretches almost the entire length of their body.

TOP 10 FASTEST FISH

FISH / SCIENTIFIC NAME / MAX. RECORDED SPEED (MPH / KM/H)

1 **Sailfish**
(*Istiophorus platypterus*)
69 / 112

2 **Striped marlin**
(*Tetrapturus audax*)
50 / 80

3 **Wahoo** (peto, jack mackerel)
(*Acanthocybium solandri*)
48 / 77

4 **Southern bluefin tuna**
(*Thunnus maccoyii*)
47 / 76

5 **Blue shark**
(*Prionace glauca*)
43 / 69

6 = **Bonefish** (*Albula vulpes*)
40 / 64

= **Swordfish** (*Xiphias gladius*)
40 / 64

8 **Atlantic needlefish**
(*Strongylura marina*)
37 / 60*

9 = **Four-winged flying fish**
(*Hirundichthys affinis*)
35 / 56*

= **Tarpon** (ox-eye herring)
(*Megalops cyprinoides*)
35 / 56*

* "Flying" or leaping through air

TOP 10 HEAVIEST MARINE MAMMALS

MAMMAL / LENGTH (FT / M) / WEIGHT (TONS)

1 **Blue whale**
(*Balaenoptera musculus*)
110.0 / 33.5   151.0

2 **Bowhead whale** (Greenland right) (*Balaena mysticetus*)
65.0 / 20.0   94.8

3 **Northern right whale** (black right) (*Balaena glacialis*)
60.0 / 18.6   85.6

4 **Fin whale** (common rorqual)
(*Balaenoptera physalus*)
82.0 / 25.0   69.9

5 **Sperm whale**
(*Physeter catodon*)
59.0 / 18.0   48.2

6 **Grey whale**
(*Eschrichtius robustus*)
46.0 / 14.0   38.5

7 **Humpback whale**
(*Megaptera novaeangliae*)
49.2 / 15.0   38.1

8 **Sei whale**
(*Balaenoptera borealis*)
60.0 / 18.5   32.4

9 **Bryde's whale**
(*Balaenoptera edeni*)
47.9 / 14.6   22.0

10 **Baird's whale**
(*Berardius bairdii*)
18.0 / 5.1   13.3

EXTREME MARINE LIFE

One specimen of the ocean quahog mollusk caught in 2007 was found to have lived 405 years, while another had a recorded lifespan of 374 years. Octopuses seldom live longer than three years, with females often dying in their second year after breeding. Several fish have lifespans that are completed within a year, among them the white goby, top minnow, and seahorse.

TOP 10 HEAVIEST SALTWATER FISH CAUGHT

FISH / SCIENTIFIC NAME	ANGLER / LOCATION / DATE	LB	OZ	KG
1 Great white shark (Carcharodon carcharias)	Alfred Dean, Ceduna, South Australia, Apr 21, 1959	2,664	0	1,208.38
2 Tiger shark (Galeocerdo cuvier)	Kevin James Clapson, Ulladulla, Australia, Mar 28, 2004	1,785	1	809.981
3 Greenland shark (Somniosus Microcephalus)	Terje Nordtvedt, Trondheimsfjord, Norway, Oct 18, 1987	1,708	9	774.99
4 Black marlin (Istiompax marlina)	Alfred C. Glassell, Jr., Cabo Blanco, Peru, Aug 4, 1953	1,560	0	707.61
5 Bluefin tuna (Thunnus thynnus)	Ken Fraser, Aulds Cove, Nova Scotia, Canada, Oct 26, 1979	1,496	0	678.58
6 Atlantic blue marlin (Makaira nigricans)	Paulo Amorim, Vitoria, Brazil Feb 29, 1992	1,402	2	636.99
7 Pacific blue marlin (Makaira nigricans)	Jay W. de Beaubien, Kaaiwi Point, Kona, Hawaii, USA, May 31, 1982	1,376	0	624.14
8 Six-gilled shark (Hexanchus griseus)	Clemens Rump, Ascension Island, Nov 21, 2002	1,298	0	588.76
9 Great hammerhead shark (Sphyrna mokarran)	Bucky Dennis, Boca Grande, Florida, USA, May 23, 2006	1,280	0	580.60
10 Shortfin mako shark (Isurus oxyrinchus)	Luke Sweeney, Chatham, Massachusetts, USA, Jul 21, 2001	1,221	0	553.84

Source: International Game Fish Association

◄ **Great bite**
The great white shark's powerful tail helps it move through the water at up to 15 mph.

THE HEAVIEST TURTLES

Average sizes and longevity of Chelonia (turtles and tortoises) remain debated by zoologists, with many extreme claims among the 265 species. The largest are marine turtles, and the Aldabra giant tortoises, found on an atoll in the Seychelles, who are the largest land-dwellers—and probably the longest-lived land creatures of all. All living examples would be dwarfed in size by prehistoric monster turtles such as *Stupendemys geographicus*, which measured up to 10 ft (3 m) in length and weighed over 4,497 lb (2,040 kg).

► **Alligator snapping turtle**
This freshwater species has an average weight of 175 lb (80 kg).

BIRD LIFE

▶ **Weighty bird**
Andean condors are so heavy that they need their huge wingspan to stay aloft.

TOP 10 **LARGEST BIRDS OF PREY***

BIRD / SCIENTIFIC NAME	MAX. LENGTH	
	IN	CM
1 Himalayan griffon vulture (*Gyps himalayensis*)	59	150
2 Californian condor (*Gymnogyps californianus*)	53	134
3 Andean condor (*Vultur gryphus*)	51	130
4 =Lammergeier (*Gypaetus barbatus*)	45	115
=Lappet-faced vulture (*Torgos tracheliotus*)	45	115
6 Eurasian griffon vulture (*Gyps fulvus*)	43	110
7 Eurasian black vulture (*Aegypus monachus*)	42	107
8 Harpy eagle (*Harpia harpyja*)	41	105
9 Wedge-tailed eagle (*Aquila audax*)	41	104
10 Ruppell's griffon (*Gyps rueppellii*)	40	101

* By length, diurnal only (hence excluding owls)

TOP 10 **FASTEST BIRDS**

BIRD / SCIENTIFIC NAME	MAX. RECORDED SPEED	
	MPH	KM/H
1 Grey-headed albatross (*Thalassarche chrysostama*)	80	127
2 Common eider (*Somateria mollissima*)	47	76
3 Bewick's swan (*Cygnus columbianus*)	45	72
4 =Barnacle goose (*Branta leucopsis*)	42	68
=Common crane (*Grus grus*)	42	68
6 Red-throated loon (*Anas platyrhynchos*)	40	65
7 =Red-throated diver (*Gavia stellata*)	38	61
=Wood pigeon (*Columba palumbus*)	38	61
9 Oystercatcher (*Haematopus ostralegus*)	36	58
10 =Ring-necked pheasant (*Phasianus colchichus*)	33	54
=White-fronted goose (*Anser albifrons*)	33	54

TOP 10 **LONGEST BIRD MIGRATIONS**

BIRD / SCIENTIFIC NAME	APPROX. DISTANCE	
	MILES	KM
1 Pectoral sandpiper (*Calidris melanotos*)	11,806	19,000*
2 Wheatear (*Oenanthe oenanthe*)	11,184	18,000
3 Slender-billed shearwater (*Puffinus tenuirostris*)	10,874	17,500*
4 Ruff (*Philomachus pugnax*)	10,314	16,600
5 Willow warbler (*Phylloscopus trochilus*)	10,128	16,300
6 Arctic tern (*Sterna paradisaea*)	10,066	16,200
7 Parasitic jaeger (*Stercorarius parasiticus*)	9,693	15,600
8 Swainson's hawk (*Buteo swainsoni*)	9,445	15,200
9 Knot (*Calidris canutus*)	9,320	15,000
10 Barn swallow (*Hirundo rustica*)	9,258	14,900

* Thought to be only half of the path taken during a whole year

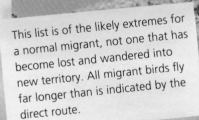

This list is of the likely extremes for a normal migrant, not one that has become lost and wandered into new territory. All migrant birds fly far longer than is indicated by the direct route.

▲ **Global traveler**
The male pectoral sandpiper has an inflatable throat sac that expands and contracts in flight, making a hollow hooting noise.

▲ **Bewick's swans**
One of the speediest birds in flight, each Bewick's swan has a unique bill pattern.

TOP 10 **BIRDS WITH THE LARGEST WINGSPANS**

BIRD*	MAX. WINGSPAN	
	IN	CM
1 Wandering albatross# (*Diomedea exulans*)	146	370
2 Great white pelican (*Pelecanus onocrotalus*)	141	360
3 Andean condor (*Vultur gryphus*)	126	320
4 Himalayan griffon vulture (*Gyps himalayensis*)	122	310
5 Eurasian black vulture (*Aegypius monachus*)	116	295
6 Marabou stork (*Leptoptilos crumeniferus*)	113	287
7 Lammergeier (*Gypaetus barbatus*)	111	282
8 Sarus crane (*Grus antigone*)	110	280
9 Kori bustard (*Ardeotis kori*)	106	270
10 Steller's sea eagle (*Haliaeetus pelagicus*)	104	265

* By species
\# The royal albatross, a close relative, is the same size

▼ *Sky wanderer*
Wandering albatrosses can live for up to 50 years and are rarely seen on land.

Extinct birds with wingspans twice as large as extant species may have been gliders and not flapping flight exponents, while some of them may have existed at times when the density of the atmosphere was higher than at present.

HEAVIEST FLIGHTLESS BIRD

The heaviest flightless bird, the ostrich, rarely needs to drink as it extracts moisture from vegetation and makes water internally by oxidizing substances in its food.

TOP 10 **HEAVIEST FLIGHTED BIRDS**

	BIRD* / SCIENTIFIC NAME	WINGSPAN		WEIGHT		
		IN	CM	LB	OZ	KG
1	Mute swan (*Cygnus olor*)	93.7	238	49	6	22.50
2	Kori bustard (*Ardeotis kori*)	106.3	270	41	8	19.00
3	= Andean condor (*Vultur gryphus*)	126.0	320	33	1	15.00
	= Great white pelican (*Pelecanus onocrotalus*)	141.7	360	33	1	15.00
5	Eurasian black vulture (*Aegypius monachus*)	116.1	295	27	5	12.50
6	Sarus crane (*Grus antigone*)	110.2	280	26	9	12.24
7	Himalayan griffon vulture (*Gyps himalayensis*)	122.0	310	26	5	12.00
8	Wandering albatross (*Diomedea exulans*)	137.8	350	24	9	11.30
9	Steller's sea eagle (*Haliaeetus pelagicus*)	104.3	265	19	8	9.00
10	Marabou stork (*Leptoptilos crumeniferus*)	113.0	287	19	6	8.90

* By species

◄ *Kori bustard*
Despite their heft, the feet of these birds are well-adapted for running.

REPTILES & AMPHIBIANS

TOP 10 COUNTRIES WITH THE MOST AMPHIBIAN SPECIES

COUNTRY / AMPHIBIAN SPECIES

1 Brazil 885

2 Colombia 747

3 Ecuador 503

4 Peru 491

5 China 368

6 Mexico 365

7 Venezuela 343

8 Indonesia 326

9 Papua New Guinea 323

10 USA 296

Source (all lists): World Conservation Monitoring Centre of the United Nations Environment Programme (UNEP-WCMC)

▲ **Brazilian tree-dweller**
The tiger-legged monkey frog is found in several South American countries, including Brazil and Colombia.

TOP 10 FROGS AND TOADS WITH THE LARGEST CLUTCH SIZES*

	SPECIES / SCIENTIFIC NAME	EGG SIZE (MM)	AVERAGE NO. OF EGGS IN CLUTCH
1	River frog (*Rana fuscigula*)	1.50	15,000
2	Crawfish frog (*Rana areolata*)	1.84	6,000
3	Gulf Coast toad (*Bufo valliceps*)	1.23	4,100
4	Bahia forest frog (*Macrogenioglottus alipioi*)	1.50	3,650
5	Giant African bullfrog (*Pyxicephalus adspersus*)	2.00	3,500
6	Marbled or veined tree frog (*Phrynohyas venulosa*)	1.60	2,920
7	Mangrove or crab-eating frog (*Rana cancrivora*)	1.25	2,527
8	Cape sand frog (*Tomopterna delalandii*)	1.50	2,500
9	Gladiator frog (*Hyla rosenbergi*)	1.95	2,350
10 =	Wood frog (*Rana sylvatica*)	1.90	1,750
=	Yosemite toad (*Bufo canorus*)	2.00	1,750

* For which data available; all eggs and larvae aquatic

TOP 10 LARGEST REPTILE FAMILIES

	FAMILY	KNOWN SPECIES
1	Colubridae (snakes)	1,747
2	Scincidae (skinks)	1,496
3	Gekkonidae (geckos)	874
4	Polychrotidae (anole lizards)	418
5	Agamidae (lizards)	411
6	Tropiduridae (lizards)	392
7	Typhlopidae (blind snakes)	383
8	Lacertidae (true lizards)	305
9	Viperidae (viperid snakes)	297
10	Gymnophthalmidae (spectacled lizards)	230

▶ **Adaptable reptile**
There are approximately 160 species of chameleon found in habitats varying from rainforests to deserts.

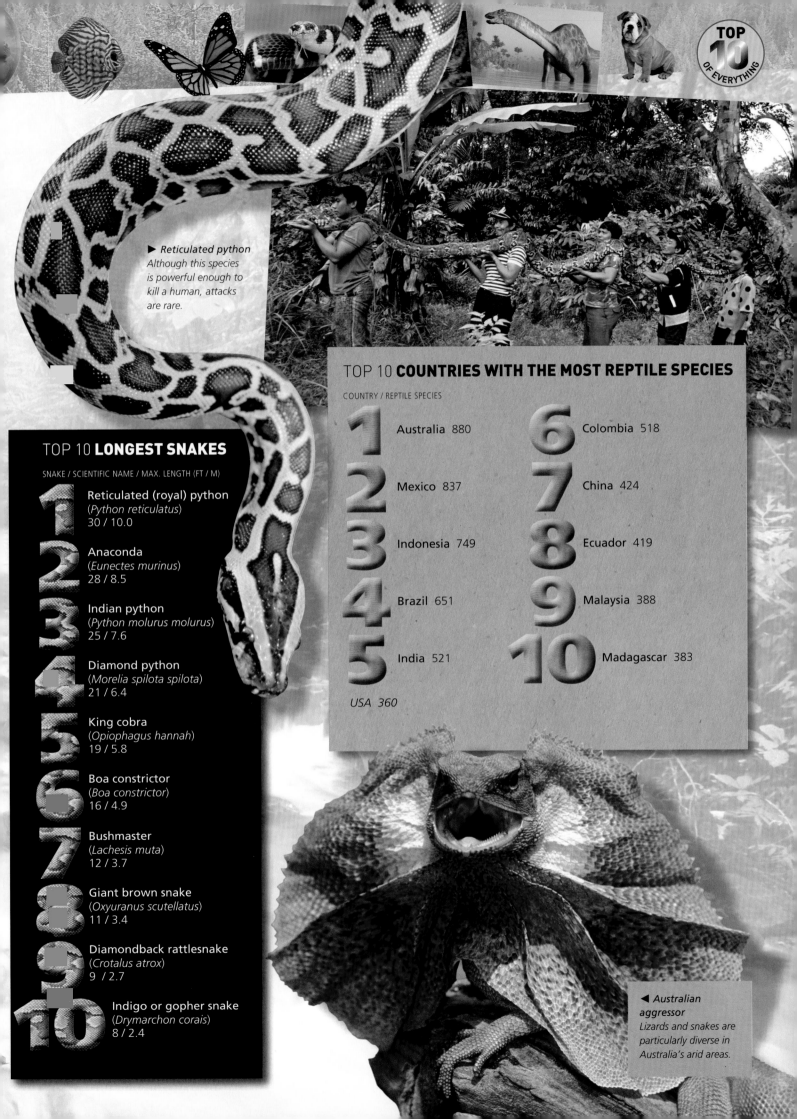

▶ **Reticulated python**
Although this species is powerful enough to kill a human, attacks are rare.

TOP 10 **LONGEST SNAKES**

SNAKE / SCIENTIFIC NAME / MAX. LENGTH (FT / M)

1 Reticulated (royal) python
(*Python reticulatus*)
30 / 10.0

2 Anaconda
(*Eunectes murinus*)
28 / 8.5

3 Indian python
(*Python molurus molurus*)
25 / 7.6

4 Diamond python
(*Morelia spilota spilota*)
21 / 6.4

5 King cobra
(*Opiophagus hannah*)
19 / 5.8

6 Boa constrictor
(*Boa constrictor*)
16 / 4.9

7 Bushmaster
(*Lachesis muta*)
12 / 3.7

8 Giant brown snake
(*Oxyuranus scutellatus*)
11 / 3.4

9 Diamondback rattlesnake
(*Crotalus atrox*)
9 / 2.7

10 Indigo or gopher snake
(*Drymarchon corais*)
8 / 2.4

TOP 10 **COUNTRIES WITH THE MOST REPTILE SPECIES**

COUNTRY / REPTILE SPECIES

1 Australia 880

2 Mexico 837

3 Indonesia 749

4 Brazil 651

5 India 521

USA 360

6 Colombia 518

7 China 424

8 Ecuador 419

9 Malaysia 388

10 Madagascar 383

◀ **Australian aggressor**
Lizards and snakes are particularly diverse in Australia's arid areas.

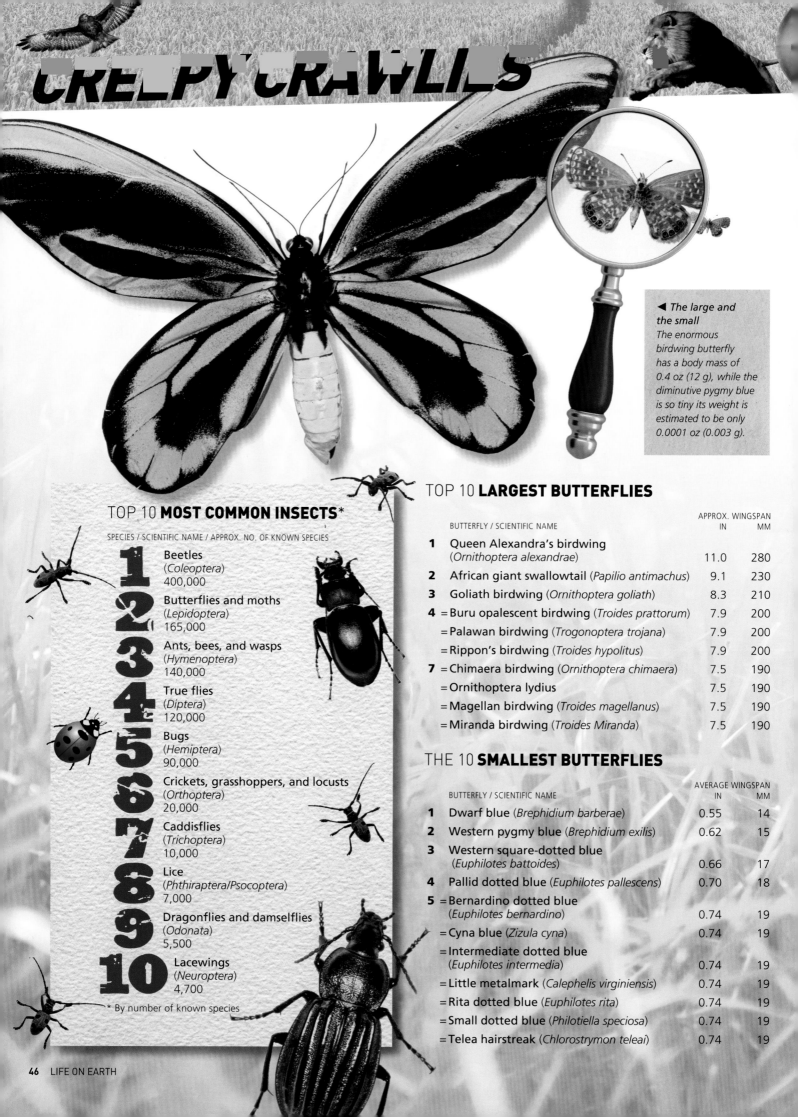

◀ **The large and the small**
The enormous birdwing butterfly has a body mass of 0.4 oz (12 g), while the diminutive pygmy blue is so tiny its weight is estimated to be only 0.0001 oz (0.003 g).

TOP 10 **MOST COMMON INSECTS***

SPECIES / SCIENTIFIC NAME / APPROX. NO. OF KNOWN SPECIES

1 Beetles
(*Coleoptera*)
400,000

2 Butterflies and moths
(*Lepidoptera*)
165,000

3 Ants, bees, and wasps
(*Hymenoptera*)
140,000

4 True flies
(*Diptera*)
120,000

5 Bugs
(*Hemiptera*)
90,000

6 Crickets, grasshoppers, and locusts
(*Orthoptera*)
20,000

7 Caddisflies
(*Trichoptera*)
10,000

8 Lice
(*Phthiraptera/Psocoptera*)
7,000

9 Dragonflies and damselflies
(*Odonata*)
5,500

10 Lacewings
(*Neuroptera*)
4,700

* By number of known species

TOP 10 **LARGEST BUTTERFLIES**

BUTTERFLY / SCIENTIFIC NAME	APPROX. WINGSPAN IN	MM
1 Queen Alexandra's birdwing (*Ornithoptera alexandrae*)	11.0	280
2 African giant swallowtail (*Papilio antimachus*)	9.1	230
3 Goliath birdwing (*Ornithoptera goliath*)	8.3	210
4 =Buru opalescent birdwing (*Troides prattorum*)	7.9	200
=Palawan birdwing (*Trogonoptera trojana*)	7.9	200
=Rippon's birdwing (*Troides hypolitus*)	7.9	200
7 =Chimaera birdwing (*Ornithoptera chimaera*)	7.5	190
=Ornithoptera lydius	7.5	190
=Magellan birdwing (*Troides magellanus*)	7.5	190
=Miranda birdwing (*Troides Miranda*)	7.5	190

THE 10 **SMALLEST BUTTERFLIES**

BUTTERFLY / SCIENTIFIC NAME	AVERAGE WINGSPAN IN	MM
1 Dwarf blue (*Brephidium barberae*)	0.55	14
2 Western pygmy blue (*Brephidium exilis*)	0.62	15
3 Western square-dotted blue (*Euphilotes battoides*)	0.66	17
4 Pallid dotted blue (*Euphilotes pallescens*)	0.70	18
5 =Bernardino dotted blue (*Euphilotes bernardino*)	0.74	19
=Cyna blue (*Zizula cyna*)	0.74	19
=Intermediate dotted blue (*Euphilotes intermedia*)	0.74	19
=Little metalmark (*Calephelis virginiensis*)	0.74	19
=Rita dotted blue (*Euphilotes rita*)	0.74	19
=Small dotted blue (*Philotiella speciosa*)	0.74	19
=Telea hairstreak (*Chlorostrymon teleai*)	0.74	19

TOP 10 **LARGEST SPIDERS**

SPECIES / LEG SPAN (IN / MM)

1 Huntsman spider
(*Heteropoda maxima*)
11.8 / 300

▶ *Huge hunter*
Common throughout
Southeast Asia and
the Caribbean, this
giant spider feeds
on cockroaches.

2 Goliath tarantula or bird-eating spider
(*Theraphosa blondi*)
11.0 / 279

3 Brazilian salmon pink
(*Lasiodora parahybana*)
10.6 / 270

4 Brazilian giant tawny red
(*Grammostola mollicoma*)
10.2 / 260

5 Wolf spider
(*Cupiennius sallei*)
10.0 / 254

6 = Purple bloom bird-eating
(*Xenesthis immanis*)
9.1 / 230

= *Xenesthis monstrosa*
9.1 / 230

8 Hercules baboon
(*Hysterocrates hercules*)
8.0 / 203

9 *Hysterocrates sp.*
7.0 / 178

10 *Tegenaria parietin*
5.5 / 140

It should be noted that although these represent the average leg spans of the world's largest spiders, their body size is often considerably smaller: that of the *Lasiodora*, found in Brazil, is around 3.6 in (92 mm), while that of the *Tegenaris parietina*, the largest spider found in Britain, may measure as little as 0.7 in (18 mm).

IMAGINE—THIS SPIDER IS AS LARGE AS THE DEPTH OF THIS PAGE!

TOP 10 **FASTEST INSECT FLYERS**

SPECIES* / SCIENTIFIC NAME / MAX. RECORDED SPEED (MPH / KM/H)

1 Hawkmoth (*Sphingidae*) 33.3 / 53.6
2 = Deer bot fly (*Cephenemyia pratti*) 30.0 / 48.0
2 = West Indian butterfly (*Nymphalidae prepona*) 30.0 / 48.0
4 Deer bot fly (*Chrysops*) 25.0 / 40.0
5 West Indian butterfly (*Hesperiidae* sp.) 18.6 / 30.0
6 Lesser emperor dragonfly (*Anax parthenope*) 17.8 / 28.6
7 = Dragonfly (*Aeschna*) 15.6 / 25.2
7 = Hornet (*Vespa*) 15.6 / 25.2
9 = Honey bee (*Apis millefera*) 13.9 / 22.4
9 = Horsefly (*Tabanus bovinus*) 13.9 / 22.4

▼ *Deer bot fly*
So called because
they attack the
nostrils of deer.

* Of those for which data is available

DEADLIEST ANIMALS

THE 10 **MOST VENOMOUS REPTILES AND AMPHIBIANS**

CREATURE* / TOXIN		FATAL AMOUNT (MG)#
1 Indian cobra — Peak V		0.009
2 Mamba — Toxin 1		0.02
3 Brown snake — Texilotoxin		0.05
4 = Inland taipan — Paradotoxin / = Mamba — Dendrotoxin		0.10
6 Taipan — Taipoxin		0.11
7 = Indian cobra — Peak X / = Poison arrow frog — Batrachotoxin		0.12
9 Indian cobra — Peak 1X		0.17
10 Krait — Bungarotoxin		0.50

* Excluding bacteria
\# Quantity required to kill an average-sized human adult

The venom of these creatures is almost unbelievably powerful: 1 mg (the approximate weight of a banknote) of Mamba Toxin 1 would be sufficient to kill 50 people. Other than reptiles, such creatures as scorpions (0.5 mg) and black widow spiders (1.0 mg) fall just outside the Top 10. Were bacteria included, 12 kg of the deadly Botulinus Toxin A (fatal dose just 0.000002 mg) would easily kill the entire population of the world. Even deadly poisons such as strychnine (35 mg) and cyanide (700 mg), seem relatively innocuous in comparison.

SNAKE BITE

Tens of thousands of people die from snake bites each year, with numbers varying greatly by geographical area. First-aid methods also vary depending on the types of snake and venom, but most guidelines advise that sucking out the venom by mouth does not work. Cutting open the bitten area is also not advised, since it can increase the risk of infection. The American Red Cross advises that the most important things to do are to keep calm, protect the victim and others from further bites, and call for medical help or get to a hospital without delay. Do not elevate the affected area or give the person anything to eat or drink, but do remove any restrictive clothing or jewelry and keep the person as still as possible.

▲ *Mamba*
A tiny dose of mamba toxin could kill a room full of people.

◄ *Poison arrow frog*
The venom from these frogs is excreted through their skin.

◄ *Deathly dance*
The Indian cobra's bite can be fatal within two hours, causing paralysis, respiratory failure, and cardiac arrest.

TOP 5 SHARK-ATTACK HOTSPOTS

LOCATION	FATAL ATTACKS	LAST FATAL ATTACK	TOTAL ATTACKS*
1 USA (excl. Hawaii)	36	2010	947
2 Australia	131	2010	417
3 South Africa	47	2010	223
4 Hawaii	8	2004	102
5 Brazil	21	2006	88

* Confirmed unprovoked attacks, including non-fatal, 1580–2010

Source: *International Shark Attack File*/American Elasmobranch Society/Florida Museum of Natural History

According to the ISAF, the average person's risk of death by shark attack is 1 in 3,748,067. In the USA, the annual risk of death from lightning is 30 times greater than that from shark attack. Between 1959 and 2010, there were 1,970 deaths by lightning in coastal USA, compared to 26 shark-attack fatalities in the same area.

KILLER SHARKS

The International Shark Attack File (ISAF) monitors worldwide incidents and has records dating back to the late 16th century. From 1580 to early 2011, the ISAF has recorded a worldwide total of 2,340 unprovoked shark attacks, 447 of which were fatal. There has been a marked increase in unprovoked attacks since the early 1990s, reflecting the increase in people engaging in scuba diving and other aquatic activities, and the increasing amount of time humans spend in the sea, rather than any observed increase in the aggressive instincts of sharks. In 2010 there were 79 unprovoked attacks and six fatalities—the highest number of attacks since 2000, and a slightly higher total of deaths from recent years (the average for the decade was 4.3 fatalities per year).

▲ *Jaws*
Despite their fearsome reputation, death by shark attack is relatively rare.

SMALL BUT DEADLY

Although deaths by shark, snake, and bear attacks tend to grab the headlines, one of the animal kingdom's greatest threats to the human population is its most tiny: the mosquito. By spreading the disease malaria, mosquitoes are responsible for more than 1 million deaths each year. No other animal comes to close to the number killed by mosquitoes, but the box jellyfish is another less obvious killer, with enough toxin in each tentacle to kill 50 humans.

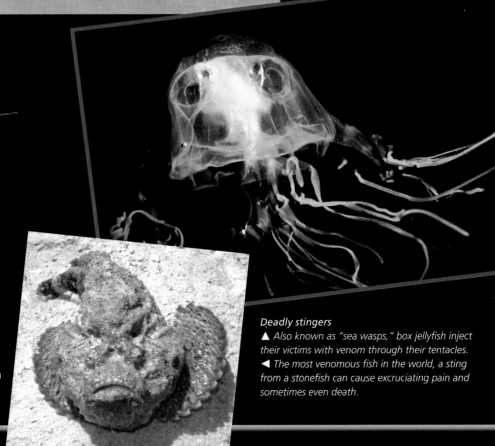

Deadly stingers
▲ *Also known as "sea wasps," box jellyfish inject their victims with venom through their tentacles.*
◄ *The most venomous fish in the world, a sting from a stonefish can cause excruciating pain and sometimes even death.*

PETS

◄ **Prickly pet**
Originally from Mexico, the tiny Chihuahua can have a hot temper.

▲ **Bright spark**
An Alsatian puppy will grow up to become an intelligent and loyal pet.

THE 10 **MOST AGGRESSIVE** DOG BREEDS

BREED

1 Dachshund

2 Chihuahua

3 Jack russell terrier

4 Akita

5 Australian cattle dog

6 Pit bull

7 Beagle

8 English springer spaniel

9 Border collie

10 German shepherd

The ranking is based on a survey of 33 dog breeds and the experiences of 6,000 dog owners conducted by researchers at the University of Pennsylvania.

TOP 10 **PEDIGREE DOG** BREEDS IN THE USA

BREED

1 Labrador retriever

2 German shepherd

3 Yorkshire terrier

4 Beagle 10,364

5 Golden retriever

6 Bulldog

7 Boxer

8 Dachshund

9 Poodle

10 Shih Tzu

Source: The American Kennel Club

TOP 10 **DOG NAMES** IN THE USA

MALE / FEMALE

1 Bear / Lady

2 Blue / Belle

3 Max / Princess

4 Duke / Mae

5 Buddy / Rose

6 Jack / Daisy

7 Prince / Grace

8 King / Baby

9 Bailey / Molly

10 Tocky / Maggie

Source: American Kennel Club

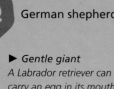

► **Gentle giant**
A Labrador retriever can carry an egg in its mouth without breaking it.

50

TOP 10 **CAT NAMES IN THE USA**

1	2	3	4	5
Max	Chloe	Bella	Oliver	Tiger

6	7	8	9	10
Smokey	Tigger	Lucy	Shadow	Angel

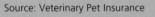

Source: Veterinary Pet Insurance

TOP 10 **PEDIGREE CAT BREEDS IN THE USA**

BREED

1 Persian
2 Maine coon
3 Exotic
4 Ragdoll
5 Sphynx
6 Siamese
7 Abyssinian
8 American shorthair
9 Cornish rex
10 Birman

Source: The Cat Fanciers' Association

TOP 10 **TYPES OF PET IN THE USA***

PET / ESTIMATED NO.

1 Cat
78,350,000

2 Dog
61,340,000

3 Small animal pets*
12,740,000

4 Parakeet
11,000,000

5 Freshwater fish
10,800,000#

6 Reptile
7,540,000

7 Finch
7,350,000

8 Cockatiel
6,320,000

9 Canary
2,580,000

10 Parrot
1,550,000

* Includes small rodents (rabbits, ferrets, hamsters, guinea pigs, and gerbils)
# No. of households owning, rather than individual specimens

◀ *True blue*
Distinguished by their piercing eyes, Ragdoll cats have silky coats and a friendly, docile nature.

LIVESTOCK & FARMING

TOP 10 NON-FOOD CROPS

CROP	PRODUCTION (TONS)*
1 Cotton	67,121,495
2 Rubber	11,267,038
3 Coffee	9,196,182
4 Tobacco	7,928,933
5 Tea	4,354,182
6 Jute	3,253,667
7 Linseed	2,340,922
8 Castor oil seed	1,635,925
9 Coir	1,220,170
10 Flax	504,758

* Latest year for which data available

▲ **Popular pigs**
Pork accounts for more than half the meat eaten in China.

TOP 10 PIG COUNTRIES

COUNTRY	PIGS*
1 China	450,880,000
2 USA	67,148,000
3 Brazil	38,045,200
4 Vietnam	27,627,700
5 Germany	26,886,500
6 Spain	26,289,600
7 Russia	16,161,860
8 Mexico	15,200,000
9 France	14,810,000
10 Poland	14,278,647
World total	941,776,122

* Latest year and countries for which data available

Source (all lists): Food and Agriculture Organization of the United Nations

TOP 10 TYPES OF LIVESTOCK

ANIMAL / WORLD STOCKS*

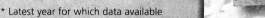

1
Chickens
18,631,409,000

* Latest year for which data available

2
Cattle
1,380,220,841

3
Ducks
1,175,595,000

4
Sheep
1,077,267,081

TOP 10 **VEGETABLE-PRODUCING COUNTRIES***

COUNTRY / PRODUCTION (TONS)

1 China 576,123,979

2 India 102,262,666

3 USA 41,702,117

4 Turkey 29,413,001

5 Egypt 22,340,390

6 Iran 19,963,882

7 Russia 16,344,036

8 Italy 15,639,042

9 Spain 14,789,292

10 Japan 11,547,563

World total 1,114,945,732

* Including watermelons; only vegetables grown for human consumption, excluding crops from private gardens

▲ *A fine flock*
Sheep are farmed in India for milk, meat, and wool.

TOP 10 **SHEEP COUNTRIES**

COUNTRY	SHEEP*
1 China	128,557,213
2 Australia	72,739,700
3 India	65,717,000
4 Iran	53,800,000
5 Sudan	51,555,000
6 Nigeria	34,687,300
7 New Zealand	32,383,600
8 UK	32,038,000
9 Pakistan	27,432,000
10 Ethiopia	25,979,900
World total	*1,077,267,081*

* Latest year and countries for which data available

TOP 10 **CATTLE COUNTRIES**

COUNTRY	CATTLE*
1 Brazil	205,292,000
2 India	172,451,000
3 USA	94,521,000
4 China	84,116,951
5 Ethiopia	50,884,000
6 Argentina	50,750,000
7 Sudan	41,563,000
8 Pakistan	33,030,000
9 Mexico	32,000,000
10 Australia	27,906,800
World total	*1,380,220,841*

* Latest year and countries for which data available

THE 25,148,136,000 ANIMALS ACCOUNTED FOR BY THE TOP 10 OUTNUMBER THE WORLD'S HUMAN POPULATION BY NEARLY 4 to 1!

5 Pigs 941,776,122

6 Goats 879,744,635

7 Turkeys 458,039,000

8 Geese and guinea fowl 357,111,000

9 Buffaloes 187,918,488

10 Horses 59,054,839

FORESTS & TREES

TOP 10 **REFORESTING COUNTRIES**

COUNTRY /
ANNUAL FOREST GAIN 2000–10: 1,000 HA/YR* / %

 1 China
2,986 / 1.57%

 2 USA
383 / 0.13%

 3 India
304 / 0.46%

 4 Vietnam
207 / 1.64%

 5 = Turkey
119 / 1.11%

 = Spain
119 / 0.68%

 7 Sweden
81 / 0.29%

 8 Italy
78 / 0.90%

 9 Norway
76 / 0.79%

 10 France
60 / 0.38%

* Hectares per year

TOP 10 **LARGEST FORESTS IN THE USA**

FOREST* / LOCATION	SQ MILES	SQ KM
1 Tongass National Forest, Sitka, AK	25,913	67,114
2 Chugach National Forest, Anchorage, AK	8,433	21,841
3 Toiyabe National Forest, Sparks, NV	5,051	13,082
4 Tonto National Forest, Phoenix, AZ	4,489	11,626
5 Gila National Forest, Silver City, NM	4,232	10,961
6 Boise National Forest, Boise, ID	4,145	10,736
7 Humboldt National Forest, Elko, NV	3,878	10,044
8 Challis National Forest, Challis, ID	3,851	9,974
9 Shoshone National Forest, Cody, WY	3,808	9,863
10 Flathead National Forest, Kalispess, MT	3,682	9,536

Source: Land Areas of the National Forest System

TONGASS FOREST IS LARGER THAN ALL 10 OF THE SMALLEST STATES AND THE DISTRICT OF COLUMBIA!

TOP 10 **TALLEST TREES IN THE USA***

TREE	LOCATION	FT	M
1 Coast redwood (*Sequoia sempervirens*)	Jedediah Smith Redwoods State Park, CA	321	97.8
2 Coast douglas fir (*Pseudotsuga menziesii var menziesii*)	Jedediah Smith Redwoods State Park, CA	301	91.7
3 Giant sequoia (*Sequoiadendron giganteum*)	Sequoia National Park, CA	274	83.5
4 Noble fir (*Abies procera*)	Mt. St. Helens National Monument, WA	272	82.9
5 Grand fir (*Abies grandis*)	Redwood National Park, CA	257	78.3
6 Port Orford cedar (*Chamaecyparis lawsoniana*)	Siskiyou National Forest, OR	242	73.8
7 Ponderosa pine (*Pinus ponderosa var. ponderosa*)	Trinity, CA	240	73.2
8 Western hemlock (*Tsuga heterophylla*)	Olympic National Park, WA	237	72.2
9 Pacific silver fir (*Abies amabilis*)	Olympic National Park, WA	218	66.4
10 California white fir (*Abies concolor var. lowiana*)	Yosemite National Park, CA	217	66.1

* Tallest known example of each species

Source:
Food and
Agriculture
Organization
of the United
Nations,
*State of
the World's
Forests*

▶ **Tree trouble**
*More than half of Indonesia's
tropical forest areas have been
earmarked for timber production.*

TOP 10 **COUNTRIES WITH THE LARGEST AREAS OF TROPICAL FOREST**

COUNTRY / AREA (SQ MILES/SQ KM)

1	**2**	**3**	**4**	**5**	**6**	**7**	**8**	**9**	**10**
Brazil	Dem. Rep. of Congo	Indonesia	Peru	Bolivia	Venezuela	Colombia	Mexico	India	Angola
1,163,222	521,512	343,029	292,032	265,012	214,730	205,352	176,700	171,622	145,035
3,012,730	1,350,7105	887,440	756,360	686,380	556,150	531,860	457,650	444,500	375,640

▼ **Remote mangroves**
*Most of Australia's
mangroves lie on
its thinly populated
northern coast.*

TOP 10 **COUNTRIES WITH THE LARGEST AREAS OF MANGROVE**

COUNTRY	MANGROVE AREA (HECTARES)
1 Indonesia	3,062,300
2 Australia	1,451,411
3 Brazil	1,012,376
4 Nigeria	997,700
5 Mexico	882,032
6 Malaysia	564,971
7 Cuba	545,805
8 Myanmar	518,646
9 Bangladesh	476,215
10 India	446,100
Top 10 total	9,957,556
World total	15,705,000

Source: Food and Agriculture Organization
of the United Nations

A total of 124 countries have been identified
as having mangroves—species of trees and
shrubs that are specially adapted to growing
in saline coasts of tropical and subtropical
regions. A survey conducted in 1980 put the
global total mangrove area as 18.8 million
hectares, so over 3 million hectares have been
lost in the past 30 years.

3

THE HUMAN WORLD

50th ANNIVERSARY OF JFK'S ASSASSINATION

On Friday November 22, 1963, President Kennedy and his wife Jackie rode in a cavalcade in an open-top car through Dealey Plaza, Dallas, Texas. At 12.30 pm the president was shot in the head by an assassin—he died in hospital shortly afterward. The sight of Jackie Kennedy in a Chanel suit and pillar-box hat covered in blood, cradling her dying husband in her arms remains a heartrendingly sad and iconic image.

The news shocked the world and stunned the nation. Grown men wept and traffic came to a halt as word spread. Everyone over a certain age can remember where they were when they first heard the news, and the question "Where were you when Kennedy was shot?" became a global conversation topic. Opinion polls show that Kennedy remains the most popular president of the past 50 years.

Last journey: Kennedy and his wife Jackie smile at the crowds gathered in Dallas, moments before the president was shot.

BODY LANGUAGE

TOP 10 LONGEST BONES IN THE HUMAN BODY

BONE / AVERAGE LENGTH (IN / CM)

4 Humerus (upper arm) 14.35 / 36.46

7 7th rib 9.45 / 24.00

8 8th rib 9.06 / 23.00

10 Sternum (breastbone) 6.69 / 17.00

6 Radius (outer lower arm) 10.40 / 26.42

5 Ulna (inner lower arm) 11.10 / 28.20

9 Innominate bone (hipbone—half pelvis) 7.28 / 18.50

1 Femur (thighbone—upper leg) 19.88 / 50.50

2 Tibia (shinbone—inner lower leg) 16.94 / 43.03

3 Fibula (outer lower leg) 15.94 / 40.50

These are average dimensions of the bones of an adult male measured from their extremities (ribs are curved, and the pelvis measurement is taken diagonally). The same bones in the female skeleton are usually 6–13% smaller, with the exception of the sternum, which is virtually identical.

▲ **The stuff of life**
Oxygen finds its way into the body via red blood cells.

THE 10 MOST COMMON ELEMENTS IN THE HUMAN BODY

	ELEMENT	SYMBOL	AVERAGE ADULT* TOTAL OZ	G
1	Oxygen#	O	1,721	48,800
2	Carbon	C	649	18,400
3	Hydrogen#	H	282	8,000
4	Nitrogen	N	73	2,080
5	Calcium	Ca	39.5	1,120
6	Phosphorus	P	31.0	880
7	= Potassium	K	5.6	160
	= Sulfur	S	5.6	160
9	Sodium	Na	4.0	112
10	Chlorine	Cl	3.4	96

* 80 kg male
# Mostly combined as water

The Top 10 elements account for more than 99% of the total, the balance comprising minute quantities of metallic elements including iron—enough (0.17 oz/4.8 g) to make a 6-in (15-cm) nail—as well as zinc, tin, and aluminum.

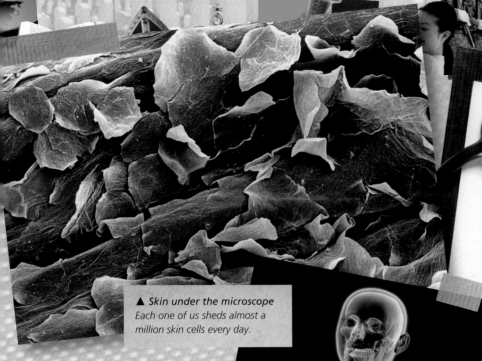

▲ Skin under the microscope
Each one of us sheds almost a million skin cells every day.

TOP 10 **LARGEST HUMAN ORGANS**

	ORGAN		AVERAGE WEIGHT	
			OZ	G
1	Skin		384.0	10,886
2	Liver		55.0	1,560
3	Brain	male	49.7	1,408
		female	44.6	1,263
4	Lungs	right	20.5	580
		left	18.0	510
		total	38.5	1,090
5	Heart	male	11.1	315
		female	9.3	265
6	Kidneys	right	4.9	140
		left	5.3	150
		total	10.2	290
7	Spleen		6.0	170
8	Pancreas		3.5	98
9	Thyroid		1.2	35
10	Prostate	male only	0.7	20

This list is based on average immediate post-mortem weights, recorded during a 10-year period. According to some definitions, the skin may be considered an organ, and at 16% of a body's total weight, it heads the Top 10.

THE 10 **MOST OBESE COUNTRIES (ADULTS)**

COUNTRY / % OF OBESE ADULTS* (MEN / WOMEN)

Nauru
84.6% / 80.5%

Tonga
64.0% / 78.1%

Micronesia
69.1% / 75.3%

Cook Islands
72.1% / 73.4%

Niue
40.7% / 64.7%

Samoa
42.2% / 60.9%

Palau
35.0% / 59.4%

Barbados
22.0% / 57.2%

Kuwait
29.6% / 55.2%

Trinidad and Tobago
19.1% / 52.7%

*Ranked by estimated percentage of obese women (those with a BMI greater than 30) aged 15–100 in those countries for which data available

Source: World Health Organization

◄ Vital organ
The liver cleans the blood of toxins and helps with digestion.

TOP 10 **COSMETIC SURGERY PROCEDURES IN THE USA**

	PROCEDURE	NO. PERFORMED*
1	Breast augmentation	318,123
2	Liposuction	289,016
3	Cosmetic eyelid surgery	152,123
4	Tummy tuck	144,929
5	Breast reduction (women)	138,152
6	Rhinoplasty	133,511
7	Facelift	127,512
8	Breast lift	121,377
9	Autologous fat	53,840
10	Forehead lift	26,514

* Latest year for which data available

Source: American Society for Aesthetic Plastic Surgery

LIFE & DEATH

▲ Long life
Japan's Jiroemon Kimura is the last known 19th-century survivor.

TOP 10 REGIONS WITH THE HIGHEST LIFE EXPECTANCY, 2013

	COUNTRY	LIFE EXPECTANCY AT BIRTH
1	Monaco	90
2 =	Japan	84
=	Singapore	84
4 =	San Marino	83
=	Andorra	83
6 =	Australia	82
=	Canada	82
=	Jersey and Guernsey	82
=	Hong Kong	82
10 =	France	81
=	Iceland	81
=	New Zealand	81
=	The Netherlands	81
=	Sweden	81
=	Switzerland	81

Source: US Census Bureau, *International Data Base*

THE 10 COUNTRIES WITH THE LOWEST BIRTH RATE

	COUNTRY	ESTIMATED BIRTH RATE*
1	Monaco	7
2 =	Germany	8
=	Japan	8
=	Singapore	8
=	South Korea	8
6 =	Austria	9
=	Bosnia and Herzegovina	9
=	Czech Republic	9
=	Italy	9
=	Slovenia	9
=	Taiwan	9
	USA	14

* Live births per 1,000, 2013

Source: US Census Bureau, *International Data Base*

THE 10 COUNTRIES WITH THE MOST BIRTHS

COUNTRY / ESTIMATED BIRTHS, 2013

1 India
24,709,000

2 China
16,535,000

3 Nigeria
6,767,000

4 Pakistan
4,591,000

5 Indonesia
4,371,000

6 USA
4,326,000

7 Ethiopia
4,086,000

8 Bangladesh
3,612,000

9 Brazil
3,535,000

10 Dem. Rep. of Congo
2,922,000

Source: US Census Bureau, *International Data Base*

▲ Baby boom
India's birth rate could make it the world's most populous country by 2030.

THE 10 **COUNTRIES WITH THE MOST DEATHS**

	COUNTRY	ESTIMATED DEATHS, 2013
1	China	9,865,000
2	India	9,022,000
3	USA	2,657,000
4	Nigeria	2,303,000
5	Russia	2,203,000
6	Indonesia	1,580,000
7	Brazil	1,329,000
8	Japan	1,180,000
9	Pakistan	1,293,000
10	Ethiopia	1,022,000

Source: US Census Bureau, *International Data Base*

▲ **Ritual fire**
The ritual burning of paper wreaths at gravesides is common in China.

▶ **A troubled country**
Drought and poor healthcare mean a shorter life for many in Chad.

THE 10 **COUNTRIES WITH THE LOWEST LIFE EXPECTANCY, 2013**

	COUNTRY	LIFE EXPECTANCY AT BIRTH
1	= Chad	49
	= South Africa	49
3	= Afghanistan	50
	= Guinea-Bissau	50
5	= Central African Republic	51
	= Somalia	51
7	= Namibia	52
	= Nigeria	52
	= Mozambique	52
10	= Tanzania	53
	= Zambia	53

PEOPLE IN THESE COUNTRIES LIVE AROUND 30 YEARS LESS THAN THOSE IN THE HIGHEST-RANKED COUNTRIES.

THE 10 **MOST COMMON CAUSES OF DEATH WORLDWIDE**

CAUSE / APPROX NO. OF DEATHS

1 Ischaemic heart disease
7,250,000

2 Cerebrovascular disease
6,150,000

3 Lower respiratory infections
3,460,000

4 Chronic obstructive pulmonary disease
3,280,000

5 Diarrheal diseases
2,460,000

6 HIV/AIDS
1,780,000

7 Trachea, bronchus, lung cancers
1,390,000

8 Tuberculosis
1,340,000

9 Diabetes mellitus
1,260,000

10 Road traffic accidents
1,210,000

Source: World Health Organization

THE 10 FIRST ROMAN EMPERORS

	EMPEROR	FATE	BORN	ACCEDED	DIED
1	Julius Caesar	Assassinated	100 BC	Oct 49 BC	Mar 15, 44 BC
2	Augustus	Died	63 BC	Jan 16, 27 BC	Aug 19, AD 14
3	Tiberius	Died	42 BC	Sep 18, AD 14	Mar 16, AD 37
4	Caligula	Assassinated	AD 12	Mar 16, AD 37	Jan 24, AD 41
5	Claudius	Assassinated	10 BC	Jan 24, AD 41	Oct 13, AD 54
6	Nero	Suicide	AD 37	Oct 13, AD 54	Jun 9, AD 68
7	Galba	Assassinated	3 BC	Jun 8, AD 68	Jan 15, AD 69
8	Otho	Suicide	AD 32	Jan 15, AD 69	Apr 16, AD 69
9	Vitellius	Assassinated	AD 15	Apr 16, AD 69	Dec 22, AD 69
10	Vespasian	Died	AD 9	Jul 1, AD 69	Jun 23, AD 79

◀ *Augustus*
Rome's second emperor was the great-nephew of Julius Caesar.

Although regarded as one of the "Twelve Caesars," the first, Julius Caesar, did not rule as emperor; if he is excluded, Titus (born December 30, AD 40, ruled from AD 79, died September AD 81) becomes No. 10.

TOP 10 MONARCHIES WITH THE MOST SUBJECTS*

COUNTRY / MONARCH / ACCESSION / POPULATION, 2012

1 Britain#
Elizabeth II (1952)
134,833,000

2 Japan
Akihito (1989)
127,368,000

3 Thailand
Bhumibol Adulyadej (1946)
67,091,000

4 Spain
Juan Carlos I (1975)
47,043,000

5 Morocco
Mohammed VI (1999)
32,309,000

6 Nepal
Gyanendra Bir Bikram
Shah Dev (2001) 29,391,883

7 Malaysia
Mizan Zainal Abidin (2006)
29,180,000

8 Saudi Arabia
Abdullah (2005)
26,535,000

9 The Netherlands
Beatrix (1980)
16,731,000

10 Cambodia
Norodom Sihamoni (1999)
14,953,000

* By population
# Total of British Commonwealth realms with monarch as head of state

Source: US Census Bureau

▲ *Long to reign*
In May 2011, Elizabeth II became the second longest-reigning British monarch.

THE LATEST MONARCHS TO ASCEND THE THRONE

In December 2011, golf enthusiast and Frank Sinatra fan Abdul Halim Mu'adzam Shah came to the throne of Malaysia at the grand age of 84, under an unusual system in which the country's nine hereditary state rulers take it in turns to be king. Other recently arrived monarchs include Emir Sheikh Sabah al-Ahmad al-Sabah of Kuwait and King Jigme Khesar Namgyal Wangchuk of Bhutan, who both inherited their respective titles in the year 2006.

TOP 10 LONGEST-REIGNING MONARCHS OF ALL TIME

	MONARCH	COUNTRY	REIGN	AGE AT ACCESSION	REIGN YEARS
1	King Louis XIV	France	1643–1715	5	72
2	King John II	Liechtenstein	1858–1929	18	71
3	Emperor Franz-Josef	Austria-Hungary	1848–1916	18	67
4	King Bhumibol Adulyadej	Thailand	1946– *	18	65
5	Queen Victoria	UK	1837–1901	18	63
6	Emperor Hirohito	Japan	1926–89	25	62
7	Emperor K'ang Hsi	China	1661–1722	7	61
8 =	King Sobhuza II#	Swaziland	1921–1982	22	60
=	Emperor Ch'ien Lung	China	1735–1796	25	60
=	Queen Elizabeth II	UK	1952– *	25	60

* Still living
# Paramount chief until 1967, when Great Britain recognized him as king with the granting of internal self-government

IN CONTRAST WITH LOUIS XIV, SHORTEST-REIGNING MONARCH LOUIS XIX OF FRANCE WAS KING FOR JUST 20 MINUTES!

▲ *Vive le Roi*
Known as the Sun King, Louis XVI outlived his eldest son and grandson.

▶ *Faithful friend*
The Thai king Bhumibol Adulyadej has written a biography of his favorite dog, Thong Daeng.

TOP 10 LONGEST-REIGNING LIVING MONARCHS

	MONARCH	COUNTRY*	ACCESSION	YRS	REIGN# MTHS	DAYS
1	Bhumibol Adulyadej	Thailand	Jun 9, 1946	65	6	21
2	Elizabeth II	UK	Feb 6, 1952	59	10	25
3	Haji Hassanal Bolkiah	Brunei	Oct 5, 1967	44	2	26
4	Sayyid Qaboos ibn Said al-Said	Oman	Jul 23, 1970	41	5	7
5	Margrethe II	Denmark	Jan 14, 1972	39	11	17
6	Carl XVI Gustaf	Sweden	Sep 15, 1973	38	3	16
7	Juan Carlos I	Spain	Nov 22, 1975	36	1	9
8	Beatrix	The Netherlands	Apr 30, 1980	31	8	1
9	Mswati	Swaziland	Mar 25, 1986	25	9	6
10	Emperor Akihito	Japan	Jan 7, 1989	22	11	24

* Sovereign states only
# As of December 31, 2011

POLITICS

TOP 10 TALLEST US PRESIDENTS

PRESIDENT	IN OFFICE	HEIGHT FT	HEIGHT IN	HEIGHT M
1 Abraham Lincoln	1861–65	6	3.75	1.92
2 Lyndon B. Johnson	1963–69	6	3.5	1.91
3 Thomas Jefferson	1801–09	6	2.5	1.89
4 = Chester A. Arthur	1881–85	6	2	1.88
= George H. W. Bush	1989–93	6	2	1.88
= Franklin D. Roosevelt	1933–45	6	2	1.88
7 = Bill Clinton	1993–2001	6	1.5	1.87
= George Washington	1789–97	6	1.5	1.87
9 = Andrew Jackson	1829–37	6	1	1.85
= Barack Obama	2009–	6	1	1.85
= Ronald W. Reagan	1981–89	6	1	1.85

At 5 ft 11.5 in (1.82 m), George W. Bush (2001–09) is the only president to be less than 6 ft 1 in (1.85 m) tall since Ronald Reagan took office in 1981. It is often claimed that the taller candidate has always won US presidential elections, but statistically this is only marginally true.

THE 10 FIRST COUNTRIES TO GIVE WOMEN THE VOTE

	COUNTRY	YEAR
1	New Zealand	1893
2	Australia (South Australia 1894; Western Australia 1898; Australia united in 1901)	1902
3	Finland (then a Grand Duchy under the Russian Crown)	1906
4	Norway (restricted franchise; all women over 25 in 1913)	1907
5	Denmark and Iceland (a Danish dependency until 1918)	1915
6	= The Netherlands	1917
	= USSR	1917
8	= Austria	1918
	= Canada	1918
	= Germany	1918
	= Great Britain and Ireland (Ireland part of the UK until 1921; women over 30 only – lowered to 21 in 1928)	1918
	= Poland	1918

THE 10 YOUNGEST US PRESIDENTS

PRESIDENT	TOOK OFFICE	AGE ON TAKING OFFICE YRS	MTHS	DAYS
1 Theodore Roosevelt	Sep 14, 1901	42	10	18
2 John F. Kennedy	Jan 20, 1961	43	7	22
3 Bill Clinton	Jan 20, 1993	46	5	1
4 Ulysses S. Grant	Mar 4, 1869	46	10	5
5 Barack Obama	Jan 20, 2009	47	5	16
6 Grover Cleveland	Mar 4, 1893	47	11	14
7 Franklin Pierce	Mar 4, 1804	48	3	9
8 James A. Garfield	Mar 4, 1881	49	3	13
9 James K. Polk	Mar 4, 1845	49	4	2
10 Millard Fillmore	Jul 10, 1850	50	6	3

▲ Heads of state
Carved into the rock face of Mount Rushmore in South Dakota are the heads of former US presidents (left to right): George Washington, Thomas Jefferson, Theodore Roosevelt, and Abraham Lincoln.

Yoweri Museveni
In 2011 the Ugandan president was voted in for a 4th term.

TOP 10 **LONGEST-SERVING PRESIDENTS TODAY**

	PRESIDENT	COUNTRY	TOOK OFFICE
1	Teodoro Obiang Nguema Mbasogo	Equatorial Guinea	Aug 3, 1979
2	José Eduardo dos Santos	Angola	Sep 21, 1979
3	Paul Biya	Cameroon	Nov 7, 1982
4	Yoweri Museveni	Uganda	Jan 29, 1986
5	Blaise Compaoré	Burkina Faso	Oct 15, 1987
6	Robert Mugabe	Zimbabwe	Dec 31, 1987
7	Islam Karimov	Uzbekistan	Mar 24, 1990
8	Nursultan Nazarbayev	Kazakhstan	Apr 24, 1990
9	Omar Hassan Ahmad Al-Bashir	Sudan	Jun 30, 1989
10	Idriss Deby	Chad	Dec 2, 1990

his list has changed dramatically in the past year. Muammar Gaddafi, president of Libya and long No. 1 on this list, was ousted from power in August 2011 and killed later that year. Former No. 2, Ali Abdullah Saleh of Yemen, was removed from office in June 2011.

THE 10 **MOST RECENTLY ELECTED FEMALE PRESIDENTS**

	PRESIDENT	COUNTRY	TOOK OFFICE
1	Atifete Jahjaga	Kosovo	Apr 7, 2011
2	Dilma Rousseff	Brazil	Jan 1, 2011
3	Laura Chinchilla	Costa Rica	May 8, 2010
4	Roza Otunbayeva	Kyrgyzstan	Apr 7, 2010
5	Dalia Grybauskaitė	Lithuania	Jul 12, 2009
6	Cristina Fernández de Kirchner	Argentina	Dec 10, 2007
7	Pratibha Patil	India	Jul 25, 2007
8	Michelle Bachelet	Chile	Mar 11, 2006*
9	Ellen Johnson-Sirleaf	Liberia	Jan 16, 2006
10	Megawati Sukarnoputri	Indonesia	Jul 23, 2001#

* Left office March 11, 2010
# Left office October 20, 2004

▶ *Laura Chinchilla*
The Costa Rican president is the first woman to hold this position in a Central American country.

▲ *A new world*
The arrival of Christopher Columbus in the Americas in 1492 led to widespread European colonization.

THE 10 FIRST EXPLORERS TO LAND IN THE AMERICAS

EXPLORER* / COUNTRY	TERRITORY	LANDED
1 Christopher Columbus, Italy	West Indies	Oct 12, 1492
2 John Cabot, Italy/England	Nova Scotia/ Newfoundland	Jun 24, 1497
3 Alonso de Ojeda, Spain	Brazil	1499
4 Vicente Yáñez Pinzón, Spain	Amazon	Jan 26, 1500
5 Pedro Alvarez Cabral, Portugal	Brazil	Apr 23, 1500
6 Gaspar Corte-Real, Portugal	Labrador	late 1500
7 Rodrigo de Bastidas, Spain	Central America	Mar 1501
8 Vasco Nuñez de Balboa, Spain	Panama	Sep 25, 1513
9 Juan Ponce de León, Spain	Florida	Apr 8, 1513
10 Juan Díaz de Solís, Spain	Río de la Plata	Jan 1, 1516

* Expedition leader only listed

THE FIRST PEOPLE TO REACH THE NORTH POLE

In September 1909, US explorer Frederick A. Cook claimed to have reached the North Pole on April 21, 1908, along with two companions. Five days later Robert E. Peary, a retired engineer from the US Navy, also claimed that he and five companions, including assistant Matthew Henson, had reached the pole on April 6, 1909, thus discrediting Cook's claims. This is generally accepted today, although some say that the only true evidence is from May 12, 1926, when Roald Amundsen successfully reached the pole.

THE 10 FIRST PEOPLE TO REACH THE SOUTH POLE

NAME / NATIONALITY / DATES

14 December 1911

1 = Roald Amundsen*
   (Norwegian; 1872–1928)

= Olav Olavson Bjaaland
   (Norwegian; 1873–1961)

= Helmer Julius Hanssen
   (Norwegian; 1870–1956)

= Sverre Helge Hassel
   (Norwegian 1876–1928)

= Oscar Wisting
   (Norwegian; 1871–1936)

* Expedition leader

17 January 1912

6 = Robert Falcon Scott*
   (British; 1868–1912)

= Henry Robinson Bowers
   (British; 1883–1912)

= Edgar Evans
   (British; 1876–1912)

= Lawrence Edward Grace Oates
   (British; 1880–1912)

= Edward Adrian Wilson
   (British; 1872–1912)

* Expedition leader

Just 33 days separate the first two expeditions to reach the South Pole. Scott's expedition was organized with its avowed goal "to reach the South Pole and to secure for the British Empire the honor of this achievement." Meanwhile, Norwegian explorer Roald Amundsen also set out for the Pole. When Scott eventually reached his goal, he discovered that the Norwegians had beaten him. Scott and his team all perished on the return journey.

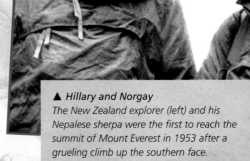

▲ Hillary and Norgay
The New Zealand explorer (left) and his Nepalese sherpa were the first to reach the summit of Mount Everest in 1953 after a grueling climb up the southern face.

THE 10 FIRST PEOPLE TO CLIMB EVEREST

	NAME	NATIONALITY	DATE
1 =	Edmund Hillary	New Zealand	May 29, 1953
=	Tenzing Norgay	Nepalese	May 29, 1953
3	Ernst Schmied	Swiss	May 29, 1953
4	Jurg Marmet	Swiss	May 29, 1953
5	Dolf Reist	Swiss	May 29, 1953
6	Hans Rudolf von Gunten	Swiss	May 29, 1953
7	Wang Fu-chou	Chinese	May 25, 1960
8	Konbu aka Gonpa	Tibetan	May 25, 1960
9	Chu Ying-hua	Chinese	May 25, 1960
10 =	Jim Whittaker	American	May 1, 1963
=	Nawang Gombu	Tibetan	May 1, 1963

THE 10 FIRST EXPEDITIONS TO REACH THE NORTH POLE OVERLAND*

	NAME[#] / COUNTRY	DATE
1	Ralph S. Plaisted, USA	Apr 19, 1968
2	Wally W. Herbert, UK	Apr 5, 1969
3	Naomi Uemura, Japan	May 1, 1978
4	Dmitri Shparo, USSR	May 31, 1979
5	Sir Ranulph Fiennes/Charles Burton, UK	Apr 11, 1982
6	Will Steger/Paul Schurke, USA	May 1, 1986
7	Jean-Louis Etienne, France	May 11, 1986
8	Fukashi Kazami, Japan	Apr 20, 1987
9	Helen Thayer, USA[†]	Apr 20, 1988
10	Robert Swan, UK	May 14, 1989

* Confirmed only
\# Expedition leader or co-leader
† New Zealand-born

▶ Naomi Uemura
Uemura made the first solo walk to the North Pole.

NOBEL PRIZES

▲ **Liu Xiaobo campaign**
The Chinese civil rights activist won the Peace Prize during his 4th term as a political prisoner.

THE 10 **LATEST WINNERS OF THE NOBEL PEACE PRIZE**

YEAR	WINNER / COUNTRY
2011	**Ellen Johnson Sirleaf, Leymah Gbowee** and **Tawakkul Karman**, Liberia and Yemen
2010	**Liu Xiaobo**, China
2009	**Barack Obama**, USA
2008	**Martti Ahtisaari**, Finland
2007	**Intergovernmental Panel on Climate Change** and **Al Gore, Jr.**, USA
2006	**Muhammad Yunus** and **Grameen Bank**, Bangladesh
2005	**International Atomic Energy Agency** and **Mohamed El Baradei**, Egypt
2004	**Wangari Maathai**, Kenya
2003	**Shirin Ebadi**, Iran
2002	**Jimmy Carter**, USA

THE 10 **LATEST WINNERS OF THE NOBEL PRIZE FOR LITERATURE**

YEAR	WINNER / COUNTRY
2011	**Tomas Tranströmer**, Sweden
2010	**Mario Vargas Llosa**, Peru and Spain
2009	**Herta Müller**, Germany
2008	**Jean-Marie Gustave Le Clézio**, France
2007	**Doris Lessing**, UK
2006	**Orhan Pamuk**, Turkey
2005	**Harold Pinter**, UK
2004	**Elfriede Jelinek**, Austria
2003	**J. M. Coetzee**, South Africa
2002	**Imre Kertész**, Hungary

THE OLDEST AND YOUNGEST TO WIN A NOBEL PRIZE

At 90 years, 3 months and 28 days, 2007 Economics winner Leonid Hurwicz is the oldest person ever to receive a Nobel Prize. He heads a Top 10 of oldest winners in which all the others are octagenarians. Other than 85-year-old Ferdinand Buisson's 1927 Peace Prize, all the oldest winners date from the last 40 years, and six of them from the last 10. By contrast, the list of youngest winners is dominated by scientists from the discovery-rich days of the early to mid 20th century. The most recent youthful winners in the Top 10 are joint 1976 Peace Prize winners Maidread Corrigan and Betty Williams, at 32 and 33 years old respectively.

THE 10 **LATEST WOMEN TO WIN A NOBEL PRIZE**

	WINNER	COUNTRY	PRIZE	YEAR
1	= Elizabeth H. Blackburn	USA	Medicine	2009
	= Carol W. Greider	USA	Medicine	2009
	= Herta Müller	Germany	Literature	2009
	= Elinor Ostrom	USA	Economics	2009
	= Ada E. Yonath	Israel	Chemistry	2009
6	Françoise Barré-Sinoussi	France	Medicine	2008
7	Doris Lessing	UK	Literature	2007
8	= Linda B. Buck	USA	Medicine	2004
	= Elfriede Jelinek	Austria	Literature	2004
	= Wangari Maathai	Kenya	Peace	2004

▶ **Herta Müller**
The Romanian-born novelist writes about life in communist Romania.

THE IG NOBEL PRIZE

Each year in October, the Ig Nobel Awards—run by the Harvard-based organization Improbable Research—parody the Nobels by honoring those scientists and academics whose work "first makes people laugh and then makes them think." The awards are made for genuine research and are handed out in a circus-like ceremony by real Nobel Laureates. (Sources: Nobel Prize/Improbable Research)

THE 5 LATEST NOBEL/IG NOBEL PHYSICS PRIZE WINNERS

2011

Nobel: Saul Perlmutter, Brian P. Schmidt, and Adam G. Riess for the discovery of the accelerating expansion of the Universe through observations of distant supernovae.

Ig Nobel: Philippe Perrin, Cyril Perrot, Dominique Deviterne, Bruno Ragaru, and Herman Kingma for determining why discus throwers become dizzy, and why hammer throwers don't.

2010

Nobel: Andre Geim and Konstantin Novoselov for their experiments regarding the two-dimensional material graphene.

Ig Nobel: Lianne Parkin, Sheila Williams, and Patricia Priest, for demonstrating that, on icy footpaths in winter, people slip and fall less often if they wear socks on the outside of their shoes.

▼ *Neverending soup*
Brian Wansink, winner of the "Nutrition Prize" demonstrates his bottomless soup bowl.

2009

Nobel: Charles Kuen Kao for achievements concerning the transmission of light in fibers for optical communication, to Willard S. Boyle and George E. Smith for the invention of an imaging semiconductor circuit–the CCD sensor.

Ig Nobel: Katherine K. Whitcome, Daniel E. Lieberman, and Liza J. Shapiro for determining why pregnant women don't tip over.

2008

Nobel: Yoichiro Nambu, Makoto Kobayashi, and Toshihide Maskawa for the discovery of the mechanism of spontaneous broken symmetry and for the discovery of the origin of the broken symmetry that predicts the existence of quarks.

Ig Nobel: Dorian Raymer and Douglas Smith for proving mathematically that heaps of string will inevitably tangle themselves up in knots.

2007

Nobel: Albert Fert and Peter Grünberg for the discovery of Giant Magnetoresistance.

Ig Nobel: L. Mahadevan and Enrique Cerda Villablanca for their study of how sheets become wrinkled.

▼ *Bird brain*
Ivan Schwab won his Ig Nobel for research on why woodpeckers don't get headaches.

MURDER & EXECUTION

◄ **Chinese justice**
The Chinese authorities have reduced the number of crimes that are capital offences.

THE 10 **COUNTRIES WITH THE MOST EXECUTIONS**

	COUNTRY	EXECUTIONS*			
1	China	>1,000#	**6**	Saudi Arabia	27
2	Iran	252	**7**	Libya	18
3	North Korea	60	**8**	Syria	17
4	Yemen	53	**9**	Bangladesh	9
5	USA	46	**10**	Somalia	8

* Latest available year; minimum estimates in most instances
\# Exact Chinese figures unavailable, but numbers estimated to be well over 1,000

Source: Amnesty International

THE 10 **FIRST COUNTRIES TO ABOLISH CAPITAL PUNISHMENT**

COUNTRY / ABOLISHED

1	Russia	1826
2	Venezuela	1863
3	San Marino	1865
4	Portugal	1867
5	Costa Rica	1877
6	Brazil	1889
7	Panama	1903
8	Norway	1905
9	Ecuador	1906
10	Uruguay	1907

Murders in the USA first exceeded 2,000 in 1910 and increased rapidly as a result of gang warfare during the Prohibition era, topping 10,000 in 1930. The total rose to over 20,000 for the first time in 1974. However, in recent years the number of murders has been in decline, with 12,996 cases of homicide in 2010.

THE 10 **WORST YEARS FOR MURDER IN THE USA**

YEAR# / MURDER RATE PER 100,000 POPULATION / TOTAL*

1 1991 9.8 / 24,703

2 1993 9.5 / 24,526

3 1992 9.3 / 23,760

4 1990 9.4 / 23,438

5 1994 9.0 / 23,326

6 1980 10.2 / 23,040

7 1981 9.8 / 22,520

8 1975 8.7 / 21,500

9 1977 9.7 / 21,460

10 1982 9.1 / 21,010

* Includes non-negligent manslaughter victims; victims of September 11, 2001 terrorist attacks are excluded

Source: Bureau of Justice Statistics

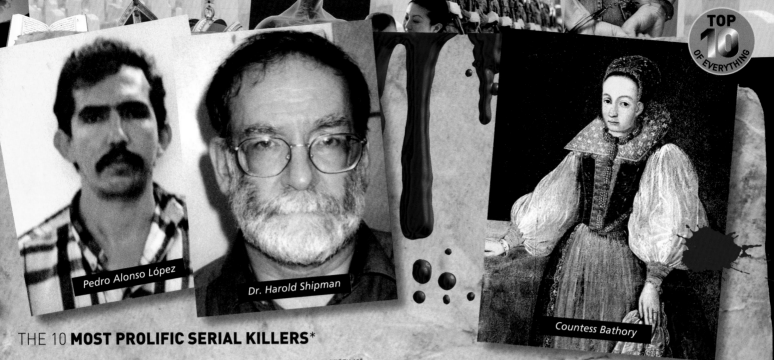

Pedro Alonso López

Dr. Harold Shipman

Countess Bathory

THE 10 **MOST PROLIFIC SERIAL KILLERS***

MURDERER / COUNTRY   VICTIMS#

1 Behram (India)   931
Behram (or Buhram) was the leader of the Thugee cult in India, which is reckoned to be responsible for the deaths of up to 2 million people. At his trial, Behram was found guilty of personally committing 931 murders between 1790 and 1830, mostly by ritual strangulation with the cult's traditional cloth, known as a *ruhmal*.

2 Countess Erszébet Báthory (Hungary)   <650
In the period up to 1610 in Hungary, Báthory (1560–1614), known as "Countess Dracula" was alleged to have murdered between 300 and 650 girls in the belief that drinking their blood would prevent her from ageing. She was eventually arrested in 1611, tried, and found guilty. She died on August 21, 1614, walled up in her own castle.

3 Pedro Alonso López (Colombia)   300
Captured in 1980, López, nicknamed the "Monster of the Andes," led police to 53 graves but confessed to killing at least 300 in Colombia, Ecuador, and Peru. He is thought to have served 14 years of a 16-year sentence before being released by the Ecuadorian government for "good behavior." His current whereabouts are unknown.

4 Dr. Harold Shipman (UK)   250
In January 2000, Manchester doctor Shipman was found guilty of the murder of 15 women patients; the official enquiry into his crimes put the figure at 218, with a probable number of victims around 250, but some authorities believe that the total could be as high as 400. Shipman hanged himself in his prison cell on January 13, 2004.

5 Luis Alfredo Garavito (Colombia)   >200
Garavito (b. 1957) confessed in 1999 to a spate of murders. Though found guilty of murdering 138 young boys, the number of his victims could actually exceed 300. The total sentences add up to 1,835 years imprisonment, but due to Colombian law, he may serve less than 30 years.

6 Henry Lee Lucas (USA)   200
Lucas (1936–2001) admitted involvement in about 600 murders, many committed with his partner-in-crime Ottis Toole, but later recanted his confessions. He died while on Death Row in Huntsville Prison, Texas.

7 Gilles de Rais (France)   <200
A fabulously wealthy French aristocrat, Gilles de Laval, Baron de Rais (1404–40) committed murders as sacrifices during black-magic rituals. Charged with a catalogue of crimes that included "the conjuration of demons," he was tried, tortured, and found guilty. He was strangled and his body burnt at Nantes on October 25, 1440.

8 Hu Wanlin (China)   196
Posing as a doctor specializing in ancient Chinese medicine, Hu Wanlin was sentenced on October 1, 2000 to 15 years imprisonment for three deaths, but authorities believe he was responsible for considerably more, an estimated 20 in Taiyuan, 146 in Shanxi, and 30 in Shangqui.

9 Hermann Webster Mudgett (USA)   <150
Also known as "H. H. Holmes," Mudgett (1860–96), a former doctor, was believed to have lured over 150 women to his Chicago "castle." This warren of secret passages was fully equipped for torturing, murdering, and dissecting his victims, and disposing of their bodies in furnaces or an acid bath. Arrested in 1894 and found guilty of the murder of an ex-partner, he confessed to killing 27, but may have murdered on up to 150 occasions. Mudgett, regarded as America's first mass murderer, was hanged on May 7, 1896.

10 Pedro Rodrigues Filho   >100
A Brazilian serial killer, convicted, and sentenced to 128 years in jail, although the maximum length of jail sentence in Brazil is 30 years. He has claimed to have killed over 100 people, at least 40 of whom were inmates.

* Includes only individual murderers; excludes murders by bandits, those carried out by terrorist groups, political and military atrocities, and gangland slayings
# Suspected victims

TOP 10 FEATURE

MOST WANTED

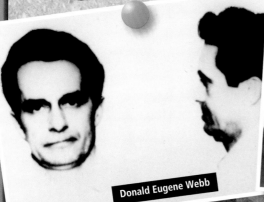

Donald Eugene Webb

Victor Manuel Gerena

Katherine Ann Power

David Daniel Keegan

THE 10 CRIMINALS LONGEST ON THE FBI'S "10 MOST WANTED" LIST

FUGITIVE / FBI NO.	CRIME	ADDED TO LIST	REMOVED FROM LIST	PERIOD ON LIST		
				YRS	MTHS	DAYS
1 Victor Manuel Gerena (386)	Armed robbery	May 14, 1984	*	27	7	18
2 Donald Eugene Webb (375)	Alleged cop killer	May 4, 1981	Mar 31, 2007	25	10	27
3 Charles Lee Heron (265)	Murder	Feb 9, 1968	Jun 18, 1986	18	4	9
4 Glen Stewart Godwin (447)	Murder	Dec 7, 1996	*	15	0	25
5 Frederick J. Tenuto (14)	Murder	May 24, 1950	Mar 9, 1964	13	9	14
6 Katherine Ann Power (315)	Bank robbery	Oct 17, 1970	Jun 15, 1984	13	7	29
7 James Joseph Bulger (458)	Murder	Aug 19, 1999	Jun 22, 2011	11	10	4
8 Arthur Lee Washington, Jr. (427)	Attempted murder	Oct 18, 1989	Dec 27, 2000	11	2	19
9 Robert William Fisher (475)	Murder	Jun 29, 2002	*	9	6	3
10 David Daniel Keegan (78)	Murder, robbery	Jun 21, 1954	Dec 13, 1963	9	5	22

* Still at large as of December 31, 2011

Source: FBI

◀ James "Whitey" Bulger
After 12 years on the run, this notorious gang boss was finally apprehended at an apartment building (below) in June 2011.

The FBI officially launched its celebrated "10 Most Wanted" list on March 14, 1950, to publicize dangerous criminals who might not otherwise receive much general attention. Since then, almost 500 criminals have figured on the list. Their names appear there until they are captured, die, or charges against them are dropped.

SHORTEST AND OLDEST

On January 8, 1969, bank robber and double cop murderer Billie Austin Bryant appeared on the list for the record shortest time—just 2 hours—before he was arrested.

James Joseph Bulger is the oldest person to have a place on the list, and his name was added in August 1999 when he was 69 years old. He was wanted for 19 counts of murder during the 1970s and 1980s, and was the former head of the notorious Boston-based Winter Hill gang. A reward of $2,000,000 was offered for information leading to his capture, and he was finally brought to justice on June 22, 2011.

MOST WANTED

OSAMA BIN LADEN

Bin Laden was added to the list on June 7, 1999, and for well over a decade was one of the most wanted men in the world. He was finally killed on May 2, 2011, by US military forces.

NET RESULT

Although the list is widely available and distributed in public places throughout the USA, in the past few years the FBI has begun to use the internet as a way of informing the public about the Most Wanted list. A minimum reward of $100,000—sometimes much more—is offered for information leading to the capture of a criminal on the list.

WANTED WOMEN

Only 8 women have ever appeared on the Most Wanted list. The first woman to earn this distinction was Ruth Eisemann-Schier, who was added in 1968 for a variety of crimes including kidnapping and extortion. The most recent was Shauntay Henderson, who was added to the list on March 31, 2007. However, she did not remain on it for long, as she was captured that same day.

PUBLIC ENEMIES

In the 1920s and 1930s, gang-related crime became common in the American Midwest around Chicago. Financial troubles caused by the Great Depression meant that many people suffered everyday hardship, but criminals made money out of bank robbery, bootlegging, and illegal sales of alcohol during the Prohibition era, using extreme violence to protect their interests. Al Capone (Public Enemy No. 1), Bonnie and Clyde, George "Baby Face" Nelson, Charles "Pretty Boy" Floyd, and John Dillinger became the most notorious figures. In 1935, J. Edgar Hoover created the FBI, whose aim was to capture the most hardened of criminals.

▲ **Al Capone**
Official mug shots of Chicago's infamous gangster.

▼ *John Dillinger*
This notorious criminal carried out a series of bank raids in Ohio in the 1930s, and became the most wanted man in America.

▲ *Bonnie and Clyde*
In the early 1930s, the couple went on a crime spree of small-scale robbery.

WORLD WARS

▼ **Dogfight**
The most successful World War I pilots became flying aces credited with shooting down many enemy aircraft during combat.

THE 10 **COUNTRIES SUFFERING THE GREATEST MILITARY LOSSES IN WORLD WAR I**

	COUNTRY	KILLED
1	Germany	1,773,700
2	Russia	1,700,000
3	France	1,357,800
4	Austria-Hungary	1,200,000
5	British Empire*	908,371
6	Italy	650,000
7	Romania	335,706
8	Turkey	325,000
9	USA	116,516
10	Bulgaria	87,500

* Including Australia, Canada, India, New Zealand, South Africa, etc.

THE 10 **YOUNGEST AIR ACES OF WORLD WAR I**

	PILOT* / TOTAL VICTORIES / BORN	FIRST KILL	AGE YRS	MTHS	DAYS
1	Edward Borgfeldt Booth (Canada) (5) Aug 31, 1899	Sep 20, 1917	18	0	20
2	Frederic Ives Lord (USA) (12) Apr 8, 1900	May 28, 1918	18	1	20
3	Richard Gordon-Bennett# (5) Mar 2, 1900	Jul 29, 1918	18	4	9
4	James Donald Innes Hardman (9) Dec 21, 1899	May 9, 1918	18	4	18
5	Risdon MacKenzie Bennett (5) Feb 12, 1900	Jul 31, 1918	18	5	19
6	Ivan Couper Sanderson (11) Dec 21, 1899	Jun 23, 1918	18	6	2
7	Francis Stephen Bowles (5) Oct 30, 1899	May 13, 1918	18	6	13
8	Charles John Sims (9) Dec 20, 1899	Jul 7, 1918	18	6	17
9	Arthur Stuart Draisey (7) Nov 21, 1899	Jul 1, 1918	18	7	10
10	Max Näther# (Ger) (26) Aug 24, 1899	May 16, 1918	18	8	22

* British unless otherwise stated
# Killed in action

THE 10 **LARGEST ARMED FORCES OF WORLD WAR I**

	COUNTRY	PERSONNEL*
1	Russia	12,000,000
2	Germany	11,000,000
3	British Empire	8,904,467
4	France	8,410,000
5	Austria-Hungary	7,800,000
6	Italy	5,615,000
7	USA	4,355,000
8	Turkey	2,850,000
9	Bulgaria	1,200,000
10	Japan	800,000

* Total at peak strength

▼ **Into battle**
British and French forces were the largest Allied contingent on the Western Front.

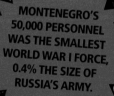

MONTENEGRO'S 50,000 PERSONNEL WAS THE SMALLEST WORLD WAR I FORCE, 0.4% THE SIZE OF RUSSIA'S ARMY.

TOP 10 **LARGEST BATTLESHIPS OF WORLD WAR II**

	NAME	COUNTRY	STATUS	LENGTH FT	M	TONNAGE
1 =	Musashi	Japan	Sunk Oct 24, 1944	862	263	72,809
=	Yamato	Japan	Sunk Apr 7, 1945	862	263	72,809
3 =	Iowa	USA	Decommissioned Oct 26, 1990	887	270	55,710
=	Missouri	USA	Decommissioned Mar 31, 1992	887	270	55,710
=	New Jersey	USA	Decommissioned Feb 8, 1991	887	270	55,710
=	Wisconsin	USA	Decommissioned Sep 30, 1991	887	270	55,710
7 =	Bismarck	Germany	Sunk May 27, 1941	823	251	50,153
=	Tirpitz	Germany	Sunk Nov 12, 1944	823	251	50,153
9 =	Jean Bart	France	Survived WWII, scrapped 1969	812	247	47,500
=	Richelieu	France	Survived WWII, scrapped 1968	812	247	47,500

▼ *USS* Missouri
Launched in 1944, this was an Iowa class vessel used to fight against the Japanese.

TOP 10 **FASTEST FIGHTER AIRCRAFT OF WORLD WAR II**

	AIRCRAFT	COUNTRY	MAX. SPEED MPH	KM/H
1	Messerschmitt Me 163	Germany	596	959
2	Messerschmitt Me 262	Germany	560	901
3	Heinkel He 162A	Germany	553	890
4	P-51-H Mustang	USA	487	784
5	Lavochkin La11	USSR	460	740
6	Spitfire XIV	UK	448	721
7	Yakolev Yak-3	USSR	447	719
8	P-51-D Mustang	USA	440	708
9	Tempest VI	UK	438	705
10	Focke-Wulf FW190D	Germany	435	700

▲ *Heinkel He 162A*
The German fighter was second only to the Messerschmitt for speed.

THE 10 **WORST ALLIED BATTLE OF BRITAIN LOSSES**

	NATIONALITY	PILOTS	KILLED
1	RAF (British/other Commonwealth)	1,822	339
2	Polish	141	29
3	Canadian	88	20
4	Australian	21	14
5	New Zealander	73	11
6 =	Fleet Air Arm	56	9
=	South African	21	9
8	Czech	86	8
9	Belgian	26	6
10	American	7	1

▲ *Call to arms*
Allied pilots sustained heavy losses against the German Luftwaffe in 1940.

THE MILITARY

▼ Chinese force
China has the world's biggest military force and its military spending is second only to the US.

TOP 10 MILITARY EXPENDITURE COUNTRIES

COUNTY / % OF WORLD TOTAL / MILITARY SPENDING ($)*

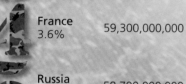
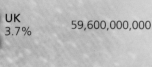

#	Country	%	Military Spending ($)
1	USA	42.8%	698,105,000,000
2	China	7.3%	119,000,000,000
3	UK	3.7%	59,600,000,000
4	France	3.6%	59,300,000,000
5	Russia	3.6%	58,700,000,000
6	Japan	3.3%	54,500,000,000
7	= Germany	2.8%	45,200,000,000
	= Saudi Arabia	2.8%	45,200,000,000
9	India	2.5%	41,300,000,000
10	Italy	2.3%	37,000,000,000

* Latest available year

World total 100.0   1,630,000,000,000

Source: The Center for Arms Control and Non-Proliferation

TOP 10 MISSILE-DEFENSE SYSTEM COUNTRIES

COUNTRY

#	Country
1	USA
2	Russia
3	China
4	India
5	UK
6	Turkey
7	South Korea
8	France
9	Japan
10	Israel

These rankings do not include nuclear capability, but are based on a conventional war, and have been arrived at after analyzing a wide variety of factors.

► India UN
As a founding member state, India contributes troops to UN peacekeeping efforts.

PEACEKEEPERS

Peacekeeping aims to create the conditions for lasting peace by the monitoring and observation of postwar areas. Operational control is established and implemented by the UN, while UN troops remain as members of their own respective forces. They may be armed but they are not expected to fight. Bangladesh, Pakistan, and India contribute the highest number of peacekeepers.

THE 10 20TH-CENTURY WARS WITH THE MOST MILITARY FATALITIES

WAR / YEARS	ESTIMATED FATALITIES
World War II 1939–45	15,843,000
World War I 1914–18	8,545,800
Korean War 1950–53	1,893,100
= Sino-Japanese War 1937–41	1,200,000
= Biafra-Nigeria Civil War 1967–70	1,000,000
Spanish Civil War 1936–39	611,000
Vietnam War 1961–75	546,000
French Vietnam War 1945–54	300,000
= India-Pakistan War 1947	200,000
= Soviet invasion of Afghanistan 1979–89	200,000
= Iran-Iraq War 1980–88	200,000

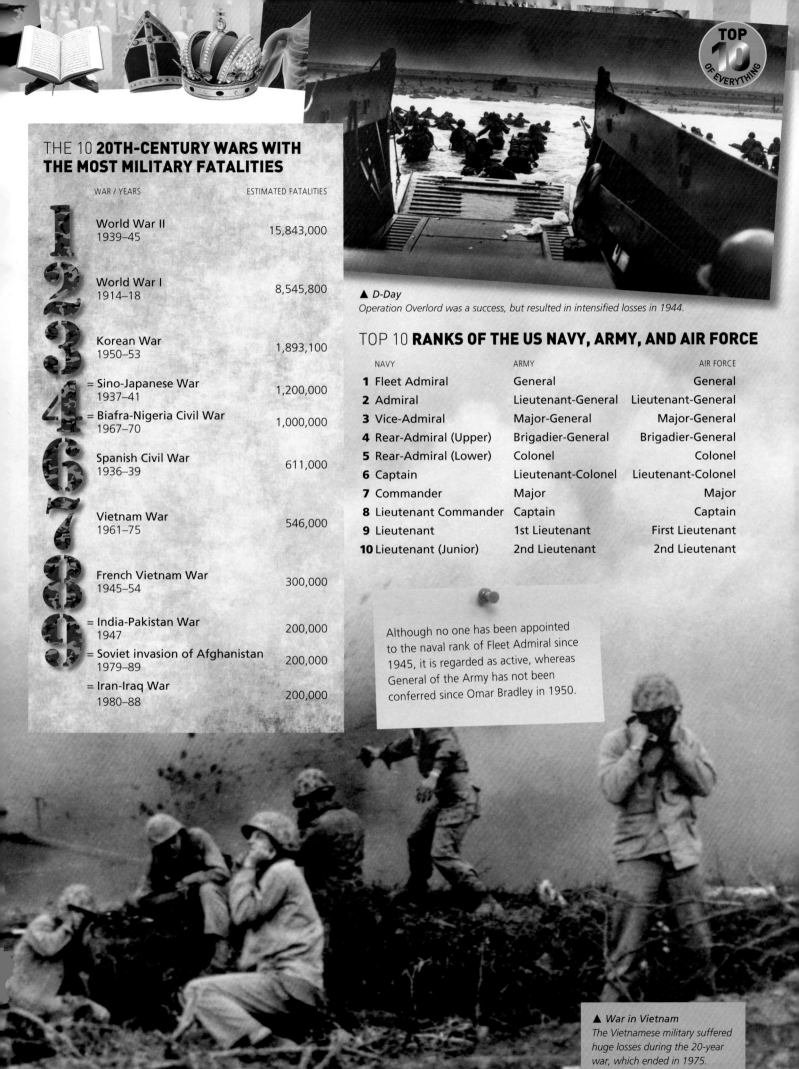

▲ D-Day
Operation Overlord was a success, but resulted in intensified losses in 1944.

TOP 10 RANKS OF THE US NAVY, ARMY, AND AIR FORCE

	NAVY	ARMY	AIR FORCE
1	Fleet Admiral	General	General
2	Admiral	Lieutenant-General	Lieutenant-General
3	Vice-Admiral	Major-General	Major-General
4	Rear-Admiral (Upper)	Brigadier-General	Brigadier-General
5	Rear-Admiral (Lower)	Colonel	Colonel
6	Captain	Lieutenant-Colonel	Lieutenant-Colonel
7	Commander	Major	Major
8	Lieutenant Commander	Captain	Captain
9	Lieutenant	1st Lieutenant	First Lieutenant
10	Lieutenant (Junior)	2nd Lieutenant	2nd Lieutenant

Although no one has been appointed to the naval rank of Fleet Admiral since 1945, it is regarded as active, whereas General of the Army has not been conferred since Omar Bradley in 1950.

▲ War in Vietnam
The Vietnamese military suffered huge losses during the 20-year war, which ended in 1975.

WORLD RELIGIONS

▼ **Thai Buddhists**
Nearly 95% of Thailand's population is of the Theravada school of Buddhism.

► **Hindu Sadhus**
These "holy men" renounce all material attachments to achieve moksha (liberation).

TOP 10 LARGEST BUDDHIST POPULATIONS

COUNTRY / BUDDHISTS

1 China 187,806,655
2 Japan 71,246,806
3 Thailand 59,917,810
4 Vietnam 43,212,172
5 Myanmar 35,750,867
6 Sri Lanka 14,378,019
7 Cambodia 12,007,108
8 India 8,225,810
9 South Korea 7,281,831
10 USA 3,955,124

Top 10 total 443,782,202
World total 463,516,919

Source: World Christian Database

TOP 10 LARGEST MUSLIM POPULATIONS

COUNTRY / MUSLIMS

1 Indonesia 190,436,400
2 India 167,486,204
3 Pakistan 166,927,482
4 Bangladesh 132,111,606
5 Iran 73,079,154
6 Nigeria 71,920,488
7 Egypt 71,738,252
8 Turkey 70,885,494
9 Algeria 34,936,806
10 Morocco 31,588,257

USA   4,695,980
Top 10 total 1,011,110,143
World total 1,533,728,688

Source: World Christian Database

TOP 10 LARGEST HINDU POPULATIONS

COUNTRY / HINDUS

1 India 895,239,610
2 Nepal 20,321,920
3 Bangladesh 14,095,750
4 Indonesia 3,538,185
5 Sri Lanka 2,721,660
6 Pakistan 2,289,607
7 Malaysia 1,780,195
8 USA 1,444,775
9 South Africa 1,195,565
10 Myanmar 818,177

Top 10 total 943,445,444
World total 949,875,210

Source: World Christian Database

THERE ARE MORE HINDUS IN INDIA THAN THERE ARE ATHEISTS AND AGNOSTICS IN THE WHOLE WORLD!

◄ **Pope in the USA**
Pope Benedict XVI celebrated mass with nearly 60,000 Catholics at Yankee Stadium.

TOP 10 **LARGEST CHRISTIAN POPULATIONS**

COUNTRY / CHRISTIANS

1 USA
247,920,130

2 Brazil
177,303,682

3 Russia
116,146,832

4 Mexico
108,721,048

5 China
107,717,161

6 Philippines
83,909,589

7 Nigeria
72,098,534

8 Dem. Rep. of Congo
62,910,134

9 Germany
57,674,094

10 India
57,264,881

Top 10 total 1,091,666,085
World total 2,269,205,835

Source: World Christian Database

TOP 10 **LARGEST JEWISH POPULATIONS**

COUNTRY / JEWS

1 Israel
5,379,493

2 USA
5,121,801

3 France
627,874

4 Argentina
501,126

5 Canada
479,824

6 UK
290,697

7 Germany
224,011

8 Russia
186,618

9 Ukraine
176,712

10 Brazil
147,046

Top 10 total 13,135,202
World total 14,760,647

Source: World Christian Database

TOP 10 **LARGEST SIKH POPULATIONS**

COUNTRY / SIKHS

1 India
22,303,343

2 UK
411,856

3 Canada
327,903

4 USA
279,346

5 Thailand
55,989

6 Saudi Arabia
52,700

7 Malaysia
47,146

8 Pakistan
44,613

9 Kenya
37,061

10 Australia
36,516

Top 10 total 23,596,473
World total 23,927,441

Source: World Christian Database

TRAVEL & TOURISM

▼ *New York, New York*
Times Square is nicknamed "The Crossroads of the World."

TOP 10 **WORLD TOURIST ATTRACTIONS**

	TOURIST ATTRACTION	LOCATION	ESTIMATED ANNUAL VISITORS
1	Times Square	New York City, USA	35,000,000
2	National Mall and Memorial Parks	Washington, DC, USA	25,000,000
3	Magic Kingdom	Lake Buena Vista, Orlando, USA	16,600,000
4	Trafalgar Square	London, UK	15,000,000
5	Disneyland Park	Anaheim, California, USA	14,700,000
6	Niagara Falls	Ontario/New York, Canada/USA	14,000,000
7	Fisherman's Wharf and Golden Gate	San Francisco, California, USA	13,000,000
8	Tokyo Disneyland and Tokyo DisneySea	Urayasu, Japan	12,900,000
9	Notre Dame de Paris	Paris, France	12,000,000
10	Disneyland Paris	Paris, France	10,600,000

Source: Forbes Traveler

◄ *French landscape*
Tourism reportedly accounts for 6% of France's annual income.

▲ *Changing of the Guard*
The ceremony at Buckingham Palace is a popular tourist attraction.

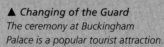

TOP 10 **MOST-VISITED CITIES**

	CITY	COUNTRY	INTERNATIONAL VISITORS*
1	LONDON	UK	14,059,000
2	BANGKOK	THAILAND	9,985,800
3	SINGAPORE	SINGAPORE	9,682,700
4	KUALA LUMPUR	MALAYSIA	9,400,000
5	ANTALYA	TURKEY	8,867,700
6	NEW YORK	USA	8,479,000
7	DUBAI	UNITED ARAB EMIRATES	7,783,000
8	PARIS	FRANCE	7,749,900
9	ISTANBUL	TURKEY	7,543,300
10	HONG KONG	CHINA	7,010,600

* Latest year for which data available   Source: Euromonitor

TOP 10 **MOST-VISITED COUNTRIES**

	COUNTRY	INTERNATIONAL VISITORS*
1	France	76,800,000
2	USA	59,700,000
3	China	55,700,000
4	Spain	52,700,000
5	Italy	43,600,000
6	UK	28,100,000
7	Turkey	27,000,000
8	Germany	26,900,000
9	Malaysia	24,600,000
10	Mexico	22,400,000

* Latest year for which data available

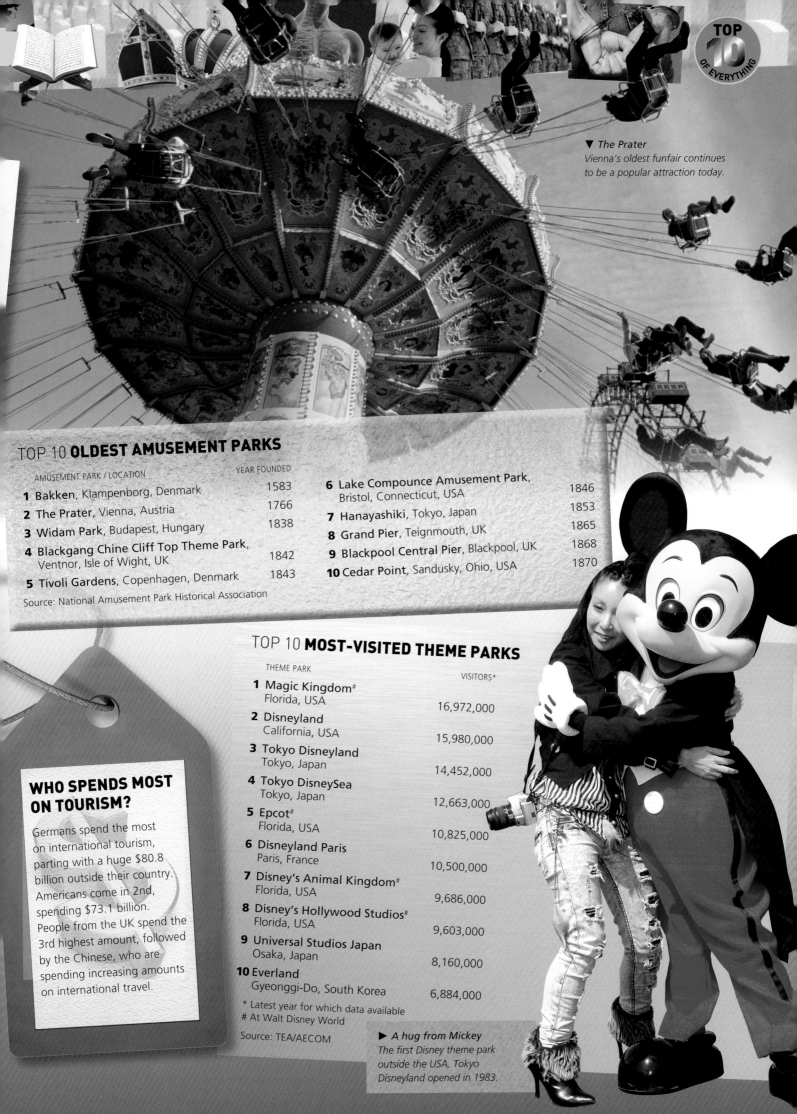

▼ The Prater
Vienna's oldest funfair continues to be a popular attraction today.

TOP 10 OLDEST AMUSEMENT PARKS

AMUSEMENT PARK / LOCATION	YEAR FOUNDED
1 Bakken, Klampenborg, Denmark	1583
2 The Prater, Vienna, Austria	1766
3 Widam Park, Budapest, Hungary	1838
4 Blackgang Chine Cliff Top Theme Park, Ventnor, Isle of Wight, UK	1842
5 Tivoli Gardens, Copenhagen, Denmark	1843
6 Lake Compounce Amusement Park, Bristol, Connecticut, USA	1846
7 Hanayashiki, Tokyo, Japan	1853
8 Grand Pier, Teignmouth, UK	1865
9 Blackpool Central Pier, Blackpool, UK	1868
10 Cedar Point, Sandusky, Ohio, USA	1870

Source: National Amusement Park Historical Association

TOP 10 MOST-VISITED THEME PARKS

THEME PARK	VISITORS*
1 Magic Kingdom# Florida, USA	16,972,000
2 Disneyland California, USA	15,980,000
3 Tokyo Disneyland Tokyo, Japan	14,452,000
4 Tokyo DisneySea Tokyo, Japan	12,663,000
5 Epcot# Florida, USA	10,825,000
6 Disneyland Paris Paris, France	10,500,000
7 Disney's Animal Kingdom# Florida, USA	9,686,000
8 Disney's Hollywood Studios# Florida, USA	9,603,000
9 Universal Studios Japan Osaka, Japan	8,160,000
10 Everland Gyeonggi-Do, South Korea	6,884,000

* Latest year for which data available
# At Walt Disney World

Source: TEA/AECOM

WHO SPENDS MOST ON TOURISM?

Germans spend the most on international tourism, parting with a huge $80.8 billion outside their country. Americans come in 2nd, spending $73.1 billion. People from the UK spend the 3rd highest amount, followed by the Chinese, who are spending increasing amounts on international travel.

▶ A hug from Mickey
The first Disney theme park outside the USA, Tokyo Disneyland opened in 1983.

4

TOWN & COUNTRY

ONE WORLD TRADE CENTER

When completed in 2013, One World Trade Center will reshape the New York City skyline. Its spire will reach to a height of 1,776 ft (541 m), making it the tallest building in the western hemisphere and the third-tallest skyscraper in the world. The new World Trade Center complex will eventually include five new skyscrapers, the National September 11 Memorial and Museum, a major city transportation hub, extensive retail areas, and a performing arts center. The Memorial opened to the public on September 11, 2011, and is set within the footprints of the original towers. The names of the 2,983 people who died in the 2001 attacks and the bombing of February 26, 1993 have been inscribed around two Memorial Pools.

Main picture: The New York City skyline as it will look on completion of the new Trade Center.
Inset: Ground Zero Memorial Pool.

CROSS COUNTRY

THE 10 LARGEST COUNTRIES

COUNTRY / AREA (SQ MILES / SQ KM) / % OF WORLD TOTAL

1 Russia
6,601,669 / 17,098,242
11.5

2 Canada
3,855,103 / 9,984,670
6.7

3 USA
3,717,813 / 9,629,091
6.5

4 China
3,705,407 / 9,596,961
6.4

5 Brazil
3,287,613 / 8,514,877
5.7

6 Australia
2,969,907 / 7,692,024
5.2

7 India
1,269,219 / 3,287,263
2.3

8 Argentina
1,073,519 / 2,780,400
2.0

9 Kazakhstan
1,052,090 / 2,724,900
1.8

10 Algeria
919,595 / 2,381,741
1.7

This list is based on the total area of a country within its borders, including offshore islands, inland water such as lakes and rivers, and reservoirs. It may thus differ from versions in which these are excluded. Antarctica has an approximate area of 5,096,549 sq miles (13,200,000 sq km), but is discounted as it is not considered a country.

Source: United Nations Statistics Division

THE 10 LARGEST COUNTRIES IN EUROPE

	COUNTRY	AREA SQ MILES	AREA SQ KM
1	Russia*	1,528,965	3,960,000
2	Ukraine	233,013	603,500
3	France	212,935	551,500
4	Spain	195,365	505,992
5	Sweden	173,860	450,295
6	Germany	137,849	357,022
7	Finland	130,559	338,145
8	Norway	125,021	323,802
9	Poland	120,728	312,685
10	Italy	116,340	301,318

* In Europe; total area 6,601,669 sq miles (17,098,242 sq km)

Source: United Nations Statistics Division

THE 10 LARGEST COUNTRIES IN OCEANIA

	COUNTRY	AREA SQ MILES	AREA SQ KM
1	Australia	2,699,907	7,692,024
2	Papua New Guinea	178,703	462,840
3	New Zealand	104,428	270,467
4	Solomon Islands	11,157	28,896
5	New Caledonia	7,358	18,575
6	Fiji	7,056	18,274
7	Vanuatu	4,706	12,189
8	French Polynesia	1,544	4,000
9	Western Samoa	1,093	2,831
10	Kiribati	280	726

Source: United Nations Statistics Division

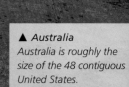

▲ Australia
Australia is roughly the size of the 48 contiguous United States.

◀ **China**
The Great Wall stretches across 5,500 miles (8,852 km) of China.

◀ **Algeria**
More than four-fifths of Algeria is covered by the Sahara Desert.

THE 10 **LARGEST COUNTRIES IN AFRICA**

	COUNTRY	AREA SQ MILES	AREA SQ KM
1	Algeria	919,595	2,381,741
2	Dem. Rep. of Congo	901,494	2,344,858
3	Sudan	728,215	1,886,068
4	Libya	679,362	1,759,540
5	Chad	495,755	1,284,000
6	Niger	489,191	1,267,000
7	Angola	481,354	1,246,700
8	Mali	478,841	1,240,192
9	South Africa	471,445	1,221,037
10	Ethiopia	426,373	1,104,300

Source: United Nations Statistics Division

THE 10 **LARGEST COUNTRIES IN THE AMERICAS**

	COUNTRY	AREA SQ MILES	AREA SQ KM
1	Canada	3,855,103	9,984,670
2	USA	3,717,813	9,629,091
3	Brazil	3,287,613	8,514,877
4	Argentina	1,073,519	2,780,400
5	Mexico	758,450	1,964,375
6	Peru	496,225	1,285,216
7	Colombia	439,737	1,138,914
8	Bolivia	424,165	1,098,581
9	Venezuela	352,145	912,050
10	Chile	291,933	756,102

Source: United Nations Statistics Division

THE 10 **LARGEST COUNTRIES IN ASIA**

	COUNTRY	AREA SQ MILES	AREA SQ KM
1	China	3,705,407	9,596,961
2	India	1,269,219	3,287,263
3	Kazakhstan	1,052,090	2,724,900
4	Saudi Arabia	830,000	2,149,690
5	Indonesia	735,358	1,904,569
6	Iran	636,372	1,648,195
7	Mongolia	603,902	1,564,100
8	Pakistan	307,374	796,095
9	Turkey	302,535	783,562
10	Myanmar	261,228	676,578

Source: United Nations Statistics Division

RUSSIA IS AROUND 39 MILLION TIMES BIGGER THAN THE SMALLEST COUNTRY IN THE WORLD, VATICAN CITY!

▲ **Canada**
With 3.3 inhabitants per sq km, Canada's population density is one of the lowest in the world.

WORLD POPULATION

▼ Hub of the world
Until 1925, London had the largest population of any city for nearly 100 years.

TOP 10 LARGEST CITIES 100 YEARS AGO

CITY / COUNTRY	POPULATION
1 London, UK	4,684,794
2 New York, USA	4,024,780
3 Paris, France	2,750,000
4 Tokyo, Japan	2,433,000
5 Berlin, Germany	2,006,850
6 Chicago, USA	1,990,750
7 Vienna, Austria	1,897,630
8 Osaka, Japan	1,765,000
9 Philadelphia, USA	1,438,318
10 St. Petersburg, Russia	1,391,000

TOP 10 WORLD CITIES IN 2015

CITY / COUNTRY	ESTIMATED POPULATION, 2015
1 Tokyo, Japan	37,050,000
2 Delhi, India	24,160,000
3 Mumbai, India	21,800,000
4 São Paulo, Brazil	21,300,000
5 Mexico City, Mexico	20,080,000
6 New York, USA	19,970,000
7 Shanghai, China	17,840,000
8 Kolkata, India	16,920,000
9 Dhaka, Bangladesh	16,620,000
10 Karachi, Pakistan	14,820,000

Source: United Nations, *World Urbanization Prospects*

TOP 10 MOST POPULATED COUNTRIES 100 YEARS AGO

COUNTRY / POPULATION

1 China 372,563,000

2 India 287,223,431

3 Russia 147,277,000

4 USA 76,356,000

5 Germany 56,345,014

6 Austro-Hungarian Empire 47,013,835

7 Japan 43,759.577

8 UK 41,605,220

9 France 38,641,333

10 Italy 32,100,000

At the beginning of the 20th century, many national boundaries were quite different from their present form: for example, India encompassed what are now Pakistan and Bangladesh, and Poland was part of Russia.

▲ Bright lights, big city
Tokyo's population swells in the daytime but decreases by about 2.5 million at night.

▲ **Indian boom**
India is currently home to over 17% of the Earth's entire population.

THERE ARE ROUGHLY THE SAME NUMBER OF PEOPLE LIVING IN MUMBAI AS THERE ARE IN THE WHOLE OF AUSTRALIA!

TOP 10 **MOST POPULATED COUNTRIES IN 2012**

	COUNTRY	POPULATION, 2012
1	China	1,343,239,923
2	India	1,205,073,612
3	USA	313,847,465
4	Indonesia	248,216,193
5	Brazil	205,716,890
6	Pakistan	190,291,129
7	Nigeria	170,123,740
8	Bangladesh	161,083,804
9	Russia	138,082,178
10	Japan	127,368,088
	World	7,023,324,899

Source: US Census Bureau, *International Data Base*

TOP 10 **MOST POPULATED COUNTRIES IN 2025**

	COUNTRY	ESTIMATED POPULATION, 2025
1	India	1,396,046,308
2	China	1,394,638,699
3	USA	351,352,771
4	Indonesia	278,502,882
5	Nigeria	234,362,895
6	Brazil	231,886,946
7	Pakistan	228,385,138
8	Bangladesh	197,673,655
9	Ethiopia	140,139,507
10	Mexico	130,198,692
	World	7,987,716,057

Source: US Census Bureau, *International Data Base*

TOP 10 **MOST POPULATED COUNTRIES IN 2050**

COUNTRY / ESTIMATED POPULATION, 2050

1 India 1,656,553,632

2 China 1,303,723,332

3 USA 439,010,253

4 Indonesia 313,020,847

5 Pakistan 290,847,790

6 Ethiopia 278,283,137

7 Nigeria 264,262,405

8 Brazil 260,692,493

9 Bangladesh 250,155,274

10 Congo (Kinshasa) 189,310,849

World 9,284,107,424

▼ **Making a splash**
One in every five people on the planet is currently a Chinese resident.

ϾOϘŁE MOVEMENT

TOP 10 EMIGRATION COUNTRIES

COUNTRY / NO. OF EMIGRANTS*

1 Mexico
11,900,000

2 India
11,400,000

3 Russia
11,100,000

4 China
8,300,000

5 Ukraine
6,600,000

6 Bangladesh
5,400,000

7 = Pakistan
4,700,000
= UK
4,700,000

9 = Philippines
4,300,000
= Turkey
4,300,000

* Latest available year

Source: World Bank

▲ **Crossing the border**
The Mexican border is the most-crossed in the world, with over 350,000 crossings to the US annually.

RECORD MIGRATIONS

Approximately 3% of the world's population are currently classed as "migrants"—meaning they live outside their place of birth—more than at any other point in history. That's one out of every 33 people in the world today. While the percentage of migrants as a share of the total population has remained fairly stable during the past 10 years, it varies vastly from country to country.

TOP 10 IMMIGRATION COUNTRIES

COUNTRY	NO. OF IMMIGRANTS (% POPULATION)
1 Qatar	86.5%
2 Monaco	71.6%
3 United Arab Emirates	70.0%
4 Kuwait	68.8%
5 Jordan	45.9%
6 Singapore	40.7%
7 Israel	40.4%
8 Bahrain	39.1%
9 Luxembourg	35.2%
10 Saudi Arabia	38.8%

Source: World Bank

▲ *The pull of Qatar*
Over 80% of Qatar's population are immigrants working in energy or construction.

PUSH AND PULL

The reasons for migration can be economic, social, political, or environmental. There can be "push" factors that encourage people to leave their home country (such as a lack of security, natural disaster, war, or poverty), or "pull" factors, which entice people to move elsewhere (such as better employment, greater wealth, or lower personal risk). Migration for work has become a way for people from developing countries to earn enough income for survival.

▼ *The push from Libya*
Thousands fled from Libya to neighboring countries due to war in 2011.

TOP 5 REMITTANCE COUNTRIES

COUNTRY / RECEIPTS, 2010 ($)	
1 India	53,100,000,000
2 China	51,300,000,000
3 Mexico	22,000,000,000
4 Philippines	21,400,000,000
5 Bangladesh	10,800,000,000

REMITTANCE RECORDS

The money sent home by migrants to family members is believed to generally reduce the level and severity of poverty, and has become an important economic factor in many developing countries. Such remittances to developing countries are estimated to have reached $325 billion in 2010, and are expected to rise further in the coming years.

MEGACITIES

TOP 10 LARGEST CAPITAL CITIES

	CITY / COUNTRY	POPULATION, 2011
1	Tokyo (including Yokohama and Kawasaki), Japan	34,300,000
2	Seoul (including Bucheon, Goyang, Incheon, Seongnam, and Suwoen), South Korea	25,100,000
3	Delhi* (including Faridabad and Ghaziabad), India	23,300,000
4	Mexico City (including Nezahualcóyotl, Ecatepec, and Naucalpan), Mexico	22,900,000
5	Manila (including Kalookan and Quezon City), Philippines	20,300,000
6	Jakarta (including Bekasi, Bogor, Depok, and Tangerang), Indonesia	18,900,000
7 =	Beijing, China	16,000,000
=	Moscow, Russia	16,000,000
9	Cairo (including Al-Jizah and Shubra al-Khaymah), Egypt	15,400,000
10	Buenos Aires (including San Justo and La Plata), Argentina	14,900,000

* Capital New Delhi

Source: Th. Brinkhoff: *The Principal Agglomerations of the World*, www.citypopulation.de

TOP 10 LARGEST CITIES IN 1950

CITY / COUNTRY / POPULATION, 1950

1	New York, USA	12,463,000
2	London, UK	8,860,000
3	Tokyo, Japan	7,000,000
4	Paris, France	5,900,000
5	Shanghai, China	5,406,000
6	Moscow, Russia	5,100,000
7	Buenos Aires, Argentina	5,000,000
8	Chicago, USA	4,906,000
9	Ruhr, Germany	4,900,000
10	Kolkatta, India	4,800,000

TOP 10 FASTEST-GROWING CITIES

CITY / COUNTRY / AVERAGE ANNUAL POPULATION GROWTH RATE* 2006–20 (%)

1	Beihai, China	10.58%
2	Ghaziabad, India	5.20%
3	Sana'a, Yemen	5.00%
4	Surat, India	4.99%
5	Kabul, Afghanistan	4.74%
6	Bamako, Mali	4.45%
7 =	Faridabad, India	4.44%
=	Lagos, Nigeria	4.44%
9	Dar es Salaam, Tanzania	4.39%
10	Chittagong, Bangladesh	4.29%

* Of urban areas with 750,000 inhabitants or more

▼ **Sprawling metropolis**
Tokyo is the largest metropolis in the world, with nearly 35 million people.

◄ *Jongno Tower*
The tower is famous for its view of Seoul, now the second-largest capital in the world.

TOP 10 COUNTRIES WITH THE MOST MILLION-PLUS CITIES

COUNTRY / CITIES WITH POPULATIONS OF OVER 1 MILLION

1 China 81

2 USA 53

3 India 48

4 Brazil 21

5 Russia 15

6 Japan 13

7 Mexico 12

8 Germany 10

9 = Pakistan 8
= UK 8

THE POPULATIONS OF GUANGZHOU AND SHANGHAI IN CHINA OUTNUMBER THAT OF THE CAPITAL BEIJING BY NEARLY 10 MILLION EACH!

▼ **Panorama of lights**
Guangzhou is merging with surrounding cities to become one of the most populous places on Earth.

TOP 10 MOST POPULOUS CITIES

	CITY / COUNTRY	POPULATION
1	Tokyo, Japan	34,300,000
2	Guangzhou, China	25,200,000
3	Seoul, South Korea	25,100,000
4	Shanghai, China	24,800,000
5	Delhi, India	23,300,000
6	Mumbai, India	23,000,000
7	Mexico City, Mexico	22,900,000
8	New York, USA	22,000,000
9	São Paulo, Brazil	20,900,000
10	Manila, Philippines	20,300,000
	Top 10 total	*241,800,000*

Source: Th. Brinkhoff: *The Principal Agglomerations of the World*, www.citypopulation.de

TOP 10 RICHEST CITIES IN 2020

	COUNTRY	EST. GDP IN 2020 ($ BILLION)
1	Tokyo, Japan	1,602
2	New York, USA	1,561
3	Los Angeles, USA	886
4	London, UK	708
5	Chicago, USA	645
6	Paris, France	611
7	Mexico City, Mexico	608
8	Philadelphia, USA	440
9	Osaka/Kobe, Japan	430
10	Washington, USA	426

▶ **LA opulence**
A Rodeo Drive Roadster, used for luxury tours in LA—one of the richest cities in the world.

MEGASTRUCTURES

TOP 10 **TALLEST MONUMENTS**

	MONUMENT	LOCATION / YEAR COMPLETED	HEIGHT FT	M
1	Gateway Arch	St. Louis, Missouri, USA, 1965	630	192
2	San Jacinto Monument	La Porte, Texas, USA, 1939	570	174
3	Crazy Horse Memorial	Thunderhead Mountain, South Dakota, USA *	563	172
4	Juche Tower	Pyongyang, North Korea, 1982	558	170
5	Washington Monument	Washington, DC, USA, 1884	555	169
6	Cruz de los Caidos	San Lorenzo de El Escorial, Spain, 1956	492	150
7	Victory Monument	Moscow, Russia, 1995	465	142
8	Pyramid of Khufu	Giza, Egypt, 2560 BC	455	139
9	National Monument	Jakarta, Indonesia, 1975	449	137
10	Pyramid of Khafre	Giza, Egypt, 2532 BC	448	136

* Under construction

▲ *Crazy Horse Memorial*
If it is ever completed, this sculpture could become the world's largest monument.

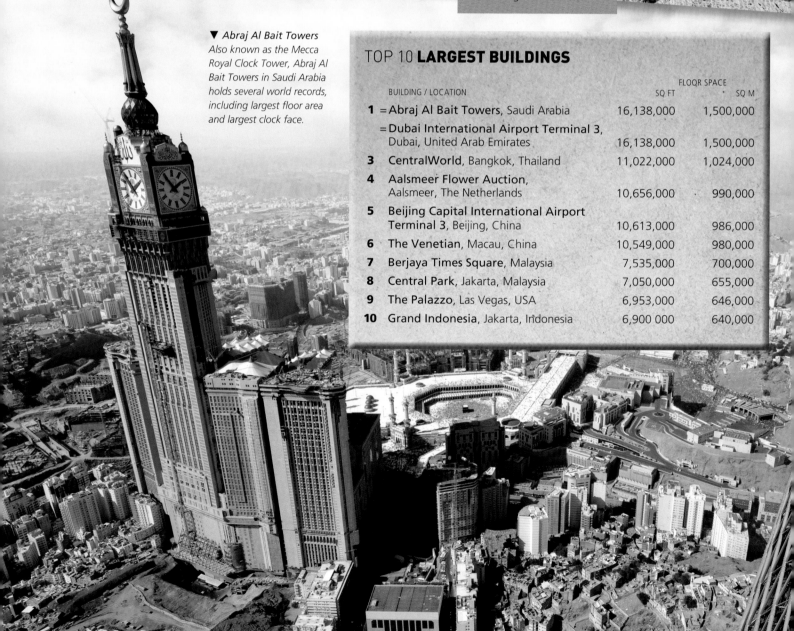

▼ *Abraj Al Bait Towers*
Also known as the Mecca Royal Clock Tower, Abraj Al Bait Towers in Saudi Arabia holds several world records, including largest floor area and largest clock face.

TOP 10 **LARGEST BUILDINGS**

	BUILDING / LOCATION	FLOOR SPACE SQ FT	SQ M
1 =	Abraj Al Bait Towers, Saudi Arabia	16,138,000	1,500,000
=	Dubai International Airport Terminal 3, Dubai, United Arab Emirates	16,138,000	1,500,000
3	CentralWorld, Bangkok, Thailand	11,022,000	1,024,000
4	Aalsmeer Flower Auction, Aalsmeer, The Netherlands	10,656,000	990,000
5	Beijing Capital International Airport Terminal 3, Beijing, China	10,613,000	986,000
6	The Venetian, Macau, China	10,549,000	980,000
7	Berjaya Times Square, Malaysia	7,535,000	700,000
8	Central Park, Jakarta, Malaysia	7,050,000	655,000
9	The Palazzo, Las Vegas, USA	6,953,000	646,000
10	Grand Indonesia, Jakarta, Indonesia	6,900 000	640,000

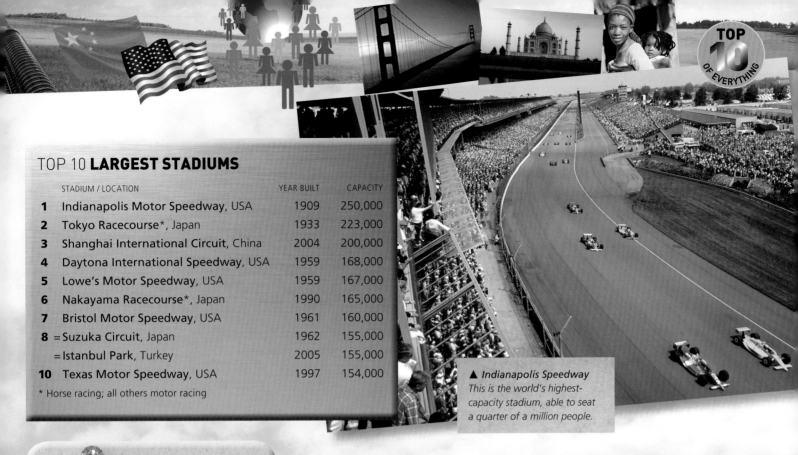

TOP 10 LARGEST STADIUMS

	STADIUM / LOCATION	YEAR BUILT	CAPACITY
1	Indianapolis Motor Speedway, USA	1909	250,000
2	Tokyo Racecourse*, Japan	1933	223,000
3	Shanghai International Circuit, China	2004	200,000
4	Daytona International Speedway, USA	1959	168,000
5	Lowe's Motor Speedway, USA	1959	167,000
6	Nakayama Racecourse*, Japan	1990	165,000
7	Bristol Motor Speedway, USA	1961	160,000
8	=Suzuka Circuit, Japan	1962	155,000
	=Istanbul Park, Turkey	2005	155,000
10	Texas Motor Speedway, USA	1997	154,000

* Horse racing; all others motor racing

▲ **Indianapolis Speedway**
This is the world's highest-capacity stadium, able to seat a quarter of a million people.

THE WORLD'S TALLEST TOWERS

The tallest tower in the world, which is freestanding and accessible, is the Tokyo Sky Tree in Japan. This steel tower, which was completed early in 2012, stands 2,080 ft (634 m) high. It is a digital radio and TV broadcasting tower and has two observation levels, with stores and restaurants that are open to the public. The Tokyo Sky Tree is taller than the Canton Tower in China, which stands at 1,969 ft (600 m) and the CT Tower in Canada, which stands at 1,814 ft (553 m) high.

TOP 10 TALLEST RELIGIOUS BUILDINGS

	BUILDING / LOCATION / YEAR COMPLETED	FT	M
1	Hassan II Mosque Casablanca, Morocco, 1993	689	210.0
2	Sagrada Família Barcelona, Spain, 2026*	558	170.0
3	Mole Antonelliana Turin, Italy, 1889	550	167.5
4	Ulm Cathedral Ulm, Germany, 1890	530	161.5
5	Our Lady of Peace Basilica Yamoussoukro, Côte d'Ivoire, 1990	518	158.0
6	Cologne Cathedral Cologne, Germany, 1880	516	157.4
7	Tianning Pagoda Changzhou, China, 2007	505	154.0
8	Notre-Dame Cathedral Rouen, France, 1876	495	151.0
9	St. Nicholas Hamburg, Germany, 1847	483	147.3
10	Notre Dame Cathedral Strasbourg, France, 1439	472	144.0

* Under construction; scheduled completion

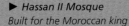

► **Hassan II Mosque**
Built for the Moroccan king Hassan II, this mosque has the tallest minaret in the world.

OVER & UNDER

TOP 10 HIGHEST BRIDGES

	BRIDGE	LOCATION / YEAR COMPLETED	HEIGHT* FT	M
1	Siduhe River	Hubei, China, 2009	1,550	472
2	Heggio Gorge	Otama, Papua New Guinea, 2005	1,289	393
3	Baluarte River	Sinaloa, Mexico, 2012	1,280	390
4	Balinghe River	Guizhou, China, 2009	1,214	370
5	Beipanjiang River	Guizhou, China, 2003	1,200	366
6 =	Aizhai	Guizhou, China, 2012	1,083	330
=	Beipanjiang River	Guizhou, China, 2009	1,083	330
8	Chenab River	Katra, Jammu-Kashmir, 2015#	1,053	321
9	Liuguanghe	Guizhou, China, 2001	975	297
10	Zhijinghe River	Hubei, China, 2009	965	294

* Clearance above water
\# Under construction; scheduled completion

▲ **Bridging the gap**
The Balinghe, China, is one of the world's highest bridges at 1,214 ft (370 m).

▼ **Twin swing**
The Spokane connects Harbor Island with West Seattle in Washington.

THE LONGEST SWING BRIDGE

Swing bridges are used throughout the world, normally where road or rail traffic crosses a busy seaway. To open, a swing bridge pivots into position on a horizontal plane. The world's longest swing bridge is the El Ferdan railway bridge in Egypt, which spans the Suez Canal from Ismailia across to Sinai. It is 1,115 ft (340 m) in length.

TOP 10 LONGEST RAIL TUNNELS

	TUNNEL / LOCATION	YEAR COMPLETED	LENGTH MILES	KM
1 =	AlpTransit Gotthard, Switzerland	2016*	35.0	57.0
=	Mont d'Ambin, France/Italy	2023*	35.0	57.0
3	Brenner Tunnel, Austria/Italy	2025*	34.2	55.0
4	Seikan, Japan	1988	33.5	53.9
5	Channel Tunnel, France/England	1994	31.3	50.5
6	Seoul Subway (Bangha-Macheon)	1996	29.6	47.6
7 °	Moscow Metro (Serpukhovsko-Timiryazevskaya line), Russia	2002	25.7	41.5
8	Madrid Metro, Spain	2003	25.5	40.9
9	Toie Oedo, Japan	2000	25.3	40.7
10	Moscow Metro (Kaluzhsko-Rizhskaya line), Russia	1990	23.4	37.6

* Under construction; scheduled completion

▲ **Tunneling On**
When completed, trains will travel through the AlpTransit tunnel at 155 mph (250 km/h).

► **World's longest**
The Akashi-Kaikyo links the Japanese Kobe-Naruto highway with the island of Awaji.

CHINA IS HOME TO 7 OUT OF THE 10 LONGEST BRIDGES IN THE WORLD!

TOP 10 LONGEST SUSPENSION BRIDGES

BRIDGE / LOCATION	YEAR COMPLETED	LENGTH OF MAIN SPAN FT	M
1 Akashi-Kaikyo Kobe-Naruto, Japan	1998	6,532	1,991
2 Xihoumen Zhoushan, China	2009	5,413	1,650
3 Great Belt Korsor, Denmark	1997	5,328	1,624
4 Gwangyang Myodo-Gwangyang, South Korea	2012*	5,069	1,545
5 Ryungyang Zhenjiang, China	2005	4,888	1,490
6 Nanjing Fourth Yangtse Nanjing, China	2012*	4,652	1,418
7 Humber Kingston-upon-Hull, UK	1981	4,625	1,410
8 Jiangyin, Jiangsu, China	1998	4,543	1,385
9 Tsing Ma, Hong Kong, China	1997	4,518	1,377
10 Verrazano-Narrows New York, USA	1964	4,260	1,298

* Under construction; scheduled completion

TOP 10 LONGEST WATER-SUPPLY TUNNELS

TUNNEL / LOCATION	YEAR COMPLETED	LENGTH MILES	KM
1 Delaware Aqueduct, New York, USA	1945	105.0	169.0
2 Päijänne, Finland	1982	74.6	120.0
3 New York Third Water Tunnel	2020*	60.0	96.6
4 Liaoning, China	2009	52.8	85.0
5 Orange-Fish, South Africa	1975	51.4	82.8
6 Bolmen, Sweden	1987	51.0	82.0
7 Thames Water Ring Main, London, UK	1994	49.7	80.0
8 West Delaware, New York, USA	1960	44.0	70.8
9 Zelivka, Czech Republic	1972	32.2	51.9
10 Central outfall, Mexico City	1975	31.1	50.0

* Scheduled completion

TOP 10 LONGEST ROAD TUNNELS

TUNNEL / LOCATION	YEAR COMPLETED	LENGTH FT	M
1 Lærdal, Norway	2000	80,413	24,510
2 Zhongnanshan, China	2007	59,186	18,040
3 St Gotthard, Switzerland	1980	55,505	16,918
4 Arlberg, Austria	1978	45,850	13,972
5 Hsuehshan, China (Taiwan)	2006	42,460	12,942
6 Fréjus, France/Italy	1980	42,306	12,895
7 Majishan, China	2009	40,321	12,290
8 Mont-Blanc, France/Italy	1965	38,094	11,611
9 Gudvangen, Norway	1991	37,493	11,428
10 Folgefonna, Norway	2001	36,581	11,150

Previous record-holders of the world's longest road tunnel include the 19,206-ft (5,854-m) Grand San Bernardo (Italy-Switzerland; 1964), the 16,841-ft (5,133-m) Alfonos XIII or Viella (Spain; 1948), the 10,620-ft (3,237-m) Queensway (Mersey) Tunnel (Liverpool and Birkenhead, UK; 1934) and the 10,453-ft (3,186-m) Col de Tende (France-Italy; 1882). The 13,780-ft (4,200-m) Ted Williams/Interstate 190 Extension tunnel, Boston, Massachusetts (1995–2003), is the USA's longest road tunnel.

5

CULTURE & LEARNING

THE LION, THE WITCH
and
THE WARDROBE

A Story for Children
by
C. S. LEWIS

NARNIA FOREVER

Although widely remembered today for his *Chronicles of Narnia*—seven classics of fantasy literature written between 1949 and 1954—C. S. Lewis was also a distinguished Oxford scholar and "media don," famed for his wartime religious broadcasts. Lewis (Jack to his friends, who included *Lord of the Rings* author J. R. R. Tolkien) died 50 years ago this year, on November 22. News coverage of this sad event was restricted, as John F. Kennedy was assassinated on the same day. Since that time, the *Narnia* series has been translated into 30 languages and adapted many times for the screen. The first of the most recent feature-film series, *The Lion, the Witch and the Wardrobe*, was among the biggest box-office successes of 2005.

WORLD LANGUAGES

TOP 10 COUNTRIES WITH THE MOST SPANISH SPEAKERS

	COUNTRY	SPEAKERS*
1	Mexico	110,651,490
2	USA	50,000,000
3	Spain	46,585,009
4	Colombia	45,830,400
5	Argentina	40,655,093
6	Venezuela	29,042,260
7	Peru	25,804,803
8	Chile	17,127,610
9	Ecuador	14,034,186
10	Guatemala	12,408,479

* As first or second/foreign language

▲ Voices of protest
Egyptians united with one voice in a wave of protest during the Arab Spring in 2011.

TOP 10 COUNTRIES WITH THE MOST ENGLISH SPEAKERS

	COUNTRY	APPROX. NO. OF ENGLISH SPEAKERS*
1	USA	225,505,953
2	UK	58,100,000
3	Canada	17,694,830
4	Australia	15,581,329
5	Ireland	4,122,100
6	Nigeria	4,000,000
7	New Zealand	3,673,679
8	South Africa	3,673,203
9	Philippines	3,427,000
10	Jamaica#	2,600,000

* People for whom English is their mother tongue; latest available data
# Includes English Creole
Source: Ethnologue

TOP 10 COUNTRIES WITH THE MOST ARABIC SPEAKERS

	COUNTRY	SPEAKERS
1	Egypt	67,367,000
2	Algeria	27,346,000
3	Saudi Arabia	22,809,000
4	Yemen	19,930,000
5	Morocco	19,390,000
6	Iraq	19,026,000
7	Sudan	18,818,000
8	Syria	15,829,000
9	Tunisia	6,911,000*
10	Libya	5,334,000

* A further 2,596,000 people speak Arabic-French

THERE ARE 6,909 LIVING LANGUAGES—ONE FOR EVERY 1,013,200 PEOPLE IN THE WORLD!

► Speaking Spanish
Spanish is the official language of nearly three-quarters of the population of Spain.

TOP 10 LANGUAGES OFFICIALLY SPOKEN IN THE MOST COUNTRIES

	LANGUAGE	COUNTRIES*
1	English	53
2	French	29
3	Arabic	25
4	Spanish	14
5	Portuguese	8
6	German	7
7	= Albanian	4
	= Italian	4
	= Russian	4
	= Serbian	4

* Independent states, excluding overseas territories and dependencies

Many countries have more than one official language—both English and French are recognized officially in Canada, for example. English is used in numerous countries as the *lingua franca*, the common language that enables people who speak mutually unintelligible languages to communicate.

Internet - http://www

File   Edit   View   History   Bookmarks   Tools   Help

http://www

Page ▼

TOP 10 ONLINE LANGUAGES

	LANGUAGE	% OF ALL INTERNET USERS	INTERNET USERS*
1	English	26.8	565,004,126
2	Chinese (Mandarin)	24.2	509,965,013
3	Spanish	7.8	164,968,742
4	Japanese	4.7	99,182,000
5	Portuguese	3.9	82,586,600
6	German	3.6	75,422,674
7	Arabic	3.3	65,365,400
8	French	3.0	59,779,525
9	Russian	3.0	59,700,000
10	Korean	2.0	39,440,800
	Top 10 languages	82.3	1,721,414,880
	Rest of world languages	17.7	350,557,483
	World total	100.0	2,071,972,363

* 2011 estimate

Source: www.internetworldstats.com

Between 2000 and 2011, internet usage grew most quickly for Arabic-speaking users, followed by Chinese and Russian-speaking users.

▼ **Mobile mandarin**
Mandarin is the official language of China, with more native speakers than any other.

TOP 10 MOST-SPOKEN LANGUAGES

	LANGUAGE	SPEAKERS*
1	Chinese (Mandarin)	845,456,760
2	Spanish	328,518,810
3	English	328,008,138
4	Arabic	221,002,544
5	Hindi	181,676,620
6	Bengali	181,272,900
7	Portuguese	177,981,570
8	Russian	143,553,950
9	Japanese	122,080,100
10	German	90,294,110

* Primary speakers only

Source: Ethnologue

EDUCATION

TOP 10 COUNTRIES WITH MOST PRIMARY-SCHOOL PUPILS

COUNTRY / PRIMARY SCHOOL PUPILS*

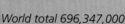
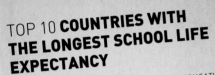

India
140,357,000

China
107,395,000

Indonesia
29,997,000

USA
24,677,000

Nigeria
21,632,000

Pakistan
18,176,000

Brazil
17,812,000

Bangladesh
16,002,000

Mexico
14,699,000

Philippines
13,145,000

World total 696,347,000

* Latest years for which data available

Source: UNESCO, *Global Education Digest 2011*

TOP 10 COUNTRIES WITH THE LONGEST SCHOOL LIFE EXPECTANCY

COUNTRY	AVERAGE NO. OF YEARS IN EDUCATION*		
	GIRLS	BOYS	TOTAL
1 New Zealand	21	20	>20
2 Australia	20	20	20
3 Iceland	20	17	>18
4 Ireland	18	18	18
5 =Norway	18	17	>17
=Monaco	17	18	>17
7 =South Korea	18	16	17
=Denmark	18	16	17
=Slovenia	18	16	17
=The Netherlands	17	17	17

* Latest year and those countries for which data available

Source: UNESCO Institute for Statistics

▼ **Indian school**
Even the most rural communities in India provide primary education for children aged 6–14.

TOP 10 COUNTRIES WITH MOST SECONDARY-SCHOOL PUPILS

COUNTRY / SECONDARY SCHOOL PUPILS*

1 China
101,448,000

2 India
96,049,000

3 USA
24,693,000

4 Indonesia
18,315,000

5 Mexico
11,444,000

6 Bangladesh
10,445,000

7 Russia
10,087,000

8 Vietnam
9,845,000

9 Pakistan
9,340,000

10 Iran
8,187,000

World total (all countries) 525,665,000

* Latest years for which data available

Source: UNESCO, *Global Education Digest 2011*

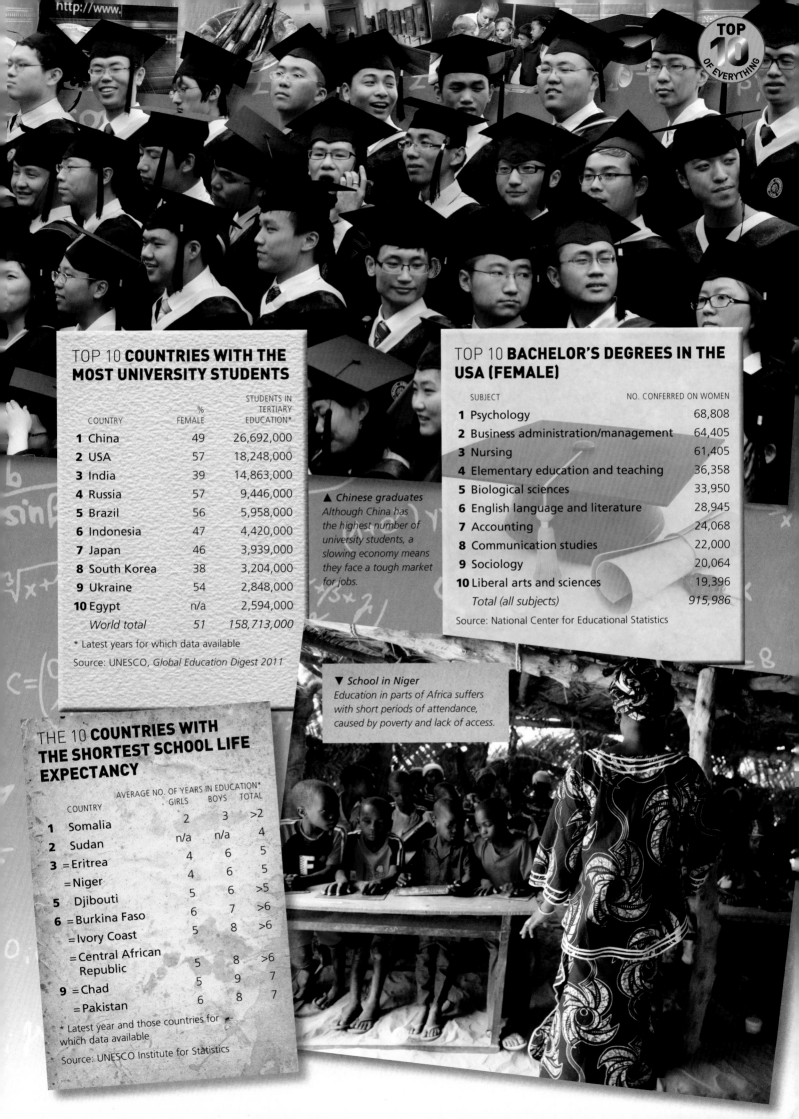

TOP 10 **COUNTRIES WITH THE MOST UNIVERSITY STUDENTS**

COUNTRY	% FEMALE	STUDENTS IN TERTIARY EDUCATION*
1 China	49	26,692,000
2 USA	57	18,248,000
3 India	39	14,863,000
4 Russia	57	9,446,000
5 Brazil	56	5,958,000
6 Indonesia	47	4,420,000
7 Japan	46	3,939,000
8 South Korea	38	3,204,000
9 Ukraine	54	2,848,000
10 Egypt	n/a	2,594,000
World total	*51*	*158,713,000*

* Latest years for which data available

Source: UNESCO, *Global Education Digest 2011*

▲ *Chinese graduates*
Although China has the highest number of university students, a slowing economy means they face a tough market for jobs.

TOP 10 **BACHELOR'S DEGREES IN THE USA (FEMALE)**

SUBJECT	NO. CONFERRED ON WOMEN
1 Psychology	68,808
2 Business administration/management	64,405
3 Nursing	61,405
4 Elementary education and teaching	36,358
5 Biological sciences	33,950
6 English language and literature	28,945
7 Accounting	24,068
8 Communication studies	22,000
9 Sociology	20,064
10 Liberal arts and sciences	19,396
Total (all subjects)	*915,986*

Source: National Center for Educational Statistics

▼ *School in Niger*
Education in parts of Africa suffers with short periods of attendance, caused by poverty and lack of access.

THE 10 **COUNTRIES WITH THE SHORTEST SCHOOL LIFE EXPECTANCY**

COUNTRY	AVERAGE NO. OF YEARS IN EDUCATION* GIRLS	BOYS	TOTAL
1 Somalia	2	3	>2
2 Sudan	n/a	n/a	4
3 =Eritrea	4	6	5
=Niger	4	6	5
5 Djibouti	5	6	>5
6 =Burkina Faso	6	7	>6
=Ivory Coast	5	8	>6
=Central African Republic	5	8	>6
9 =Chad	5	9	7
=Pakistan	6	8	7

* Latest year and those countries for which data available

Source: UNESCO Institute for Statistics

LIBRARIES

TOP 10 **BOOKS FOUND IN MOST LIBRARIES**

	BOOK	TOTAL LIBRARY HOLDINGS*
1	The Bible	796,882
2	US Census	460,628
3	Mother Goose	67,663
4	Dante Alighieri, Divine Comedy	62,414
5	Homer, The Odyssey	45,551
6	Homer, The Iliad	44,093
7	Mark Twain, Huckleberry Finn	42,724
8	J. R. R. Tolkien, Lord of the Rings (trilogy)	40,907
9	William Shakespeare, Hamlet	39,521
10	Lewis Carroll, Alice's Adventures in Wonderland	39,277

* Based on WorldCat listings of all editions of books held in 53,000 libraries in 96 countries

Source: Online Computer Library Center

◄ **The Bible and Mother Goose**
From Mother Goose to the Bible, the world's libraries are an eclectic treasure trove of fact and fiction.

TOP 10 **MOST-BORROWED FICTION TITLES IN THE USA**

AUTHOR / TITLE

1 **Dan Brown**, The Lost Symbol
2 **Kathryn Stockett**, The Help
3 **Michael Connelly**, Nine Dragons
4 **David Baldacci**, True Blue
5 **Nicholas Sparks**, The Last Song
6 **James Patterson**, I, Alex Cross
7 **James Patterson and Richard DiLallo**, Alex Cross's Trial
8 **Audrey Niffenegger**, The Time Traveler's Wife
9 **Patricia Cornwell**, The Scarpetta Factor
10 **John Sandford**, Rough Country

Source: Library Journal

TOP 10 **MOST-BORROWED NONFICTION TITLES IN THE USA**

Source: Library Journal

AUTHOR / TITLE

1 **Mitch Albom**
Have a Little Faith: a True Story

2 **Edward M. Kennedy**
True Compass

3 **Steven D. Levitt and Stephen J. Dubner**
Super Freakonomics

4 **Malcolm Gladwell**
Outliers: The Story of Success

5 **Malcolm Gladwell**
What the Dog Saw: and Other Adventures

6 **Sarah Palin**
Going Rogue: An American Life

7 **James Patterson and Martin Dugard**
The Murder of King Tut

8 **Andre Agassi**
Open: An Autobiography

9 **Steve Harvey**
Committed: Act Like a Lady, Think Like a Man

10 **Jon Krakauer**
Where Men Win Glory: The Odyssey of Pat Tillman

◄ *Palace of books*
The Austrian National library in the Hofburg Palace, Vienna, was once home to the country's emperors.

▼ *Tome home*
France's new national library in Paris, the Bibliotheque Nationale, contains over 10 million volumes.

THE LARGEST LIBRARY IN THE WORLD IS THE LIBRARY OF CONGRESS IN WASHINGTON, DC, WITH 32,124,000 BOOKS.

TOP 10 OLDEST NATIONAL LIBRARIES

LIBRARY / LOCATION	FOUNDED
1 Národní Knihovna Ceské Republiky National Library of the Czech Republic, Prague, Czech Republic	1366
2 Österreichische Nationalbibliothek National Library of Austria, Vienna, Austria	1368
3 Biblioteca Nazionale Marciana, Venice, Italy	1468
4 Bibliothèque Nationale de France National Library of France, Paris, France	1480
5 National Library of Malta, Valetta, Malta	1555
6 Bayericsche Staatsbibliothek, Munich, Germany	1558
7 Bibliothèque Royale Albert 1er National Library of Belgium, Brussels, Belgium	1559
8 Nacionalna i Sveucilišna Knjižnica Zagreb National and University Library, Zagreb, Croatia	1606
9 Helsingin Yliopisto Kirjasto National Library of Finland, Helsinki, Finland	1640
10 Det Kongeligie Bibliotek National Library of Denmark, Copenhagen, Denmark	1653

What may claim to be the world's first national library was that in Alexandria, Egypt, founded in about 307 BC by King Ptolemy I Soter. It assembled the world's largest collection of scrolls, which were totally destroyed by Arab invaders in AD 642—an event that is considered one of the greatest losses to world scholarship.

TOP 10 LARGEST PUBLIC LIBRARIES IN THE USA

LIBRARY / LOCATION	BOOKS
1 Boston Public Library*	24,079,520
2 New York Public Library*	16,640,294
3 Public Library of Cincinnati and Hamilton County	8,959,303
4 Queens Borough Public Library	7,384,276
5 Detroit Public Library	7,252,846
6 Los Angeles Public Library	6,434,367
7 Chicago Public Library	5,743,002
8 Free Library of Philadelphia	4,970,401
9 Hannepin Public Library	4,793,215
10 Cleveland Public Library	4,565,137

* Branches and research, including private collections

Source: American Library Association

TOP 10 BESTSELLING BOOK SERIES*

SERIES / AUTHOR / INSTALMENTS	ESTIMATED SALES*
1 Harry Potter, J. K. Rowling, 7	450,000,000
2 Goosebumps, R. L. Stine, 62+ spin off series	350,000,000
3 Perry Mason, Erle Stanley Gardner, 82	300,000,000
4 Berenstain Bears, Stan and Jan Berenstain, 300+	260,000,000
5 = The Railway Series, Rev. W. Awdry and Christopher Awdry, 41	200,000,000
= Noddy, Enid Blyton, 24	200,000,000
7 The Baby-sitters Club, Ann Martin, 335	172,000,000
8 Peter Rabbit, Beatrix Potter, 6	150,000,000
9 Chicken Soup for the Soul, Jack Cranfield and Mark Victor Hansen, 105	130,000,000
10 Frank Merriwell, Gilbert Patten, 209	125,000,000

* By one or two known authors
# Including translations

Many of the bestselling book series would be classed as children's literature or young-adult fiction. If book series written by various "ghost writers" were included, the *Sweet Valley High* series and *Choose Your Own Adventure* would tie for 5th place, with approximate sales of 250 million each. C. S. Lewis's much-loved series, *The Chronicles of Narnia*, comes in just shy of the Top 10 with 120 million in sales, and the *Twilight* series by Stephenie Meyer continues to gain ground, with around 116 million sold.

▼ *Pottermania*
The Harry Potter tales continue to hold the rapt attention of fans both young and old.

▶ *Never the Twain*
The cunning Tom Sawyer is one of Mark Twain's most popular characters.

TOP 10 MOST DOWNLOADED ENGLISH-LANGUAGE AUTHORS

AUTHOR	DOWNLOADS*
1 Mark Twain	65,912
2 Arthur Conan Doyle	60,937
3 Charles Dickens	49,480
4 Jane Austen	44,120
5 William Shakespeare	42,741
6 Edgar Allan Poe	36,529
7 Richard Francis Burton	32,835
8 H. G. Wells	29,478
9 Lewis Carroll	26,723
10 P. G. Wodehouse	24,500

* Based on a 30-day sample on Project Gutenberg

TOP 10 MOST-TRANSLATED AUTHORS

AUTHOR / COUNTRY / DATES	TRANSLATIONS*
1 Agatha Christie (UK; 1890–1976)	7,003
2 Jules Verne (France; 1828–1905)	4,579
3 William Shakespeare (England; 1564–1616)	4,037
4 Enid Blyton (UK; 1897–1968)	3,719
5 V. I. Lenin (Russia; 1870–1924)	3,644
6 Barbara Cartland (UK; 1901–2000)	3,554
7 Danielle Steele (USA; b.1947)	3,273
8 Hans Christian Andersen (Denmark; 1805–75)	3,231
9 Stephen King (USA; b.1947)	3,014
10 Jakob Grimm (Germany; 1785–1863)	2,770

* 1979–2011; all languages and world regions

Source: *Index Translationum*, UNESCO

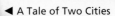

▲ **Found in translation**
Agatha Christie's murder mysteries have a truly global appeal.

▶ **Sci-fi pioneer**
Jules Verne's stories foresaw space travel and underwater exploration.

TOP 10 BESTSELLING NOVELS*

AUTHOR / TITLE / FIRST PUBLISHED / ESTIMATED SALES#

1 Charles Dickens,
A Tale of Two Cities, 1859
>200,000,000

2 J. R. R. Tolkien,
The Lord of the Rings†, 1954–55
150,000,000

3 = J. R. R. Tolkien, The Hobbit, 1937
>100,000,000

= Cao Xueqin, Dream of the Red Chamber,
18th century >100,000,000

5 Agatha Christie,
And Then There Were None, 1939
100,000,000

6 C. S. Lewis, The Lion, the Witch and
the Wardrobe, 1950
85,000,000

7 H. Rider Haggard,
She, 1887
83,000,000

8 = Antoine de Saint-Exupery,
Le Petit Prince, 1943 80,000,000

= Dan Brown, The Da Vinci Code, 2003
80,000,000

10 J. D. Salinger
The Catcher in the Rye, 1951
65,000,000

◀ **A Tale of Two Cities**
Dickens' classic tale set during the French Revolution has sold in excess of 200 million copies.

THE 10 LATEST WINNERS OF THE PULITZER PRIZE FOR FICTION

YEAR   AUTHOR / TITLE

2011 Jennifer Egan
A Visit from the Goon Squad

2010 Paul Harding Tinkers

2009 Elizabeth Strout
Olive Kitteridge

2008 Junot Diaz
The Brief Wondrous Life
of Oscar Wao

2007 Cormac McCarthy
The Road

2006 Geraldine Brooks
March

2005 Marilynne Robinson
Gilead

2004 Edward P. Jones
The Known World

2003 Jeffrey Eugenides
Middlesex

2002 Richard Russo Empire Falls

* Single-volume novels
# Including translations
† Written as a single book—figure is an estimate of copies of the full story sold, whether published as one volume or three

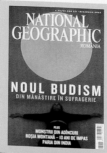

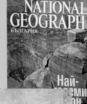

▲ NG birthday

National Geographic *magazine* celebrates its 125th anniversary in 2013.

TOP 10 MAGAZINES

	MAGAZINE*	AVERAGE YEARLY CIRCULATION#
1	Better Homes & Gardens	7,648,900
2	Game Informer (USA)	5,954,884
3	Reader's Digest	5,653,440
4	National Geographic	4,445,603
5	Good Housekeeping	4,336,711
6	Woman's Day (USA)	3,863,710
7	Family Circle	3,816,958
8	People	3,556,753
9	Time	3,376,226
10	Ladies' Home Journal	3,267,239

* Independently bought magazines in English-speaking countries
\# Based on first half of 2011

Source: Audit Bureau of Circulations

TOP 10 MAGAZINE GENRES IN THE USA

	GENRE	NO. OF PUBLICATIONS, 2011
1	Medicine	1,100
2	Regional interest	939
3	Travel	829
4	Religion and theological	784
5	Business and industry	613
6	College and alumni	569
7	Health and fitness	508
8	College student press	425
9	Education	387
10 =	Computers and automation	381
=	Lifestyle	381

Source: National Directory of Magazines

TOP 10 SUNDAY NEWSPAPERS IN THE USA

	NEWSPAPER	AVERAGE CIRCULATION*
1	The New York Times	1,438,585
2	Los Angeles Times	1,055,076
3	Washington Post	866,057
4	Chicago Tribune	864,845
5	New York News	674,104
6	Detroit News & Free Press	605,369
7	Houston Chronicle	584,164
8	Philadelphia Inquirer	556,426
9	Star Tribune (Minneapolis)	520,828
10	The Boston Globe	503,659

* Latest period for which data available

Source: Audit Bureau of Circulations

The number of magazines devoted to medicine and fitness has increased over the last five years, and education and lifestyle magazines have become more popular. Just short of the Top 10 are women's magazines. Magazines devoted to cars and music have fallen out of the Top 10.

▶ *Japanese Sun*
The Asahi Shimbun *("Morning Sun") was launched in Osaka, Japan, in 1879.*

TOP 10 **DAILY NEWSPAPERS**

NEWSPAPER	COUNTRY	AVERAGE DAILY CIRCULATION*
1 Yomiuri Shimbun	Japan	10,021,000
2 Asahi Shimbun	Japan	8,054,000
3 Mainichi Shimbun	Japan	3,945,646
4 Bild	Germany	3,548,000
5 Canako Xiaoxi (Beijing)	China	3,183,000
6 The Times of India	India	3,146,000
7 Nihon Keizai Shimbun	Japan	3,034,481
8 The Sun	UK	3,026,556
9 People's Daily	China	2,808,000
10 Chunichi Shimbun	Japan	2,763,602

* Latest period for which data available; morning edition if published twice daily

Source: World Association of Newspapers

COUNTRIES WITH THE LEAST PRESS FREEDOM

The dictatorships of Eritrea, Turkmenistan, and North Korea usually finish at the bottom of the annual press freedom index issued by Reporters Without Borders, which campaigns for the free flow of news. Syria, Iran, China, Vietnam, and Bahrain are little better, with no independent media outlets.

▼ *The big read*
Over 4,000 new newspaper titles are registered in India every year.

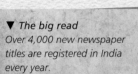

TOP 10 **ENGLISH-LANGUAGE DAILY NEWSPAPERS**

NEWSPAPER	COUNTRY	AVERAGE DAILY CIRCULATION
1 The Times of India	India	3,146,000
2 The Sun	UK	3,026,556
3 USA Today	USA	2,293,310
4 Daily Mail	UK	2,157,085
5 The Wall Street Journal	USA	2,011,999
6 The Mirror	UK	1,295,972
7 Hindustan Times	India	1,143,000
8 The Hindu	India	1,102,783
9 Deccan Chronicle	India	1,003,171
10 The New York Times	USA	1,000,665

Source: World Association of Newspapers/Audit Bureau of Circulations

ART ON SHOW

▲ Popular painting
Seurat's The Bathers *(1884) was a major attraction at the Manet to Picasso show.*

EXHIBITION	YEAR	TOTAL ATTENDANCE
1 Manet to Picasso	2006–07	1,110,044
2 Seeing Salvation: The Image of Christ	2000	355,175
3 Velázquez	2006–07	302,520
4 Vermeer and the Delft School	2001	276,164
5 Titian	2003	267,939
6 Raphael: From Urbino to Rome	2004–05	230,649
7 Picasso Prints: Challenging the Past	2009	227,831
8 Kienholz: The Hoerengracht	2009–10	223,183
9 El Greco	2004	219,000
10 Picasso: Challenging the Past	2009	204,862

* In the 21st century

TOP 10 MOST-VISITED GALLERIES AND MUSEUMS, 2011

GALLERY / LOCATION	TOTAL ATTENDANCE
1 Louvre Museum, Paris, France	8,880,000
2 Metropolitan Museum of Art, New York, USA	6,004,254
3 British Museum, London, UK	5,848,534
4 National Gallery, London, UK	5,253,216
5 Tate Modern, London, UK	4,802,287
6 National Gallery of Art, Washington, DC, USA	4,392,252
7 National Palace Museum, Taipei, China	3,849,577
8 Centre Pompidou, Paris, France	3,613,076
9 National Museum of Korea, Seoul, South Korea	3,239,549
10 Musée d'Orsay, Paris, France	3,154,000

Source: *The Art Newspaper*

▲ Mona's eye view
Leonardo da Vinci's famous Mona Lisa *is the biggest visitor attraction at the Louvre gallery in Paris, drawing hundreds of thousands of visitors every year.*

TOP 10 BEST-ATTENDED EXHIBITIONS AT THE METROPOLITAN MUSEUM OF ART, NEW YORK

	EXHIBITION	YEARS	ATTENDANCE
1	The Treasures of Tutankhamun	1978–79	1,226,467
2	Mona Lisa	1963	1,007,521
3	The Vatican Collection: The Papacy and Art	1983	896,743
4	Glory of Russian Costume	1976–77	835,862
5	Origins of Impressionism	1994–95	794,108
6	Romantic and Glamorous Hollywood	1974–75	788,665
7	The Horses of San Marco	1980	742,221
8	Man and the Horse	1984–85	726,523
9	Picasso in the Metropolitan Museum of Art	2010	703,256
10	Masterpieces of Fifty Centuries	1979–81	690,471

TOP 10 BEST-ATTENDED ART EXHIBITIONS, 2011

	EXHIBITION*	VENUE / CITY / DATES	ATTENDANCE# DAILY AVERAGE	TOTAL
1	Abstract Impressionist New York	Museum of Modern Art, New York, Oct 3, 2010–Apr 25, 2011	5,655	1,159,229
2	Landscape Reunited	National Palace Museum, Taipei Jun 2–Sep 5, 2011	8,828	847,509
3	Counter Space	Museum of Modern Art, New York, Sep 15, 2010–May 2, 2011	3,570	821,145
4	Tutenkhamun and Golden Age of the Pharaohs	Melbourne Museum, Melbourne, Apr 8–Dec 4, 2011	3,318	796,277
5	The Saved Gods of the Palace of Tell Hafaf	Pergamonmuseum, Berlin, Jan 28–Aug 14, 2011	3,920	780,000
6	Newspeak: British Art Now	Saatchi Gallery, London, Oct 27, 2010–Apr 30, 2011	4,122	708,984
7	Bill Fontana: The More Things Change	SF Museum of Modern Art, San Francisco, Nov 20, 2010–Nov 6, 2011	2,357	706,627
8	Alexander McQueen: Savage Beauty	Metropolitan Museum of Art, New York, May 4–Aug 7, 2011	8,025	661,509
9	Te Ao Maori: Maori Treasures	Shanghai Museum, Shanghai, Jul 21–Nov 6, 2011	5,660	611,287
10	The Magical World of Escher	Centro Cultural Banco do Brasil, Rio de Janeiro, Jan 18–Mar 27, 2011	9,677	573,691

* With longest part of run in 2011
\# Approximate totals provided by museums

Source: *The Art Newspaper*

▲ **Golden boy**
The tomb treasures of the Egyptian boy-king Tutankhamun have fascinated the public since their discovery.

◄ **Guan Yin**
Set by the South China Sea, the Guan Yin statue stands at 354 ft (108 m).

THE WORLD'S TALLEST STATUES

At 420 ft (128 m), the Spring Temple Buddha at Jiuhua Mountain in central China is currently the world's tallest statue. It may be overtaken by the monument to the Native American warrior Crazy Horse in South Dakota; a work in progress since 1948, this is planned to top out at 564 ft (172 m) when complete.

THE CRAZY HORSE MEMORIAL IS NEARLY TWICE THE HEIGHT OF THE STATUE OF LIBERTY!

ART ON SALE

TOP 10 MOST EXPENSIVE PAINTINGS EVER SOLD AT AUCTION

PAINTING / ARTIST / SALE	PRICE ($)
1 Nude, Green Leaves and Bust, Pablo Picasso (Spanish; 1881–1973), Christie's, New York, May 4, 2010	106,482,500
2 Garçon à la pipe, Pablo Picasso, Sotheby's, New York, May 5, 2004	104,168,000
3 Dora Maar au chat, Pablo Picasso, Sotheby's, New York, May 3, 2006	95,216,000
4 Portrait of Adele Bloch-Bauer II, Gustav Klimt (Austrian; 1862–1918), Christie's, New York, Nov 8, 2006	87,936,000
5 Triptych, Francis Bacon (Irish; 1909–92), Sotheby's, New York, May 14, 2008	86,281,000
6 Portrait du Dr Gachet, Vincent van Gogh (Dutch; 1853–90), Christie's, New York, May 15, 1990	82,500,000
7 Le Bassin aux Nymphéas, Claude Monet (French; 1840–1926), Christie's, London, Jun 24, 2008	80,643,507 (£40,921,250)
8 Bal au Moulin de la Galette, Montmartre, Pierre-Auguste Renoir (French; 1841–1919), Sotheby's, New York, May 17, 1990	78,100,000
9 The Massacre of the Innocents, Sir Peter Paul Rubens (Flemish; 1577–1640), Sotheby's, London, Jul 10, 2002	75,930,440 (£49,506,648)
10 White Center (Yellow, pink and lavender on rose), Mark Rothko (American; 1903–70), Sotheby's, New York, May 15, 2007	72,840,000

▲ A patron's privilege
Adele Bloch-Bauer was the only subject to be painted twice by Gustav Klimt.

TOP 10 MOST EXPENSIVE WORKS OF ART BY LIVING ARTISTS*

PAINTING / ARTIST / MEDIUM	SALE / DATE	PRICE ($)
1 Benefits Supervisor Sleeping, Lucian Freud, (British; 1922–2011), painting	Christie's, New York, May 13, 2008	33,641,000
2 Flag, Jasper Johns (American; b. 1930), painting	Christie's, New York, May 11, 2010	28,642,500
3 Balloon Flower – Magenta, Jeff Koons, (American; b. 1955), sculpture	Christie's, London, Jun 30, 2008	25,765,204 (£12,921,250)
4 Hanging Heart – Magenta/Gold, Jeff Koons, sculpture	Sotheby's, New York, Nov 14, 2007	23,561,000
5 Naked Portrait with Reflection, Lucian Freud, painting	Christie's, London, Jun 30, 2008	23,531,904 (£11,801,250)
6 Abstraktes Bild, Gerhard Richter (German; b. 1932), painting	Sotheby's, New York, Nov 9, 2011	20,802,500
7 IB and Her Husband, Lucian Freud, painting	Christie's, New York, Nov 13, 2007	19,361,000
8 Lullaby Spring, Damien Hirst (British; b. 1965), sculpture	Sotheby's, London, Jun 21, 2007	19,230,922 (£9,652,000)
9 The Golden Calf, Damien Hirst, sculpture	Sotheby's, London, Sep 15, 2008	18,603,218 (£10,345,250)
10 Gudrun, Gerhard Richter, painting	Sotheby's, New York, Nov 9, 2011	18,002,500

* Artist still living at time of sale

▶ An eye for anatomy
Famed for his nude portraits, Lucian Freud painted on ever-larger canvases.

◀ **Venetian view**
Turner's Guidecca superbly
evokes the light and color
of a famous seascape.

▲ **Back in vogue**
Madonna is a fan of Polish
painter Tamara de Lempicka,
pictured here in 1929.

TOP 10 MOST EXPENSIVE OLD MASTER PAINTINGS

PAINTING / ARTIST / SALE / DATE	PRICE ($)
1 Massacre of the Innocents, Sir Peter Paul Rubens (Flemish; 1577–1640), Sotheby's, London, Jul 10, 2002	76,529,058 (£49,506,648)
2 Modern Rome – Camp Vaccino, Joseph Mallord William Turner (British; 1775–1851), Sotheby's, London, Jul 7, 2010	45,101,996 (£29,721,250)
3 Venice, A View of the Rialto Bridge, Looking North, From The Fondamenta Del Carbon, Francesco Guardi (Italian; 1712–93), Sotheby's, London, Jul 6, 2011	42,739,627 (£26,697,250)
4 Portrait of Lorenzo de' Medici, Duke of 'Urbino, three-quarter-length, Raphael (Italian; 1483–1520), Christie's, London, Jul 5, 2007	37,277,500 (£18,500,000)
5 Gimcrack on Newmarket Heath, with a trainer, a jockey and a stable lad, George Stubbs (British; 1724–1806), Christie's, London, Jul 5, 2012	36,038,403 (£22,441,250)
6 Giudecca, Donna della Salute and San Giorgio, Venice, Joseph Mallord William Turner, Christie's, New York, Apr 6, 2006	35,656,000
7 Portrait of Duke Cosimo I de Medici, Jacopo da Carucci (Pontormo) (Italian; 1494–1557), Christie's, New York, May 31, 1989	35,200,000
8 Portrait of a man with arms akimbo, Rembrandt van Rijn (Dutch; 1606–69), Christie's, London, Dec 8, 2009	32,855,313 (£20,201,250)
9 Grand Canal looking Northeast from Palazzo Balbi to the Rialto Bridge, Venice, Canaletto (Italian; 1697–1768), Sotheby's, London, Jul 7, 2005	32,746,478 (£18,600,000)
10 Young woman seated at virginals, Johannes (van Delft) Vermeer (Dutch; 1632–75), Sotheby's, London, Jul 7, 2004	30,140,259 (£16,245,600)

TOP 10 MOST EXPENSIVE WORKS OF ART BY WOMEN ARTISTS*

PAINTING / ARTIST / SALE / DATE	PRICE ($)
1 Les Fleurs, Natalia Goncharova (Russian; 1881–1962) Christie's, London, Jun 24, 2008	10,896,492 (£5,529,250)
2 Spider, Louise Bourgeois (American, French; 1911–2010) Christie's, New York, Nov 8, 2011	10,722,500
3 Espagnole, Natalia Goncharova Christie's, London, Feb 2, 2010	10,273,974 (£6,425,250)
4 Picking Apples, Natalia Goncharova Christie's, London, Jun 18, 2007	9,778,656 (£4,948,000)
5 Untitled, Joan Mitchell (American; 1926–92) Sotheby's, New York, Nov 9, 2011	9,322,500
6 Le Rêve (Rafaëla Sur Fond Vert), Tamara de Lempicka (Polish; 1898–1980) Sotheby's, New York, Nov 2, 2011	8,482,500
7 Wild Indigenous Tree and Shrubbery in Early Johannesburg, Ruth Squibb (South African, b. 1928) Stephan Weiz & Co., South Africa, Aug 4, 2009	6,663,880 (51,778,405 ZAR)
8 Oozewald, Cady Noland (American; b. 1956) Sotheby's, New York, Nov 9, 2011	6,578,500
9 La Dormeuse, Tamara de Lempicka Sotheby's, London, Jun 22, 2011	6,537,973 (£4,073,250)
10 Les Arbres en Fleurs (Pommiers en Fleurs), Natalia Goncharova Christies, London, Feb 9, 2011	6,372,066 (£3,961,250)

* Sold at auction

TOP 10 FEATURE

AUCTION TREASURES

TOP 10 **MOST EXPENSIVE ITEMS SOLD AT AUCTION**

CATEGORY / ITEM / SALE / PRICE ($)

1
Painting
Nude, Green Leaves and Bust, Pablo Picasso, Christie's New York, May 4, 2010
$106,482,500

2
Sculpture
L'Homme qui march I, Alberto Giacometti, Sotheby's London, Feb 3, 2010
$103,700,000

3
Jewel
The Graff Pink Diamond, 24.78 carat pink diamond mounted in a ring, Sotheby's Geneva, Nov 16, 2010
$46,000,000

6
Car
1957 Ferrari 250 Testa Rossa Pebble Beach Concours d'Elegance, Gooding & Company, Aug 20–21, 2011
$16,390,000

7
Musical instrument
1721 "Lady Blunt" Stradivarius violin, Tarisio Auction House (online auction), June 20, 2011
$15,894,000

8
Clothing
Marilyn Monroe's white dress from the 1955 film The Seven Year Itch, Auction of Debbie Reynolds' Hollywood memorabilia, Jun 19, 2011
$4,600,000

THE GRAFF PINK

The most expensive single jewel ever sold at auction, the Graff Pink was named by its new owner, Laurence Graff, after its 2010 purchase. With a pre-sale estimate of $27–38 million, the emerald-cut pink diamond had been sold by American jeweler Harry Winston to a private collector in the 1950s.

MARILYN MONROE'S DRESS

Film icons simply don't get any bigger than Marilyn Monroe, as proven by her record-breaking wardrobe. The image of Monroe standing above a New York subway grate as her white dress billows around her bare legs is one of the most memorable in movie history, and the dress did not disappoint when it came up for auction. Designed by William Travilla, it was acquired by actress Debbie Reynolds in 1971 when she bought Monroe's wardrobe from 20th Century Fox. The dress was actually not the first of Monroe's wardrobe to break auction records—back in 1999, the figure-hugging dress she wore to seductively serenade John F. Kennedy with "Happy Birthday, Mr. President" became the most expensive piece of clothing when it sold at auction for $1,267,500.

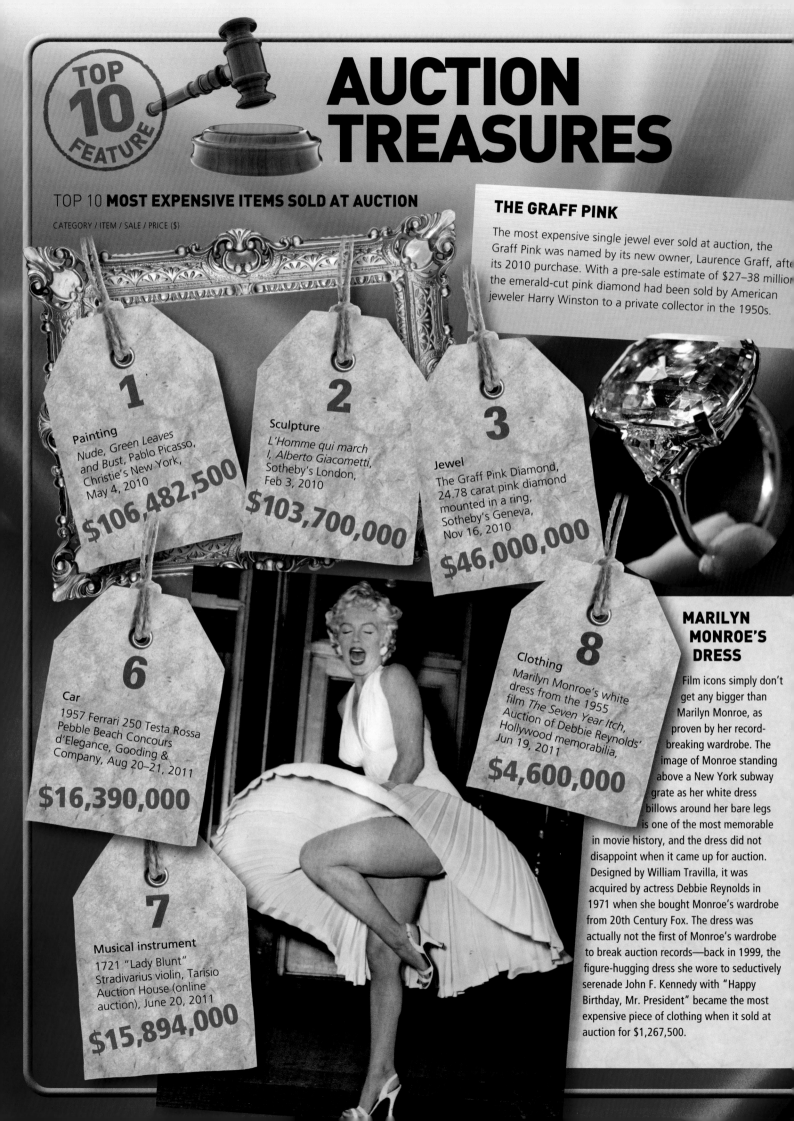

4

Furniture

18th-century badminton cabinet, ebony wood inlaid with precious gems, Christie's, Dec 9, 2004

36,662,106

5

Book/manuscript

The Codex Leicester, Leonardo da Vinci's notebook 1994 (purchased by Bill Gates)

$30,802,500

THE CODEX LEICESTER

Leonardo da Vinci has often been described as the ultimate Renaissance man—not only considered one of the greatest painters of all time, but also a scientist, mathematician, engineer, inventor, botanist, and musician. During his lifetime, Leonardo meticulously recorded his thoughts, ideas, and sketches in journals, and *The Codex Leicester* is probably the most famous of these. When Bill Gates purchased the 72-page handwritten document in 1994 it became the most expensive book ever sold. Three years after buying it, Gates released a digitally scanned version to be distributed as wallpaper and screensaver files.

10

Comic book

Action Comics No. 1, 1938 edition, featuring Superman's debut, ComicConnect.com, Mar 29, 2010

$1,500,000

9

Sports memorabilia

Mark McGwire's 70th home run baseball, 1999

$3,005,000

eBay

One of the most expensive items ever auctioned on eBay was a "gigayacht," which sold for a record-breaking $168 million. The 405-ft boat was designed by naval architect Frank Mulder and sold by a Florida company called 4Yacht. It came complete with a helicopter garage and 14 multilevel VIP suites.

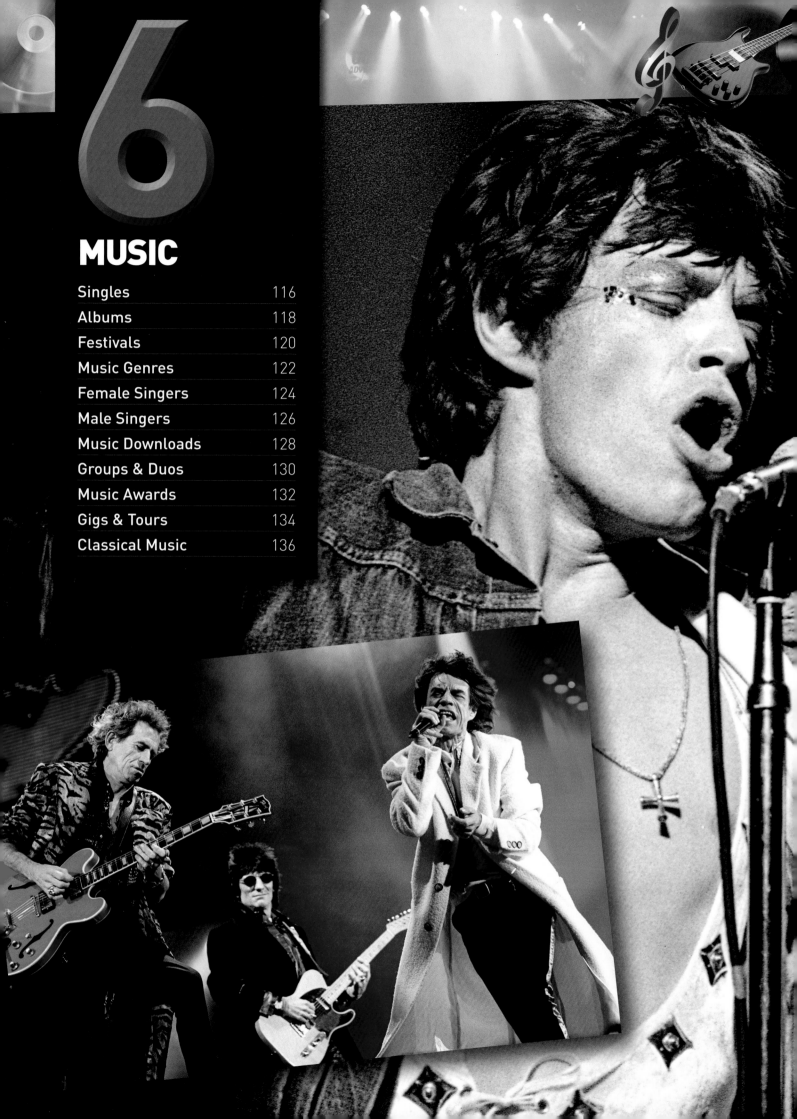

6

MUSIC

STILL ROCKING, STILL ROLLING

Rolling Stones icons Mick Jagger and Keith Richards both celebrate their 70th birthdays in 2013, on July 26 and December 18 respectively. Both grew up in Dartford, Kent, UK, and their chance meeting at the town's railway station in October 1951 led to the formation of one of the best-known bands in the world, selling an estimated 170 million albums globally. The songwriting partnership of Jagger and Richards was the driving force behind this success, and they are now the only original members of the Stones—drummer Charlie Watts, who celebrates 50 years with the group in 2013, is a relative newcomer. After half a century, the Rolling Stones are still pulling the crowds and making serious money: their A Bigger Bang tour made a staggering $558 million in total.

SINGLES

TOP 10 BESTSELLING SINGLES ARTISTS OF THE PAST FIVE YEARS IN THE USA

ARTIST

1. Taylor Swift
2. Rihanna
3. Eminem
4. Lady Gaga
5. Britney Spears
6. Black Eyed Peas
7. Kanye West
8. Michael Jackson
9. Katy Perry
10. Beyoncé

Source: Music Information Database

TOP 10 SINGLES IN THE USA IN 2011

TITLE / ARTIST

1. "Rolling in the Deep"
Adele
2. "Party Rock Anthem"
LMFAO feat. Lauren Bennett and GoonRock'
3. "E.T."
Katy Perry feat. Kanye West
4. "Moves Like Jagger"
Maroon 5 feat. Christina Aguilera
5. "Give Me Everything"
Pitbull feat. Nayer, Afrojack, and Ne-Yo
6. "Pumped Up Kicks"
Foster the Apple
7. "Someone Like You"
Adele
8. "F**k You (Forget You)"
Cee Lo Green
9. "Super Bass"
Nicki Minaj
10. "Born This Way"
Lady Gaga

Source: Nielsen Soundscan

▼ *Triple triumph*
"Grenade" was Bruno Mars's 3rd No. 1 single in both the US and UK.

◀ *Not so rainy*
Rihanna's "Umbrella" spent weeks at No. 1 and sold 6.6 million copies worldwide.

TOP 10 SINGLES OF ALL TIME

	TITLE / ARTIST	YEAR OF ENTRY	SALES EXCEED
1	"White Christmas" Bing Crosby	1942	50,000,000
2	"Candle in the Wind (1997)"/"Something About the Way You Look Tonight" Elton John	1997	33,000,000
3	= "Rock Around the Clock" Bill Haley and His Comets	1954	25,000,000
	= "Little Drummer Boy" The Harry Simeone Chorale	1958	25,000,000
5	= "It's Now or Never" Elvis Presley	1960	20,000,000
	= "We Are the World" USA for Africa	1985	20,000,000
7	"Yes Sir, I Can Boogie" Baccara	1977	18,000,000
8	"Wind of Change" The Scorpions	1991	14,000,000
9	"Sukiyaki" Kyu Sakamoto	1963	13,000,000
10	= "I Want to Hold Your Hand" The Beatles	1963	12,000,000
	= "I Will Always Love You" Whitney Houston	1992	12,000,000

Source: Music Information Database

TOP 10 SINGLES IN THE USA IN THE PAST FIVE YEARS

TITLE / ARTIST / YEAR

1 "Boom Boom Pow" Black Eyed Peas 2009
2 "I Gotta Feeling" Black Eyed Peas 2009
3 "California Gurls" Katy Perry feat. Snoop Dogg 2010
4 "Poker Face" Lady Gaga 2009
5 "Hey, Soul Sister" Train 2010
6 "Love the Way You Lie" Eminem feat. Rihanna 2010
7 "Right Round" Flo Rida feat. Ke$ha 2009
8 "E.T." Katy Perry feat. Kanye West 2011
9 "Rolling in the Deep" Adele 2011
10 "Dynamite" Taio Cruz 2010

Source: Nielsen Soundscan

▼ A good night
The Black Eyed Peas have performed at the Grammies and at the Super Bowl.

TOP 10 ARTISTS WITH THE MOST NO. 1 SINGLES IN THE USA

	ARTIST / TOTAL CHART HITS	NO. 1 SINGLES
1	Elvis Presley (122)	22
2	The Beatles (70)	20
3	Mariah Carey (44)	18
4	Michael Jackson (48)	13
5	= Madonna (55)	12
	= The Supremes (45)	12
7	= Whitney Houston (39)	11
	= Rihanna (35)	11
9	= Janet Jackson (39)	10
	= Stevie Wonder (63)	10

Source: Music Information Database

ALBUMS

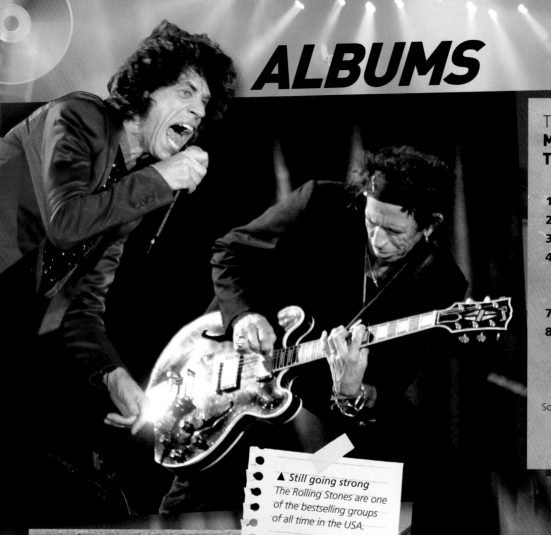

TOP 10 ARTISTS WITH THE MOST NO. 1 ALBUMS IN THE USA

	ARTIST / TOTAL CHART ALBUMS	NO. 1 ALBUMS
1	The Beatles (50)	19
2	Jay-Z (20)	12
3	Elvis Presley (119)	10
4	=Barbra Streisand (50)	9
	=Bruce Springsteen (30)	9
	=The Rolling Stones (48)	9
7	Garth Brooks (16)	8
8	=Elton John (42)	7
	=Madonna (21)	7
	=Led Zeppelin (19)	7
	=U2 (19)	7

Source: Music Information Database

▲ **Still going strong**
The Rolling Stones are one of the bestselling groups of all time in the USA.

TOP 10 ALBUMS OF ALL TIME

	TITLE / ARTIST / YEAR OF ENTRY	ESTIMATES SALES (MILLIONS)
1	Thriller, Michael Jackson (1982)	100
2	Back in Black, AC/DC (1980)	49
3	The Dark Side of the Moon, Pink Floyd (1973)	45
4	Bat out of Hell, Meat Loaf (1977)	43
5	= Their Greatest Hits (1971–1975), Eagles (1976)	42
	=Dirty Dancing, Various Artists (1987)	42
	= The Bodyguard, Whitney Houston/Various Artists (1992)	42
8	= Millennium, Backstreet Boys (1999)	40
	=Saturday Night Fever, Various Artists (1977)	40
	=Rumours, Fleetwood Mac (1977)	40

ALBUMS THAT STAYED LONGEST AT US NO. 1 IN THE PAST FIVE YEARS

In November 2011, British singing superstar Adele clocked up 13 weeks at US No. 1 with her album *21*, thereby completing the longest residence in the top spot for 40 years. Another Brit—reality-show participant Susan Boyle—also took the US by storm and her album *I Dreamed a Dream* stayed on the top spot for 6 weeks in 2010. Taylor Swift boasts two longstanding No. 1 albums with *Fearless* (11 weeks) and *Speak Now* (4 weeks).

▲ **Video star**
The title track of Michael Jackson's Thriller had a 14-minute promotional video.

TOP 10 **ALBUMS IN THE USA IN THE PAST FIVE YEARS***

TITLE / ARTIST / YEAR

1 **21**, Adele
2011

2 Recovery,
Eminem
2010

3 **Noel**, Josh Groban
2007

4 Speak Now,
Taylor Swift
2010

5 Fearless,
Taylor Swift
2009

6 I Dreamed a Dream,
Susan Boyle
2009

7 Need You Now,
Lady Antebellum
2010

8 High School Musical 2,
Soundtrack
2007

9 Tha Carter III, Lil Wayne
2008

10 Long Road Out of
Eden, The Eagles
2007

Source: Nielsen Soundscan

TOP 10 **BESTSELLING ALBUM ARTISTS IN THE USA IN THE PAST FIVE YEARS**

ARTIST

1 Taylor Swift

2 Michael Jackson

3 Lady Gaga

4 Eminem

5 Susan Boyle

6 Justin Bieber

7 Adele

8 Michael Bublé

9 Carrie Underwood

10 The Beatles

Source: Music Information Database

TOP 10 **ALBUMS IN THE USA IN 2011**

ALBUM / ARTIST

1 21, Adele

2 Tha Carter IV Lil Wayne

3 Born This Way
Lady Gaga

4 My Kinda Party
Jason Aldean

5 Sigh No More
Mumford & Sons

6 Watch the Throne
Jay-Z and Kanye West

7 4 Beyoncé

8 Own the Night
Lady Antebellum

9 Doo Wops & Hooligans,
Bruno Mars

10 Never Say Never:
The Remixes (EP)
Justin Bieber

Source: Nielsen Soundscan

▲ *London lady*
While achieving astonishing record sales, Adele has wowed the critics, too.

▲ *Poker face*
Lady Gaga has sold over 23 million albums worldwide.

FESTIVALS

TOP 10 **MUSIC FESTIVALS**

FESTIVAL / LOCATION / APPROX. AVERAGE
DAILY ATTENDANCE (2011)

An atmospheric place
The country around Glastonbury has many prehistoric sites and is linked to Arthurian legend.

1 Glastonbury Festival
Pilton, Somerset, England / 145,000
Festival organizer Michael Eavis began hosting a music festival on his dairy farm in the early 1970s, when entry cost £1. The festival features special areas such as the Dance Village, the Green Fields, the Theatre and Circus fields, and Strummerville, alongside the main music stages. The next Glastonbury festival will take place in the summer of 2013, with 2012 being declared a "fallow" year.

2 Roskilde Festival
Roskilde, Denmark / 110,000
This four-day Danish festival has existed since 1971 and is one of the biggest in Europe. The Roskilde Foundation runs the annual event as a non-profit organization for the development and support of music, culture, and humanism. The once mainly Scandinavian crowd is now more international, with a 2011 festival attendee average age of 22.8 years.

3 Rock al Parque
Bogotá, Colombia / 88,600
The only South American festival to make the Top 10, this free three-day festival has been taking place since 1995. Originally devoted to rock and metal music, Rock al Parque has gradually diversified to represent other genres, including ska, punk, and reggae, with an average of 50 national and international bands performing each year.

4 Reading and Leeds Festival
Reading, UK / 86,999 Leeds, UK / 74,999
Advertised as Europe's biggest and best dual-site event, this pair of annual music festivals take place at different ends of England and shares the same bill over the same weekend in August. The Reading Festival is the world's oldest popular music festival still in existence, and the original venue.

5 T in the Park
Balado, Kinross-shire, Scotland / 85,000
The three-day T in the Park music festival is Scotland's most successful outdoor music event. At 18 years old in 2011, the festival featured over 200 artists performing across 11 stages—more than four times its original size.

6 Rock Werchter
Werchter, Belgium / 83,000
Belgium's largest festival, and one of the biggest rock festivals in Europe, began in 1974 as a one-day event. Since 2003, the festival has spanned four days. Featured artists in 2011 included Linkin Park, Coldplay, Kings of Leon, Portishead, A-Trak, and Iron Maiden.

7 Oxegen
Punchestown, Co. Kildare, Ireland / 80,000
First held in 2004, Oxegen is widely regarded as Ireland's top music festival. Beyoncé, Foo Fighters, Arctic Monkeys, and Coldplay were among the headliners of the 2011 three-day event, which also featured "The Headphone Disco" and a campsite cinema.

8 Summerfest

Milwaukee, Wisconsin, USA / 79,876

Located in the heart of the American Midwest, Summerfest is also known as "The Big Gig" and is held along Milwaukee's lakefront. Lasting up to 11 days, this eclectic festival is make up of 11 stages with performances from over 700 bands.

9 Coachella

Indio, California, USA / 75,000

First held in 1999 in the grounds of a polo club and headlined by such acts as Beck, Morrissey, Tool, and Rage Against the Machine, the event will expand to two weekends in its 13th year, with the same lineups for both weekends.

10 = Sziget Festival

Budapest, Hungary / 60,000

With more than 1,000 performances from a range of different genres, the nearly week-long Sziget Festival has been described as the "Burning Man" Festival (Nevada, USA) of Europe, and enjoys a reputation as an arts and music festival. Held every August on an island of the Danube River in the middle of Budapest, the festival is popular with west Europeans.

= Pinkpop Festival

Landgraaf, Netherlands / 60,000

One of the world's oldest music festivals, and the Netherlands' best-known festival, Pinkpop has been rocking since 1970. Over the three days, approximately 40 artists perform across three stages.

WOODSTOCK

The mother of all modern-day music festivals, Woodstock was a moment in music history that has gripped the world ever since. Thirty-two acts, including such greats as Jimi Hendrix, Janis Joplin, the Grateful Dead, the Who, and Crosby, Stills, Nash & Young, performed over four days in August 1969 to a crowd of over half a million people on a dairy farm in rural Bethel, New York. The festival was one of the biggest rock events of all time and encapsulated the antiwar sentiments and flower-power culture of the era. Originally conceived by four young men as a business venture, it was eventually opened up to the public as a free concert when organizers feared they could not control the far-bigger crowds than expected. Remarkable given the massive numbers of revellers, Woodstock has become an icon of the 1960s hippie counterculture of peace, love, and rock 'n' roll.

WOODSTOCK
MUSIC & ART FAIR
presents

AN
AQUARIAN
EXPOSITION
in
WHITE LAKE, N.Y

3 DAYS
of PEACE
& MUSIC

AUGUST
15, 16, 17

MUSIC GENRES

TOP 10 ALL TIME ROCK SINGLES IN THE USA

SINGLE / ARTIST / YEAR

1 "Hey, Soul Sister"
Train
2010

2 "Viva La Vida"
Coldplay
2008

3 "Apologize"
Timbaland feat. OneRepublic
2007

4 "Gives You Hell"
All-American Rejects
2009

5 "Hound Dog"/
"Don't Be Cruel"
Elvis Presley 1956

6 "How to Save a Life"
The Fray
2006

7 "Eye of the Tiger"
Survivor
1982

8 "Chasing Cars"
Snow Patrol
2006

9 "Hey There Delilah"
Plain White T's
2007

10 "Use Somebody"
Kings of Leon
2009

▲ Loud onstage, quiet off...
*Despite his onstage persona,
Guns N' Roses singer Axl Rose is
notoriously shy of the media.*

TOP 10 COUNTRY ALBUMS IN THE USA

TITLE / ARTIST / YEAR

1 Come on Over
Shania Twain
1997

2 No Fences
Garth Brooks
1990

3 WRopin' the Wind
Garth Brooks
1991

4 Wide Open Spaces
Dixie Chicks
1998

5 The Woman in Me
Shania Twain
1995

6 Up!
Shania Twain
2002

7 Double Live
Garth Brooks
1992

8 Fly
Dixie Chicks
1999

9 Garth Brooks
Garth Brooks
1990

10 The Hits
Garth Brooks
1994

TOP 10 HEAVY METAL ALBUMS IN THE USA

ALBUM / ARTIST / YEAR

1 Led Zeppelin IV
Led Zeppelin
1971

2 Back in Black
AC/DC
1980

3 Appetite for Destruction
Guns N' Roses
1987

4 Boston
Boston
1976

5 Physical Graffiti
Led Zeppelin
1975

6 Metallica
Metallica
1991

7 Bat Out of Hell
Meat Loaf
1977

8 Hysteria
Def Leppard
1987

9 Slippery When Wet
Bon Jovi
1986

10 Led Zeppelin II
Led Zeppelin
1973

Source (all lists): Music Information Database

◄ Come on Eileen
*Born Eileen Edwards, Shania
Twain's appeal goes far
beyond the country fanbase.*

▶ *Shapeshifter*
Like David Bowie, Madonna's capacity for reinvention appears to be unlimited.

TOP 10 HIP HOP/RAP SINGLES IN THE USA*

SINGLE / ARTIST / YEAR

1 "E.T. "
Katy Perry feat. Kanye West
2011

2 "Love the Way You Lie"
Eminem feat. Rihanna
2010

3 "Right Round"
Flo Rida feat. Ke$ha
2009

4 "Airplanes"
B.o.B feat. Hayley Williams
2010

5 "Not Afraid"
Eminem
2010

6 "F**k You (Forget You)"
Cee Lo Green
2011

7 "Lollipop"
Lil Wayne feat. Static Major
2008

8 "Down"
Jay Sean feat. Lil Wayne
2009

9 "Low"
Flo Rida feat. T-Pain
2008

10 "Crank That"
Soulja Boy Tell 'Em
2007

* In the past five years

TOP 10 R&B/DANCE ALBUMS IN THE USA

ALBUM / ARTIST / YEAR

1 Thriller
Michael Jackson
1982

2 The Bodyguard (Soundtrack)
Whitney Houson
1992

3 Whitney Houston
Whitney Houston
1985

4 Purple Rain (Soundtrack)
Prince
1984

5 II
Boyz II Men
1994

6 Crazysexycool
TLC
1994

7 Can't Slow Down
Lionel Richie
1983

8 The Immaculate Collection
Madonna
1990

9 Please Hammer Don't Hurt 'Em
MC Hammer 1990

10 Like a Virgin
Madonna
1984

TOP 10 RAP ALBUMS IN THE USA

ALBUM / ARTIST / YEAR

1 Speakerboxxx/ The Love Below
Outkast, 2003

2 The Marshall Mathers LP
Eminem
2000

3 The Eminem Show
Eminem
2002

4 Life After Death
The Notorious B.I.G.
1997

5 Greatest Hits
2Pac
1998

6 All Eyez on Me
2Pac
1996

7 Licensed to Ill
The Beastie Boys
1987

8 Big Willie Style
Will Smith
1997

9 Country Grammar
Nelly
2000

10 Get Rich or Die Tryin'
50 Cent, 2003

▶ *Lucky man*
50 Cent survived a shooting to make a six-times platinum album.

FEMALE SINGERS

TOP 10 FEMALE SINGERS WITH THE MOST US NO. 1 SINGLES

	SINGER / TOTAL CHART HITS	NO. 1 SINGLES
1	Mariah Carey (44)	18
2	Madonna (55)	12
3 =	Whitney Houston (39)	11
=	Rihanna (34)	11
5 =	Janey Jackson (39)	10
6 =	Diana Ross (40)	6
=	Paula Abdul (15)	6
=	Katy Perry (13)	6
9 =	Barbra Streisand (41)	5
=	Britney Spears (28)	5
=	Olivia Newton-John (36)	5
=	Christina Aguilera (25)	5
=	Beyoncé (30)	5

Source: Music Information Database

◀ **Global appeal**
Since Destiny's Child disbanded, Beyoncé has sold over 75 million albums worldwide.

▼ **Breakfast from America**
Christina Aguilera's "Lady Marmalade" is her biggest US success.

TOP 10 SINGLES BY FEMALE SINGERS IN THE USA

	SINGLE / SINGER	YEAR
1	"Just Dance" Lady Gaga (feat. Colby O'Donis)	2009
2	"Poker Face" Lady Gaga	2009
3	"Tik-Tok" Ke$ha	2010
4	"Rolling in the Deep" Adele	2011
5	"Hot N Cold" Katy Perry	2008
6	"California Gurls" Katy Perry feat. Snoop Dogg	2010
7	"Firework" Katy Perry	2010
8	"Love Story" Taylor Swift	2009
9	"E.T." Katy Perry feat. Kanye West	2011
10	"Single Ladies (Put a Ring on It)" Beyoncé	2006

Source: Music Information Database

TOP 10 **FEMALE ALBUMS IN THE USA IN THE 21ST CENTURY**

ALBUM / ARTIST / YEAR

1 **Some Hearts,** Carrie Underwood
2006

2 **Fearless,**
Taylor Swift
2009

3 **21,** Adele
2011

4 **Taylor Swift,**
Taylor Swift
2008

5 **I Dreamed a Dream,**
Susan Boyle
2009

6 **The Fame,**
Lady Gaga
2010

7 **Speak Now,**
Taylor Swift
2010

8 **As I Am,** Alicia Keys
2007

9 **The Duchess,**
Fergie
2007

10 **B'day,** Beyoncé
2006

Source: Music Information Database

▶ **Crazy name**
It is said that Lady Gaga got her stage name from a mistake with predictive text.

TOP 10 **FEMALE SINGERS WITH THE MOST PLATINUM ALBUMS IN THE USA**

SINGER / TOTAL ALBUMS	PLATINUM ALBUMS
1 Mariah Carey (14)	64
2 Madonna (18)	63
3 Barbra Streisand (49)	61
4 Whitney Houston (8)	55
5 Celine Dion (13)	49
6 Shania Twain (5)	48
7 Reba McEntire (26)	38
8 Britney Spears (6)	33
9 Linda Ronstadt (19)	29
10 Janet Jackson (8)	26

Source: RIAA

THE 10 **YOUNGEST FEMALE SINGERS TO HAVE A NO. 1 SINGLE IN THE USA IN THE 21ST CENTURY**

ARTIST / SINGLE / YEAR	AGE YRS	MTHS	DAYS
1 Rihanna "SOS" 2006	18	2	23
2 Ciara feat. Petey Pablo "Goodies" 2009	18	10	17
3 Fantasia "I Believe" 2004	20	0	10
4 Kelly Clarkson "A Moment Like This" 2002	20	5	11
5 Alicia Keys "Fallin'" 2001	20	6	24
6 Ja Rule feat. Ashanti* "Always on Time" 2002	21	4	10
7 P!nk "Lady Marmalade" 2001	21	8	25
8 P!Mya "Lady Marmalade" 2001	21	9	23
9 Beyoncé feat. Jay-Z "Crazy in Loce" 2003	21	10	8
10 LMFAQ feat. Lauren Bennett and GoonRock "Party Rock Anthem" 2011	22	0	23

* Ashanti had a chart-topper in her her own right ("Foolish"), 2 months later

Source: Music Information Database

MALE SINGERS

▲ *From King to Kingston*
Sean Kingston's "Beautiful Girls" samples the Ben E. King classic "Stand By Me."

THE 10 YOUNGEST MALE SOLO SINGERS TO HAVE A NO. 1 SINGLE IN THE USA IN THE PAST FIVE YEARS

	SINGLE / ARTIST	YEAR	YRS	AGE* MTHS	DAYS
1	"Crank That Soulja Boy" Soulja Boy	2007	17	1	18
2	"Kiss Kiss" Chris Brown	2007	18	6	5
3	"Whatcha Say" Jason Derulo	2009	20	1	24
4	"Fireflies" Owl City (Adam Young)	2009	23	4	2
5	"Black and Yellow" Wiz Khalifa	2011	23	5	11
6	"Just the Way You Are" Bruno Mars	2010	24	11	24
7	"What Goes Around ... Goes Around" Justin Timberlake	2007	26	1	3
8	"Whatever You Like" T.I.	2008	27	11	12
9	"This Is Why I'm Hot" Mims	2007	27	11	16
10	"Right Round" Flo Rida	2009	29	2	12

* During first week of debut No. 1 single Source: Music Information Database

TOP 10 MALE SINGERS WITH THE MOST PLATINUM ALBUMS IN THE USA

Platinum albums in the USA are those that have achieved sales of 1 million.

	ARTIST / GOLD TOTAL	PLATINUM ALBUMS			ARTIST / GOLD TOTAL	PLATINUM ALBUMS
1	Garth Brooks (16)	145		6	George Strait (38)	61
2	Elvis Presley (94)	104		7	Bruce Springsteen (21)	52
3	Billy Joel (18)	80		8	Kenny Rogers (31)	45
4	Michael Jackson (11)	70		9	Eric Clapton (25)	41
5	Elton John (38)	65		10=	Neil Diamond (40)	40
				10=	Allan Jackson (18)	40

Source: RIAA

► *Jason Derulo*
Miami-born Jason Derulo altered the spelling of his last name from Desrouleaux.

THE 10 LAST FOREIGN MALE SOLO SINGERS TO HAVE A NO. 1 SINGLE IN THE USA*

	SINGLE / ARTIST	COUNTRY	DATE AT NO. 1
1	"Beautiful Girls" Sean Kingston	Jamaica	Aug 11, 2007
2	"Bad Day" Daniel Powter	Canada	Apr 8, 2006
3	"Temperature" Sean Paul	Jamaica	Apr 1, 2006
4	"Get Busy" Sean Paul	Jamaica	May 10, 2003
5	"Angel" Shaggy (feat. Rayvon)	Jamaica	Mar 31, 20018
6	"It Wasn't Me" Shaggy (feat. RikRok)	Jamaica	Feb 3, 2001
7	"Be With You" Enrique Iglesias	Spain	Jun 24, 2000
8	"Bailamos" Enrique Iglesias	Spain	Sep 4, 1999
9	"Livin' La Vida Loca" Ricky Martin	Puerto Rico	May 8, 1999
10	"Here Comes the Hotstepper" Ini Kamoze	Jamaica	Dec 17, 1994

* Excluding UK singers

Source: Music Information Database

TOP 10 **BESTSELLING ALBUMS BY MALE SOLO ARTISTS IN THE USA IN THE PAST FIVE YEARS**

ALBUM / ARTIST / YEAR

1 **Christmas**
Michael Bublé, 2011

2 **Noel**
Josh Groban, 2007

3 **Recovery**
Eminem, 2010

4 **Tha Carter III**
Lil' Wayne, 2008

5 **Number Ones**
Michael Jackson, 2009

6 **Rock N Roll Jesus**
Kid Rock, 2008

7 **My World 2.0**
Justin Bieber, 2010

8 **My Christmas**
Andrea Bocelli, 2009

9 **Graduation**
Kanye West, 2007

10 **Tha Carter IV**
Lil' Wayne, 2011

Source: Music Information Database

▶ *Eminem*
Rapper Eminem's first international hit album was Slim Shady, back in 1999.

◀ *Brass nerve*
The son of a preacher, B.o.B. played the trumpet in his North Carolina school band.

TOP 10 **BESTSELLING SINGLES BY MALE SOLO ARTISTS IN THE USA IN THE PAST FIVE YEARS**

SINGLE / ARTIST / YEAR

1 "Low"
Flo Rida (feat. T-Pain), 2007

2 "I'm Yours"
Jason Mraz, 2008

3 "Dynamite"
Taio Cruz, 2010

4 "Love the Way You Lie"
Eminem (feat. Rihanna), 2010

5 "Apologize"
Timbaland
(feat. OneRepublic), 2007

6 "Right Round"
Flo Rida, 2009

7 "Crank That"
Soulja Boy Tell 'Em, 2007

8 "Stronger"
Kanye West, 2007

9 "Airplanes"
B.o.B (feat. Hayley Williams), 2010

10 "Lollipop"
Lil Wayne (feat. Static Major), 2008

Source: Music Information Database

MUSIC DOWNLOADS

TOP 10 DIGITAL SINGLES STAYING LONGEST AT NO. 1 IN THE USA

SINGLE / ARTIST	DATE	WEEKS
1 "Low" Flo Rida feat. T-Pain	Dec 15, 2007–Mar 8, 2008	13
2 = "Boom Boom Pow" Black Eyed Peas	Apr 18–Jun 20, 2009	10
= "I Gotta Feeling" Black Eyed Peas	Jun 27–Sep 26, 2009	10
4 "Hollaback Girl" Gwen Stefani	Apr 30–Jul 16, 2005	9
= "Gold Digger" Kanye West feat. Jamie Foxx	Sep 17–Nov 19, 2005	9
6 = "Candy Shop" 50 Cent feat. Olivia	Feb 19–Apr 19, 2005	8
7 = "Bad Day" Daniel Powter	Apr 1–June 3, 2006	7
= "Love the Way You Lie" Eminem feat. Rihanna	Jul 10–Aug 28, 2010	7
= "E.T." Katy Perry feat. Kanye West	Mar 26–May 14, 2011	7
10 = "I Kissed A Girl" Katy Perry	Jul 5–Aug 9, 2008	6
= "Right Round" Flo Rida feat. Ke$ha	Feb 28–Apr 4, 2009	6
= "Party in the U.S.A." Miley Cyrus	Aug 29–Oct 17, 2009	6
= "TiK ToK" Ke$ha	Jan 2–Feb 13, 2010	6
= "Rolling in the Deep" Adele	May 21–Jun 25, 2011	6
= "Party Rock Anthem" LMFAO feat. Lauren Bennett & GoonRock	Jul 16–Aug 20, 2011	6

Source: Music Information Database

◀ **Early success**
Katy Perry's first single was the one of the biggest-selling of 2008.

TOP 10 DIGITAL SINGLES IN THE USA

	SINGLE / ARTIST
1	"I Gotta Feeling" Black Eyed Peas
2	"Low" Flo Rida feat. T-Pain
3	"Just Dance" Lady Gaga feat. Colby O'Donis
4	"Rolling in the Deep" Adele
5	"Dynamite" Taio Cruz
6	"Boom Boom Pow" Black Eyed Peas
7	"Poker Face" Lady Gaga
8	"I'm Yours" Jason Mraz
9	"Viva La Vida" Coldplay
10	"TiK ToK" Ke$ha

Source: Nielsen Soundscan

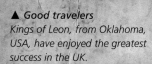

▲ **Good travelers**
Kings of Leon, from Oklahoma, USA, have enjoyed the greatest success in the UK.

TOP 10 ALBUM DOWNLOADS IN THE USA IN 2011

ALBUM / ARTIST

1 21, Adele

2 Born this Way, Lady Gaga

3 Sigh No More, Mumford & Sons

4 Songs for Japan, Various Artists

5 Lasers, Lupe Fiasco

6 Lungs, Florence + the Machine 2009

7 Femme Fatale, Britney Spears

8 Loud, Rihanna

9 Teenage Dream, Katy Perry

10 Doo-Wops and Hooligans, Bruno Mars

Source: Nielsen Soundscan

▲ **International reach**
Florence + the Machine's Lungs ranked in the Top 10 downloads in both the UK and the US.

TOP 10 DIGITAL ALBUMS IN THE USA

ALBUM / ARTIST / YEAR

1 21
Adele 2011

2 Recovery
Eminem 2010

3 Sigh No More
Mumford & Sons 2011

4 The Fame
Lady Gaga 2010

5 Viva La Vida or
Death and All His Friends
Coldplay 2008

6 Fearless
Taylor Swift 2008

7 Only by the Night
Kings of Leon 2008

8 Twilight
Soundtrack 2008

9 E.N.D. (Energy Never Dies)
Black Eyed Peas 2009

Source: Official Charts Company

10 Speak Now
Taylor Swift 2010

Source: Nielsen Soundscan

TOP 10 BESTSELLING DIGITAL ARTISTS IN THE USA

ARTIST

1 Taylor Swift

2 Black Eyed Peas

3 Rihanna

4 Eminem

5 Lady Gaga

6 Kanye West

7 Beyoncé

8 Nickelback

9 Michael Jackson

10 Katy Perry

▶ **Go west**
With 2007's "Stronger" Kanye West scored a chart No. 1.

AROUND 40 BILLION SONGS ARE DOWNLOADED ILLEGALLY EVERY YEAR—THAT'S 90% OF ALL MUSIC DOWNLOADS!

GROUPS & DUOS

TOP 10 GROUPS AND DUOS WITH THE MOST NO. 1 ALBUMS IN THE USA

ARTIST / NO. 1 SINGLES

1 The Beatles 19

2 The Rolling Stones 9

3 = Led Zeppelin 7

4 = U2 7

The Eagles 6

6 = Paul McCartney and Wings 5

8 = Herb Alpert and the Tijuana Press 5

= Chicago 5

10 = The Kingston Trio 5

= Pink Floyd 5

= Van Halen 5

= Metallica 5

Source: Music Information Database

▲ **Close harmony**
Paul McCartney, John Lennon, and George Harrison shared vocal duties in the Beatles.

TOP 10 ALBUMS BY GROUPS AND DUOS IN THE USA IN THE PAST FIVE YEARS

ALBUM	ARTIST
1 Long Road Out of Eden	The Eagles
2 Need You Now	Lady Antebellum
3 Daughtry	Daughtry
4 Dark Horse	Nickelback
5 Viva La Vida (Or Death And All His Friends)	Coldplay
6 Minutes to Midnight	Linkin Park
7 Love on the Inside	Sugarland
8 E.N.D. (Energy Never Dies)	Black Eyed Peas
9 Sigh No More	Mumford and Sons
10 Black Ice	AC/DC

Source: Music Information Database

▶ **Classic cover**
Pink Floyd associate George Hardie did the artwork for The Dark Side of the Moon.

▶ *Three decades of success*
U2's first No. 1 album was
War in 1983 and 30 years
on they are still popular.

TOP 10 **GROUPS AND DUOS WITH THE MOST NO. 1 SINGLES IN THE USA**

ARTIST / WEEKS AT NO. 1

1 The Beatles 20

2 The Supremes 12

3 The Bee Gees 9

4 The Rolling Stones 8

5 = Hall and Oates 6
= Paul McCartney and Wings 6

= Boyz II Men* 5
= The Eagles 5
= The Four Seasons 5
= KC and the Sunshine Band 5

* ...ng one with Mariah Carey

Source: Music Information Database

TOP 10 **GROUPS AND DUOS SPENDING THE MOST WEEKS AT NO. 1 IN THE USA**

ARTIST / WEEKS AT NO. 1

1 The Beatles 59

2 Boyz II Men 50

3 The Bee Gees 27

4 = The Supremes 22
= Santana 22

6 = The Four Seasons 18
= TLC 18

8 = The Rolling Stones 17
= Destiny's Child 17

10 The Everly Brothers 6

Source: Music Information Database

TOP 10 **SINGLES BY GROUPS AND DUOS IN THE USA IN THE PAST FIVE YEARS**

SINGLE / ARTIST

1 "I Gotta Feeling"
Black Eyed Peas

2 "Just Dance"
Lady Gaga feat. Colby O'Donis

3 "Boom Boom Pow"
Black Eyed Peas

4 "Party Rock Anthem"
LMFAO feat. Lauren Bennett and GoonRock

5 "Hey, Soul Sister"
Train

6 "Love the Way You Lie"
Eminem feat. Rihanna

7 "Need You Now"
Lady Antebellum

8 "Viva La Vida"
Coldplay

9 "California Gurls"
Katy Perry feat. Snoop Dogg

10 "Right Round"
Flo Rida feat. Ke$ha

Source: Music Information Database

MUSIC AWARDS

The Ivor Novello Awards have been presented annually since 1955, mainly rewarding songwriting achievements. Paul McCartney and John Lennon each received one award as members of the Beatles; their other awards were won either in partnership or individually.

TOP 10 WINNERS OF THE MOST IVOR NOVELLO AWARDS

	WINNER / AWARDS	
1	Paul McCartney	20
2 =	John Lennon	14
=	Andrew Lloyd Webber	14
4	Elton John	13
5	Tim Rice	13
6 =	Barry Gibb	9
=	Robin Gibb	9
8 =	Matt Aitken	8
=	Maurice Gibb	8
=	Tony MacAulay	8
=	Mike Stock	8
=	Bernie Taupin	8
=	Pete Waterman	8

Source: British Academy of Songwriters, Composers and Authors

▲ **Fab Four win**
John Lennon won the first of his "Ivors'" as part of the Beatles in 1964.

THE 10 ARTISTS WITH MOST MTV AWARDS

	ARTIST	AWARDS
1	Madonna	20
2	Lady Gaga	15
3	Peter Gabriel	13
4	R.E.M.	12
5 =	Beyoncé	11
=	Eminem	11
=	Green Day	11
8	Aerosmith	10
9 =	Fatboy Slim	9
=	Janet Jackson	9

Source: MTV

◄ **All over now**
R.E.M. broke up in September 2011 after 31 years together.

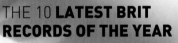

THE 10 **LATEST GRAMMY RECORDS OF THE YEAR**

RECORD / ARTIST

2012
"Rolling in the Deep" Adele

2011
"Need You Now" Lady Antebellum

2010
"Use Somebody" Kings of Leon

2009
"Please Read the Letter"
Alison Krauss and Robert Plant

2008
"Rehab" Amy Winehouse

2007
"Not Ready to Make Nice" Dixie Chicks

2006
"Boulevard of Broken Dreams" Green Day

2005
"Here We Go Again"
Ray Charles and Norah Jones

2004
"Clocks" Coldplay

2003
"Don't Know Why" Norah Jones

Source: NARAS

▲ **Country cousins**
In total, Lady
Antebellum claimed an
impressive five Grammy
Awards in 2011.

▶ **Tragic talent**
The profits from Amy
Winehouse's final
album will go to help
vulnerable people.

THE 10 **LATEST BRIT RECORDS OF THE YEAR**

YEAR	RECORD / ARTIST
2012	"What Makes You Beautiful", One Direction
2011	"Pass Out", Tinie Tempah
2010	"Beat Again", JLS
2009	"The Promise", Girls Aloud
2008	"Shine", Take That
2007	"Patience", Take That
2006	"Speed of Sound", Coldplay
2005	"Your Game", Will Young
2004	"White Flag", Dido
2003	"Just a Little", Liberty X

Source: BRITS

The Grammy Awards ceremony
has been held annually since its
inauguration on May 4, 1959,
and the awards are considered
the most prestigious in the
music industry. They are given
retrospectively, thus the 54th
awards presented in 2012
were in recognition of musical
accomplishments during 2011.

TOP 10 **COUNTRY MUSIC ASSOCIATION AWARD WINNERS**

	ARTIST	AWARDS
1	George Strait	22
2	Brooks and Dunn	19
3	Vince Gill	18
4	Alan Jackson	16
5	Brad Paisley	14
6 =	Garth Brooks	11
=	Tim McGraw	11
8	Dixie Chicks	10
9 =	Alabama	9
=	Chet Atkins	9
=	Tony Brown	9
=	Johnny Cash	9
=	The Judds	9
=	Willie Nelson	9
=	Dolly Parton	9
=	Statler Brothers	9

Source: Country Music Association

TOP 10 BEST-ATTENDED CONCERTS OF THE 2000s

ARTIST / VENUE / DATE	GROSS ($)	ATTENDANCE
1 Take That Wembley Stadium, London, England Jun 30, Jul 1–2, 4–6, 8–9, 2011	61,713,184	623,737
2 Bruce Springsteen & the E Street Band Giants Stadium, East Rutherford, NJ Jul 15–Aug 31, 2003	38,684,050	566,560
3 Take That City of Manchester Stadium, Manchester, England Jun 3–5, 7–8, 10–12, 2011	44,183,145	443,223
4 Prince O2 Arena, London Aug 1–Sep 21, 2007	22,052,026	351,527
5 Lollapalooza Grant Park, Chicago, IL Aug 5–7, 2011	19,902,224	270,000
6 U2, Muse Estadio do Morumbi, Sao Paulo, Brazil Apr 9–10, 13, 2011	32,754, 065	269,491
7 Bruce Springsteen & the E Street Band Giants Stadium, East Rutherford, NJ Sep 30–Oct 9, 2009	22,570,336	260,668
8 The Spice Girls O2 Arena, London Dec 15, 2006–Jan 22, 2007	33,829,250	256,647
9 U2 Croke Park, Dublin Jun 24–27, 2005	21,163,695	246,743
10 U2 Croke Park, Dublin Jul 24–27, 2009	28,815,352	243,198

Source: *Billboard*

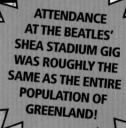

▼ The Boss's place
New Jersey-born Bruce Springsteen regarded the now-demolished Giants Stadium as his home turf.

ATTENDANCE AT THE BEATLES' SHEA STADIUM GIG WAS ROUGHLY THE SAME AS THE ENTIRE POPULATION OF GREENLAND!

▼ Noises off
The screaming of ecstatic fans drowned out the Beatles at Shea Stadium.

TOP 10 BEST-ATTENDED BEATLES CONCERTS

VENUE	DATE	ATTENDANCE
1 Shea Stadium, New York, NY	Aug 15, 1965	55,600
2 Rizal Memorial Football Stadium, Manila	Jul 4, 1966	50,000
3 Dodger Stadium, Los Angeles, CA	Aug 28, 1966	45,000
4 Shea Stadium, New York, NY	Aug 23, 1966	44,600
5 White Sox Park, Chicago, IL	Aug 10, 1965	37,000
6 DC Stadium, Washington, DC	Aug 15, 1966	32,164
7 Atlanta Stadium, Atlanta, GA	Aug 18, 1965	30,000
8 Candlestick Park, San Francisco, CA	Aug 29, 1966	25,000
9 Metropolitan Stadium, Bloomington, MN	Aug 21, 1965	25,000
10 Busch Stadium, St. Louis, MO	Aug 21, 1966	23,000

Source: Music Information Database

TOP 10 **HIGHEST-GROSSING TOURS OF 2011**

ARTIST	GROSS ($ MILLION)
1 U2	293
2 Bon Jovi	193
3 Take That	185
4 Roger Waters	150
5 Taylor Swift	97
6 Kenny Chesney	85
7 Usher	75
8 Lady Gaga	72
9 Andre Rieu	67
10 Sade	50

Source: Billboard

▲ **High roller**
According to Billboard magazine, Taylor Swift was the most financially successful music artist of 2011.

◄ **The greatest**
Readers of Q magazine voted U2 the best musical act of the last quarter-century.

TOP 10 **BEST-ATTENDED MADONNA CONCERTS**

VENUE / DATE	ATTENDANCE
1 Estadio River Plate, Buenos Aires, Argentina Dec 4–8, 2008	263,693
2 Estadio Nacional, Santiago, Chile Dec 10–11, 2008	146,242
3 Stade de France, Paris, France Sep 20–21, 2008	138,163
4 Ullevi Stadion, Goteborg, Sweden Aug 8–9, 2009	119,709
5 Estadio do Marcana, Rio de Janeiro, Brazil Dec 14–15, 2008	107,000
6 Foro Sol, Mexico City, Mexico Nov 29–30, 2008	104,270
7 Amsterdam Arena, Amsterdam, Holland Sep 3–4, 2006	102,330
8 Hayarkon Park, Tel Aviv, Israel Sep 1–2, 2009	99,674
9 Madison Square Garden, New York, NY Jun 28–Jul 19, 2006	91,841
10 Madison Square Garden, New York, NY Jun 16–24, 2004	88,625

Source: Music Information Database

TOP 10 **BEST-ATTENDED LADY GAGA CONCERTS**

VENUE / DATE	ATTENDANCE
1 Madison Square Garden, New York Jul 6, 7, 9, 2010	45,461
2 Rod Laver Arena, Melbourne, Australia Mar 23–24, Apr 9, 2010	39,299
3 Sydney Entertainment Centre, Sydney Mar 17–18, Apr 7, 2010	35,460
4 O2 Arena, London, England May 30–31, 2010	34,159
5 O2 Arena, London, England Feb 26–27, 2010	33,636
6 Sportpaleis, Antwerp, Belgium Nov 22–23, 2010	31,941
7 Sportpaleis, Antwerp, Belgium May 17–18, 2010	31,818
8 Palais Omnisports Bercy, Paris, France May 21–22, 2010	31,474
9 Estadio Tres de Marzo, Guadalajara, Mexico May 3, 2011	29,047
10 Madison Square Garden, New York Feb 21–22, 2011	28,949

CLASSICAL MUSIC

TOP 10 BESTSELLING CLASSICAL ARTISTS IN THE USA

ARTIST

1. Andrea Bocelli
2. Luciano Pavarotti
3. Placido Domingo
4. José Carreras
5. Charlotte Church
6. Mario Lanza
7. Van Cliburn
8. Benedictine Monks of Santo Domingo de Silos
9. Royal Philharmonic Orchestra
10. Neville Marriner

Source: Music Information Database

THE 10 LATEST BEST CLASSICAL ALBUM GRAMMIES

YEAR	TITLE / COMPOSER
2011	Requiem, Giuseppe Verdi
2010	Symphony No. 8/Adagio from Symphony No. 10, Gustav Mahler
2009	Rise and Fall of the City of Mahagonny, Kurt Weill
2008	Made in America, Joan Tower
2007	Symphony No. 7, Gustav Mahler
2006	Songs of Innocence and of Experience, William Bolcom
2005	On the Transmigration of Souls, John Adams
2004	Symphony No. 3, Gustav Mahler
2003	A Sea Symphony, Ralph Vaughan Williams
2002	Les Troyens, Hector Berlioz

Source: NARAS

TOP 10 VERDI OPERAS MOST FREQUENTLY PERFORMED AT THE METROPOLITAN OPERA HOUSE, NEW YORK

OPERA	PERFORMANCES
1 Aïda	1,122
2 La Traviata	977
3 Rigoletto	841
4 Il Trovatore	625
5 Otello	314
6 Un Ballo In Maschera	287
7 La Forza Del Destino	230
8 Falstaff	175
9 Simon Boccanegra	139
10 Macbeth	98

Source: Metropolitan Opera

▶ *If at first...*
La Traviata was first performed in 1853.

▼ *Luciano Pavarotti*
Pavarotti's 1990 rendition of Nessun Dorma brought him fame around the world.

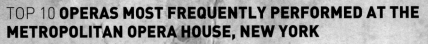

TOP 10 OPERAS MOST FREQUENTLY PERFORMED AT THE METROPOLITAN OPERA HOUSE, NEW YORK

	OPERA	COMPOSER	TOTAL*
1	La Bohème	Giacomo Puccini	1,253
2	Aïda	Giuseppi Verdi	1,122
3	La Traviata	Giuseppi Verdi	977
4	Carmen	Georges Bizet	971
5	Tosca	Giacomo Puccini	925
6	Madama Butterfly	Giacomo Puccini	842
7	Rigoletto	Giuseppi Verdi	841
8	Faust	Charles Gounod	747
9	Pagliacci	Ruggero Leoncavallo	712
10	Cavalleria Rusticana	Mascagni	671

Source: Metropolitan Opera

▶ **Musical legacy**
The composer George Bizet died shortly after the premiere of Carmen.

◀ **Crossover appeal**
Charlotte Church has had pop hits too, and hosted a chat show.

TOP 10 CLASSICAL ALBUMS IN THE USA

	TITLE	PERFORMER/ORCHESTRA	YEAR
1	The Three Tenors in Concert	José Carreras, Placido Domingo, Luciano Pavarotti	1990
2	Romanza	Andrea Bocelli	1997
3	Sogno	Andrea Bocelli	1999
4	Voice of an Angel	Charlotte Church	1999
5	Chant	Benedictine Monks of Santo Domingo De Silos	1994
6	The Three Tenors in Concert 1994	José Carreras, Placido Domingo, Luciano Pavarotti	1994
7	Sacred Arias	Andrea Bocelli	1999
8	Tchaikovsky: Piano Concerto No. 1	Van Cliburn	1958
9	Amore	Andrea Bocelli	2006
10	Cieli Di Toscana	Andrea Bocelli	2001

Source: Music Information Database

Sales of classical music boomed to unprecedented heights at the end of the 1980s and in the early 1990s. Records by a select band of superstars—tenors José Carreras, Placido Domingo, and Luciano Pavarotti (particularly the latter, who even had a Top 3 single with *Nessun Dorma*), and young-gun violinist Nigel Kennedy— soared way ahead of the field.

7

ENTERTAINMENT

40 YEARS OF CGI

The evolution of computer-generated imagery (CGI) has had a huge impact on the world of entertainment over the past four decades, and has given us some of the biggest-grossing movies in recent years. While 2D CGI was first used in the film *Westworld* in 1973, the first fully computer-generated feature film, *Toy Story*, was released in 1995. Thanks to the advancements in computer-processing power, the CGI animation bar has been rising ever since, bringing us such modern classics as the *Toy Story* and *Shrek* series, *Up*, and *Finding Nemo*. With the expected releases of *Monsters University*, the prequel to *Monsters, Inc.*, *Leafmen* (a new animated film from the director of *Ice Age* and *Robots*), and *Despicable Me 2*, 2013 looks set to be another exciting year in the life of CGI animation.

Main image: Toy Story
Inset: Westworld

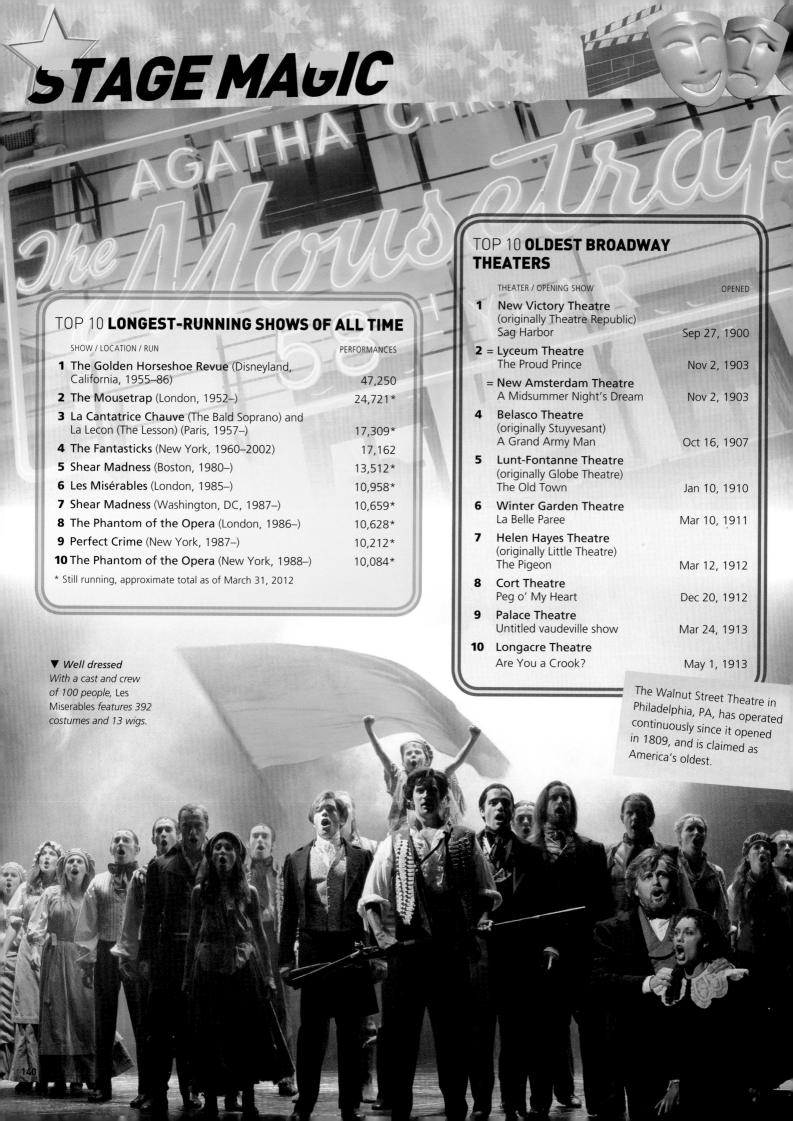

STAGE MAGIC

TOP 10 LONGEST-RUNNING SHOWS OF ALL TIME

SHOW / LOCATION / RUN	PERFORMANCES
1 The Golden Horseshoe Revue (Disneyland, California, 1955–86)	47,250
2 The Mousetrap (London, 1952–)	24,721*
3 La Cantatrice Chauve (The Bald Soprano) and La Lecon (The Lesson) (Paris, 1957–)	17,309*
4 The Fantasticks (New York, 1960–2002)	17,162
5 Shear Madness (Boston, 1980–)	13,512*
6 Les Misérables (London, 1985–)	10,958*
7 Shear Madness (Washington, DC, 1987–)	10,659*
8 The Phantom of the Opera (London, 1986–)	10,628*
9 Perfect Crime (New York, 1987–)	10,212*
10 The Phantom of the Opera (New York, 1988–)	10,084*

* Still running, approximate total as of March 31, 2012

▼ **Well dressed**
With a cast and crew of 100 people, Les Miserables features 392 costumes and 13 wigs.

TOP 10 OLDEST BROADWAY THEATERS

THEATER / OPENING SHOW	OPENED
1 New Victory Theatre (originally Theatre Republic) Sag Harbor	Sep 27, 1900
2 = Lyceum Theatre The Proud Prince	Nov 2, 1903
= New Amsterdam Theatre A Midsummer Night's Dream	Nov 2, 1903
4 Belasco Theatre (originally Stuyvesant) A Grand Army Man	Oct 16, 1907
5 Lunt-Fontanne Theatre (originally Globe Theatre) The Old Town	Jan 10, 1910
6 Winter Garden Theatre La Belle Paree	Mar 10, 1911
7 Helen Hayes Theatre (originally Little Theatre) The Pigeon	Mar 12, 1912
8 Cort Theatre Peg o' My Heart	Dec 20, 1912
9 Palace Theatre Untitled vaudeville show	Mar 24, 1913
10 Longacre Theatre Are You a Crook?	May 1, 1913

The Walnut Street Theatre in Philadelphia, PA, has operated continuously since it opened in 1809, and is claimed as America's oldest.

140

THE 10 **LATEST TONY AWARDS FOR A PLAY**

YEAR	PLAY	PLAYWRIGHT
2011	War Horse	Nick Stafford
2010	Red	John Logan
2009	God of Carnage	Yasmina Reza
2008	August: Osage County	Tracy Letts
2007	The Coast of Utopia	Tom Stoppard
2006	The History Boys	Alan Bennett
2005	Doubt	John Patrick Shanley
2004	I Am My Own Wife	Doug Wright
2003	Take Me Out	Richard Greenberg
2002	The Goat or Who is Sylvia?	Edward Albee

The Tony Awards honor outstanding Broadway plays and musicals, actors and actresses, music, costume, and other contributions.

THE 10 **LATEST TONY AWARDS FOR A MUSICAL**

YEAR	MUSICAL
2011	The Book of Mormon
2010	Memphis
2009	Billy Elliot, The Musical
2008	In the Heights
2007	Spring Awakening
2006	Jersey Boys
2005	Monthy Python's Spamalot
2004	Avenue Q
2003	Hairspray
2002	Thoroughly Modern Millie

▼ *History man*
Richard Griffiths in Alan Bennett's multi award-winning The History Boys.

▼ *Stage to celluloid*
Robert Redford also starred in the 1967 film of Barefoot in the Park.

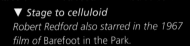

TOP 10 **LONGEST-RUNNING COMEDIES* ON BROADWAY**

	COMEDY	RUN	PERFORMANCES
1	Life with Father	Nov 8, 1939–Jul 12, 1947	3,224
2	Abie's Irish Rose	May 23, 1922–Oct 1, 1927	2,327
3	Gemini	May 21, 1977–Sep 6, 1981	1,819
4	Harvey	Nov 1, 1944–Jan 15, 1949	1,775
5	Born Yesterday	Feb 4, 1946–Dec 31, 1949	1,642
6	Mary, Mary	Mar 8, 1961–Dec 12, 1964	1,572
7	The Voice of the Turtle	Dec 8, 1943–Jan 3, 1948	1,557
8	Barefoot in the Park	Oct 23, 1963–Jun 25, 1967	1,530
9	Same Time, Next Year	Mar 14, 1975–Sep 3, 1978	1,453
10	Arsenic and Old Lace	Jan 10, 1941–Jun 17, 1944	1,444

* Plays only; not including musical comedies

MOVIE BUSINESS

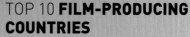

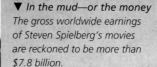
◄ *Bollywood blockbuster*
Ra One broke Indian box-office records on its first weekend release in 2011.

TOP 10 FILM-PRODUCING COUNTRIES

COUNTRY / FEATURE FILMS PRODUCED

#	Country	Feature films produced
1	India	1,288
2	USA	677
3	China	456
4	Japan	448
5	France	230
6	Spain	186
7	Germany	150
8	South Korea	139
9	Italy	131
10	UK	126

Source: Screen Digest

TOP 10 BILLION-DOLLAR DIRECTORS

#	DIRECTOR / MOVIES	HIGHEST-EARNING MOVIE	TOTAL GROSS ($)*
1	Steven Spielberg 25	E.T.: The Extra-Terrestrial	7,827,700,000
2	George Lucas 6	Star Wars	3,525,700,000
3	Robert Zemeckis 15	Forrest Gump	3,340,200,000
4	Ron Howard 20	How the Grinch Stole Christmas	2,924,300,000
5	James Cameron 9	Avatar	2,877,400,000
6	Chris Columbus 14	Home Alone	2,720,700,000
7	Tim Burton 15	Alice in Wonderland	2,491,500,000
8	Richard Donner 16	Superman	2,491,000,000
9	Michael Bay 9	Transformers: Revenge of the Fallen	2,361,400,000
10	Clint Eastwood 31	Unforgiven	2,295,100,000

* Of all movies

▼ *In the mud—or the money*
The gross worldwide earnings of Steven Spielberg's movies are reckoned to be more than $7.8 billion.

TOP 10 COUNTRIES WITH MOST CINEMA ADMISSIONS PER CAPITA

#	COUNTRY	ADMISSIONS PER CAPITA*
1	Iceland	5.4
2	Singapore	4.5
3	Australia	4.3
4	USA	3.9
5	= Ireland	3.6
	= New Zealand	3.6
7	France	3.3
8	Canada	3.1
9	South Korea	3.0
10	India	2.9

* Latest available year

TOP 10 **YEARS FOR CINEMA ADMISSIONS IN THE USA***

	YEAR	ADMISSIONS
1	1946	4,067,300,000
2	1945	3,664,400,000
3	1944	3,422,700,000
4	1943	3,168,500,000
5	1948	3,017,500,000
6	1942	2,840,100,000
7	1947	2,777,700,000
8	1949	2,630,600,000
9	1950	2,270,400,000
10	1951	2,072,300,000

* 1946–present

1955 was the last year on record that US movie attendance was greater than 2 billion. From 1956 onward, admissions declined, reaching a low of 820,300,000 in 1971. The downward trend was not reversed until 1991, when they began to increase again.

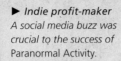

▶ *Indie profit-maker*
A social media buzz was crucial to the success of Paranormal Activity.

TOP 10 **MOST PROFITABLE MOVIES OF ALL TIME***

MOVIE / YEAR	BUDGET ($)	TOTAL WORLD GROSS ($)*	PROFIT RATIO
1 Paranormal Activity 2009	15,000	196,681,656	13,112.11
2 The Blair Witch Project 1999	35,000	248,662,839	7,104.65
3 Rocky 1976	1,100,000	225,000,000	204.55
4 American Graffiti 1973	750,000	140,000,000	186.66
5 Snow White and the Seven Dwarfs 1937	1,488,000	187,670,866	126.12
6 The Rocky Horror Picture Show 1975	1,200,000	139,876,417	116.56
7 Gone With the Wind 1939	3,900,000	390,525,192	100.13
8 Saw 2004	1,200,000	103,096,345	85.91
9 E.T.: The Extra-Terrestrial 1982	10,500,000	792,910,554	75.52
10 My Big Fat Greek Wedding 2002	5,000,000	368,744,044	73.75

* Movies grossing more than $100 million worldwide

▲ *Aaaagh—it's a turkey!*
A critical mauling preceded the commercial disaster of The Adventures of Pluto Nash.

THE BIGGEST FILM FLOPS OF ALL TIME

The pirate movie *Cutthroat Island* (1995) is often cited as the biggest film flop ever; it lost nearly 84% of its massive budget, and tipped its studio into bankruptcy. If marketing expenses are discounted, however, the battle of the bombs is fought between the sci-fi thriller *Eye See You* and the comedy howler *The Adventures of Pluto Nash* (both 2002). But in terms of absolute losses, unadjusted for inflation, the dubious honor of biggest movie flop goes to *Mars Needs Moms* (2011), which is estimated to have lost over $136 million. Some celebrated box-office failures—such as *Waterworld* (1995)—have actually shown a profit over time.

BLOCKBUSTERS

THE 10 HIGHEST-EARNING MOVIES OF THE LAST 10 DECADES

DECADE / MOVIE / YEAR / ESTIMATED BUDGET ($) / ESTIMATED WORLD TOTAL GROSS ($)

2010s
Harry Potter and the Deathly Hallows Part 2 (2011)
$250,000,000
$1,328,111,219

2000s
Avatar (2009)
$237,000,000
$2,782,275,172

1990s
Titanic (1997)
$200,000,000
$1,848,880,000

1980s
ET: The Extra-Terrestrial (1982)
$10,500,000
$792,900,000

1970s
Star Wars (1977)
$13,000,000
$797,900,000

1960s
One Hundred and One Dalmatians (1961)
$4,000,000
$215,800,000

1950s
Peter Pan (1953)
$4,000,000
$145,000,000

1940s
Bambi (1942)
$2,000,000
$268,000,000

1930s
Gone With the Wind (1939)
$3,850,000
$390,000,000

1920s
The Big Parade (1925)
$245,000
$20,000,000

▲ **Wading in profit**
Moviegoers' enthusiasm for the Pirates of the Caribbean franchise remains high.

THE MOST EXPENSIVE MOVIES

Some consider *Avatar* to be the most expensive movie ever made, but in fact it ranks only 9th. Officially, *Pirates of the Caribbean: At World's End*—which was produced together with *Dead Man's Chest* on a combined budget of $450 million—is the most expensive film, at $300 million. This is followed by the two *Hobbit* movies produced in 2012 and 2013, then the animated *Tangled* at No. 4. However, budget figures for movies can be unreliable, so are only estimates. Film studios often try to keep such information to themselves, and will use accounting tricks to inflate or reduce budgets.

▶ **Hair raising**
Tangled *took six years to make and cost $260 million.*

TOP 10 HIGHEST-GROSSING MOVIES, 2011

	MOVIE	WORLD GROSS ($)
1	Harry Potter and the Deathly Hallows Part 2	1,328,111,219
2	Transformers: Dark of the Moon	1,123,746,996
3	Pirates of the Caribbean: On Stranger Tides	1,043,871,802
4	The Twilight Saga: Breaking Dawn Part 2	652,252,000
5	The Hangover Part 2	581,464,305
6	Kung Fu Panda 2	655,692,281
7	Fast Five	626,137,675
8	The Smurfs	562,547,576
9	Cars 2	551,852,396
10	Rio	484,635,760

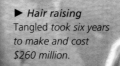

TOP 10 **MOVIES OF ALL TIME**

MOVIE / YEAR / ESTIMATED WORLD GROSS (US$)

1 Avatar (2009)
$2,782,275,172

2 Titanic (1997)
$1,843,201,268

3 Harry Potter and the Deathly Hallows Part 2 (2011)
$1,328,111,219

4 Transformers: Dark of the Moon (2011)
$1,123,746,996

5 The Lord of the Rings: The Return of the King (2003)
$1,119,110,941

6 Pirates of the Caribbean: Dead Man's Chest (2006)
$1,066,179,725

7 Toy Story 3 (2010)
$1,063,171,911

8 Pirates of the Caribbean: On Stranger Tides (2011)
$1,043,871,802

9 Alice in Wonderland (2010)
$1,024,299,904

10 The Dark Knight (2008)
$1,001,921,825

* Unadjusted grosses from box-office receipts

▼ *Fast earner*
Avatar grossed $1 billion worldwide in a record-breaking 19 days.

AVATAR'S CUMULATIVE TAKINGS ARE EQUIVALENT TO THE GROSS DOMESTIC PRODUCT OF GUYANA!

◄ *50 years of 007
From Sean Connery to Daniel Craig, the name Bond, James Bond, has meant movie blockbuster.*

TOP 10 **MOVIE FRANCHISES OF ALL TIME**

	FRANCHISE	MOVIES	YEARS	TOTAL WORLD GROSS ($)
1	Harry Potter	8	2001–11	7,705,165,743
2	James Bond	24	1963–2010	5,116,147,171
3	Star Wars	7	1977–2005	4,279,632,749
4	Pirates of the Caribbean	4	2003–11	3,723,435,967
5	Shrek	5	2001–10	3,287,285,005
6	The Lord of the Rings	4	2001–03	2,945,626,609
7	Transformers	4	2007–11	2,675,610,116
8	Batman	6	1989–2008	2,633,156,7759
9	Spider-Man	3	2002–07	2,496,346,518
10	The Twilight Saga	4	2008–10	2,453,822,671

OPENING WEEKENDS

TOP 10 ANIMATED MOVIE OPENING WEEKENDS

MOVIE / YEAR / OPENING WEEKEND GROSS ($)

1 Shrek the Third
2007
$121,629,270

2 Toy Story 3
2010
$110,307,189

3 Shrek 2
2004
$108,037,878

4 The Simpsons Movie
2007
$74,036,787

5 Shrek Forever After
2010
$70,838,207

6 The Incredibles
2004
$70,467,623

7 Finding Nemo
2003
$70,251,710

8 Up
2009
$68,108,790

9 Ice Age: The Meltdown
2006
$68,033,544

10 Cars 2
2011
$66,135,507

▲ *It's elementary*
Director Guy Ritchie scored his biggest hit to date with Sherlock Holmes.

TOP 10 CHRISTMAS OPENING WEEKENDS

MOVIE / YEAR / OPENING WEEKEND GROSS ($)

1 Sherlock Holmes
2009
$62,304,277

2 Marley and Me
2008
$36,357,586

3 Catch Me If You Can
2002
$30,053,627

4 Cheaper by the Dozen
2003
$27,557,647

5 Bedtime Stories
2008
$27,450,296

6 The Curious Case of Benjamin Button 2008
$26,853,816

7 Patch Adams
1998
$25,262,280

8 It's Complicated
2009
$22,100,820

9 Valkyrie
2008
$21,027,007

10 Ali
2001
$14,710,892

▶ *Hidden star*
Toy Story star Sheriff Woody Pride is voiced by Tom Hanks.

► *Gone too soon*
The Dark Knight was the last film that Heath Ledger lived to complete.

★ ★ ★ ★ ★

TOP 10 FASTEST FILMS TO GROSS $150 MILLION

MOVIE / YEAR	DAYS TO $150 MILLION
1 = Harry Potter and the Deathly Hallows Part 2, 2011	3
= The Dark Knight, 2008	3
= Spider-Man 3, 2007	3
4 = Transformers: Revenge of the Fallen, 2009	4
= Star Wars: Episode III – Revenge of the Sith, 2005	4
= Pirates of the Caribbean: Dead Man's Chest, 2006	4
= The Twilight Saga: New Moon 2009	4
= Pirates of the Caribbean: At World's End, 2007	4
9 = Harry Potter and the Half-Blood Prince, 2009	5
= The Twilight Saga: Eclipse, 2010	5
= Spider-Man 2, 2004	5
= Indiana Jones and the Kingdom of the Crystal Skull, 2008	5

TOP 10 MOVIES THAT STAYED LONGEST AT NO. 1

MOVIE / YEAR	CONSECUTIVE NO. 1 WEEKENDS
1 ET: The Extra-Terrestrial 1982	16
2 Titanic 1997	15
3 Tootsie 1982	14
4 Beverly Hills Cop 1984	13
5 Home Alone 1990	12
6 Back to the Future 1985	11
7 Ghostbusters 1984	10
8 = Crocodile Dundee 1986	9
= Good Morning, Vietnam 1987	9
10 = Fatal Attraction 1987	8
= Porky's 1982	8

► *Funny guy*
Eddie Murphy made the transition from stand-up comic to leading man.

TOP 10 OPENING WEEKENDS FOR MOVIES NOT AT NO. 1

MOVIE / YEAR / OPENING WEEKEND GROSS ($)

1 The Day After Tomorrow 2004
$68,743,584

2 Sherlock Holmes 2009
$62,304,277

3 Wanted 2008
$50,927,085

4 Alvin and the Chipmunks: The Squeakquel 2009
$48,875,415

5 Tangled 2010
$48,767,052

6 Kung Fu Panda 2 2011
$47,656,302

7 The Longest Yard 2005
$47,606,480

8 Madagascar 2005
$47,224,594

9 Alvin and the Chipmunks 2007
$44,307,417

10 Terminator Salvation 2009
$42,558,390

TOP 10 MOVIES OF THE 1950s

MOVIE	YEAR
1 Lady and the Tramp*	1955
2 Peter Pan*	1953
3 Cinderella*	1950
4 The Ten Commandments	1956
5 Ben-Hur#	1959
6 Sleeping Beauty*	1959
7 Around the World in 80 Days	1956
8 This is Cinerama	1952
9 South Pacific	1958
10 The Robe	1953

* Animated
\# Winner of Best Picture Academy Award

▶ *Singing success*
The Sound of Music *was a No. 1 box-office hit in 1965. For the first time, each of the Top 10 films of the decade earned more than $100 million globally.*

While the popularity of animated films continued, the 1950s was outstanding as the decade of the "big" picture: not only were many of the most successful films enormous in terms of cast and scale, but also the magnitude of the subjects they tackled: three were major biblical epics, with *The Robe* the first film to offer CinemaScope.

▼ *Love at first sight*
Lady and the Tramp *has become a Walt Disney classic.*

TOP 10 MOVIES OF THE 1960s

MOVIE	YEAR
1 One Hundred and One Dalmatians*	1961
2 The Jungle Book*	1967
3 The Sound of Music#	1965
4 Thunderball	1965
5 Goldfinger	1964
6 Doctor Zhivago	1965
7 You Only Live Twice	1967
8 The Graduate	1968
9 Butch Cassidy and the Sundance Kid	1969
10 Mary Poppins	1964

* Animated
\# Winner of Best Picture Academy Award

TOP 10 MOVIES OF THE 1970s

MOVIE	YEAR
1 Star Wars*	1977
2 Jaws	1975
3 Grease	1978
4 Close Encounters of the Third Kind	1977
5 The Exorcist	1973
6 Superman	1978
7 Saturday Night Fever	1977
8 Jaws 2	1978
9 Moonraker	1979
10 The Spy Who Loved Me	1977

* Later retitled *Star Wars: Episode IV—A New Hope*

▼ Star Wars
In the 1970s, the arrival of the two prodigies, Steven Spielberg and George Lucas, set the scene for high-adventure blockbusters.

TOP 10 **MOVIES OF THE**
1980s

MOVIE	YEAR
1 E.T.: The Extra-Terrestrial	1982
2 Return of the Jedi*	1983
3 The Empire Strikes Back#	1980
4 Indiana Jones and the Last Crusade	1989
5 Rain Man†	1988
6 Raiders of the Lost Ark	1981
7 Batman	1989
8 Back to the Future	1985
9 Who Framed Roger Rabbit	1988
10 Top Gun	1986

* Later retitled *Star Wars: Episode VI— Return of the Jedi*
\# Later retitled *Star Wars: Episode V— The Empire Strikes Back*
† Winner of Best Picture Academy Award

▼ Indiana Jones
The 1980s was clearly the decade of the adventure movie, with George Lucas and Steven Spielberg carving up the Top 10 between them, variously as director, writer, or producer of no fewer than seven of the Top 10.

▲ Asteroid impact
The disaster movie Armageddon became the highest-grossing movie of 1998.

TOP 10 **MOVIES OF THE**
1990s

MOVIE	YEAR
1 Titanic*	1997
2 Star Wars: Episode I— The Phantom Menace	1999
3 Jurassic Park	1993
4 Independence Day	1996
5 The Lion King#	1994
6 Forrest Gump*	1994
7 The Sixth Sense	1999
8 Jurassic Park: The Lost World	1997
9 Men in Black	1997
10 Armageddon	1998

* Winner of Best Picture Academy Award
\# Animated

Each of the Top 10 movies of the 1990s has earned more than $550 million around the world, a total of more than 8.4 billion between them.

TOP 10 **MOVIES OF THE**
2000s

MOVIE	YEAR
1 Avatar	2009*
2 The Lord of the Rings: Return of the King	2003
3 Pirates of the Caribbean: Dead Man's Chest	2006
4 Toy Story 3	2010
5 Alice in Wonderland	2010
6 The Dark Knight	2008
7 Harry Potter and the Sorcerer's Stone	2001
8 Pirates of the Caribbean: At World's End	2007
9 Harry Potter and the Order of the Phoenix	2007
10 Harry Potter and the Half-Blood Prince	2009

* Multiple releases

► Lord of the Rings
This hugely ambitious and successful film trilogy (2001–03) was the 6th highest-grossing series of all time.

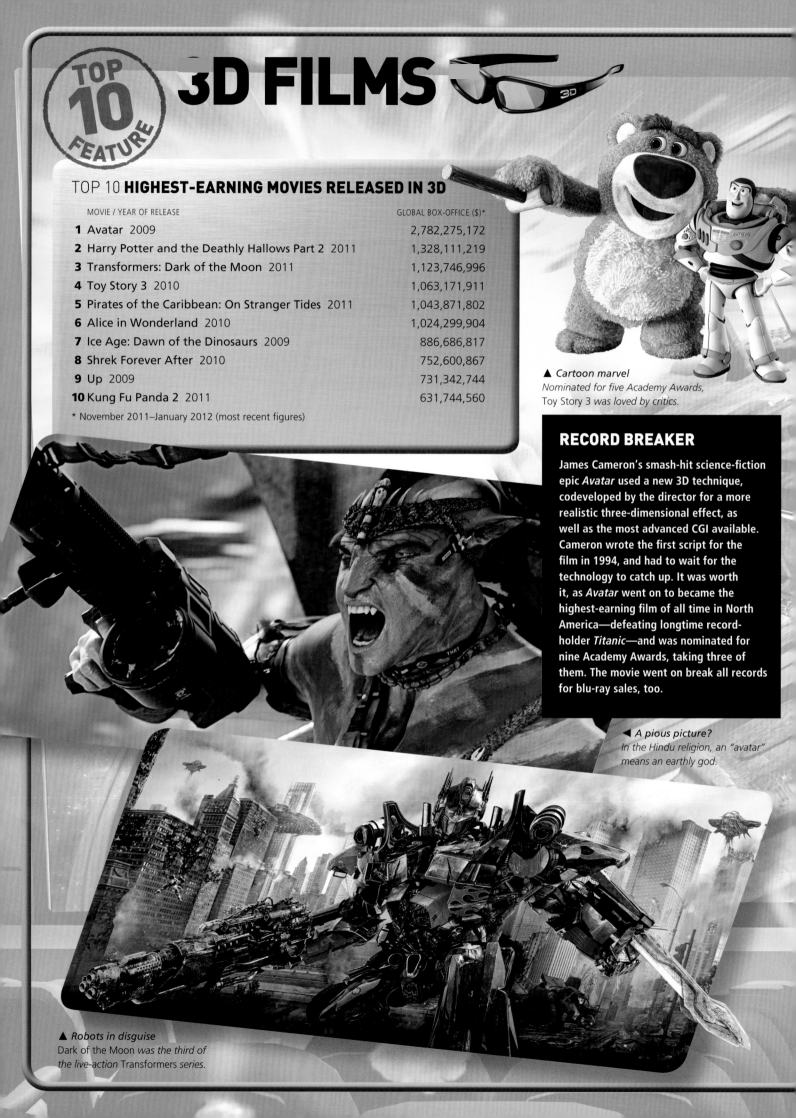

3D FILMS

TOP 10 HIGHEST-EARNING MOVIES RELEASED IN 3D

MOVIE / YEAR OF RELEASE	GLOBAL BOX-OFFICE ($)*
1 Avatar 2009	2,782,275,172
2 Harry Potter and the Deathly Hallows Part 2 2011	1,328,111,219
3 Transformers: Dark of the Moon 2011	1,123,746,996
4 Toy Story 3 2010	1,063,171,911
5 Pirates of the Caribbean: On Stranger Tides 2011	1,043,871,802
6 Alice in Wonderland 2010	1,024,299,904
7 Ice Age: Dawn of the Dinosaurs 2009	886,686,817
8 Shrek Forever After 2010	752,600,867
9 Up 2009	731,342,744
10 Kung Fu Panda 2 2011	631,744,560

* November 2011–January 2012 (most recent figures)

▲ *Cartoon marvel*
Nominated for five Academy Awards,
Toy Story 3 was loved by critics.

RECORD BREAKER

James Cameron's smash-hit science-fiction epic *Avatar* used a new 3D technique, codeveloped by the director for a more realistic three-dimensional effect, as well as the most advanced CGI available. Cameron wrote the first script for the film in 1994, and had to wait for the technology to catch up. It was worth it, as *Avatar* went on to became the highest-earning film of all time in North America—defeating longtime record-holder *Titanic*—and was nominated for nine Academy Awards, taking three of them. The movie went on break all records for blu-ray sales, too.

◄ *A pious picture?*
In the Hindu religion, an "avatar"
means an earthly god.

▲ *Robots in disguise*
Dark of the Moon was the third of
the live-action Transformers series.

THE 5 **BEST 3D MOVIES**

MOVIE / YEAR OF RELEASE

1 Ávatar 2009

2 How to Train Your Dragon 2010

3 Journey to the Center of the Earth 2008

4 Beowulf 2007

5 Toy Story 3 2012

▲ *Dragon training*
Hiccup rides Toothless the dragon.

THE ORIGINS OF 3D FILM

In a 3D film, an optical illusion of depth is achieved by using two images shot from slightly different perspectives. The technique goes back as far as 1838, when the English scientist Sir Charles Wheatstone invented the stereoscope (above), which enabled still images to be viewed three-dimensionally. Film pioneer William Friese-Greene patented the application of stereoscopy to moving pictures in 1894, but his technique was cumbersome. The first 3D feature film was *The Power of Love*, which premiered in Los Angeles in 1922 and used the anaglyph system, which required the audience to wear glasses with different-colored lenses.

A 3D FUTURE?

The success of recent 3D movies, led by *Avatar*, has caused observers to predict that they represent the future of the feature film. Some critics, however, say that the format is more about style than content, and health concerns have also been raised, with some 3D moviegoers complaining of headaches and eyestrain, or even nausea and dizziness. The box-office failure of the 3D animated action comedy *Mars Needs Moms* (2011) may indicate that the recent boom in 3D movies is—like the one in the 1950s—not destined to last.

FANTASTIC SIGHTS LEAP AT YOU IN **3-DIMENSION**

AMAZING! EXCITING! SPECTACULAR!

IT CAME FROM OUTER SPACE

Monster appeal
In the 1950s, cinema audiences donned their 3D specs and thrilled to oddball fantasies like The Creature from the Black Lagoon *(1954).*

ACTORS

MOVIE / YEAR

1 The Perfect Storm 2000
2 Planet of the Apes 2001
3 The Departed 2006
4 The Other Guys 2010
5 The Italian Job 2003
6 Date Night 2010
7 The Fighter 2010
8 Four Brothers 2005
9 The Happening 2008
10 Three Kings 1999

After his breakthrough in *Boogie Nights* (1997), Mark Wahlberg established himself as a performer to be reckoned with in *Three Kings* (1999) and then the summer hit *The Perfect Storm* (2000).

◄ **Metal man**
Robert Downey Jr. reprised his successful Iron Man role in the 2010 sequel.

TOP 10 **ROBERT DOWNEY JR. MOVIES**

MOVIE / YEAR

1 Iron Man 2008
2 Iron Man 2 2010
3 Sherlock Holmes 2009
4 The Incredible Hulk 2008
5 Tropic Thunder 2008
6 Sherlock Holmes: A Game of Shadows 2011
7 Due Date 2010
8 Back to School 1986
9 Bowfinger 1999
10 The Shaggy Dog 2006

TOP 10 **DANIEL CRAIG** MOVIES

MOVIE / YEAR

1 Quantum of Solace 2008
2 Casino Royale 2006
3 Lara Croft: Tomb Raider 2001
4 Road to Perdition 2002
5 Cowboys & Aliens 2011
6 The Golden Compass 2007
7 Munich 2005
8 The Girl with the Dragon Tattoo 2011
9 Elizabeth 1998
10 Defiance 2008

► **Cowboys & Aliens**
Daniel Craig plays a cowboy hero in this movie that combines sci-fi and western.

TOP 10 BRAD PITT MOVIES

MOVIE / YEAR

1 Mr & Mrs Smith 2005
2 Ocean's Eleven 2001
3 Megamind 2010
4 Troy 2004
5 The Curious Case of Benjamin Button 2008
6 Ocean's Twelve 2004
7 Inglourious Basterds 2009
8 Ocean's Thirteen 2007
9 Interview with the Vampire 1994
10 Se7en 1995

◀ Mr & Mrs Smith
Brad Pitt's top movie grossed $500 million worldwide.

TOP 10 TOM HANKS MOVIES

MOVIE / YEAR

1 Toy Story 3* 2010
2 Forrest Gump 1994
3 Toy Story 2* 1999
4 Cast Away 2000
5 The Da Vinci Code 2006
6 Saving Private Ryan 1998
7 Toy Story* 1995
8 The Polar Express* 2004
9 Apollo 13 1995
10 Catch Me if You Can 2002

* Voice

▲ *Twilight star Pattinson's roles in the Twilight Saga trio made him one of Hollywood's highest-paid actors.*

TOP 10 ROBERT PATTINSON MOVIES

MOVIE / YEAR

1 The Twilight Saga: Eclipse 2010
2 The Twilight Saga: New Moon 2009
3 Harry Potter and the Order of the Phoenix 2007
4 Harry Potter and the Goblet of Fire 2005
5 The Twilight Saga: Breaking Dawn Part 1 2011
6 Twilight 2008
7 Water for Elephants 2011
8 Remember Me 2010
9 Little Ashes 2009
10 Bel Ami 2012

TOP 10 ADAM SANDLER MOVIES

MOVIE / YEAR

1 Big Daddy 1999
2 Grown Ups 2010
3 The Waterboy 1998
4 The Longest Yard 2005
5 Click 2006
6 Anger Management 2003
7 Mr Deeds 2002
8 50 First Dates 2004
9 I Now Pronounce You Chuck and Larry 2007
10 Bedtime Stories 2008

ACTRESSES

▲ The Blind Side
Sandra Bullock starred in the first movie to gross over $200 million with only one top-billed female star.

► Monster hit
Reese Witherspoon voiced one of the characters in the animated Monsters Vs. Aliens, which heads her list of box-office successes.

TOP 10 SANDRA BULLOCK MOVIES

MOVIE / YEAR

1 The Blind Side 2009
2 The Proposal 2009
3 Speed 1994
4 A Time to Kill 1996
5 Miss Congeniality 2000
6 The Prince of Egypt* 1998
7 Two Weeks Notice 2002
8 While You Were Sleeping 1995
9 Divine Secrets of the Ya-Ya Sisterhood 2002
10 Demolition Man 1998

* Voice

TOP 10 SARAH JESSICA PARKER MOVIES

MOVIE / YEAR

1 Sex and the City 2008
2 The First Wives Club 1996
3 Sex and the City 2 2010
4 Failure to Launch 2006
5 Footloose 1984
6 The Family Stone 2005
7 New Year's Eve 2011
8 Hocus Pocus 1993
9 Mars Attacks! 1996
10 Honeymoon in Vegas 1992

Sarah Jessica Parker's first Sex and the City movie earned $415 million and she still makes a good income from repeats of the TV show. The second film (2010) wasn't such a big hit, but it still brought in $290 million.

TOP 10 REESE WITHERSPOON MOVIES

MOVIE / YEAR

1 Monsters Vs. Aliens* 2009
2 Sweet Home Alabama 2002
3 Four Christmases 2008
4 Walk the Line 2005
5 Legally Blonde 2001
6 Legally Blonde 2: Red, White and Blonde 2003
7 Water for Elephants 2011
8 Just Like Heaven 2005
9 Pleasantville 1998
10 Little Nicky 2000

* Voice

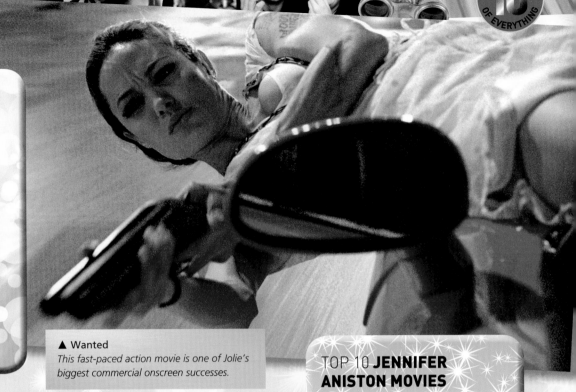

TOP 10 **ANGELINA JOLIE MOVIES**

MOVIE / YEAR

1 Kung Fu Panda* 2008
2 Mr & Mrs Smith 2005
3 Kung Fu Panda 2* 2011
4 Shark Tale* 2004
5 Wanted 2008
6 Lara Croft: Tomb Raider 2001
7 Salt 2010
8 Gone in 60 Seconds 2000
9 Beowulf 2007
10 The Tourist 2010

* Voice

▲ **Wanted**
This fast-paced action movie is one of Jolie's biggest commercial onscreen successes.

TOP 10 **CAMERON DIAZ MOVIES**

MOVIE / YEAR

1 Shrek 2* 2004
2 Shrek the Third* 2007
3 Shrek* 2001
4 Shrek Forever After* 2010
5 There's Something About Mary 1998
6 My Best Friend's Wedding 1997
7 Charlie's Angels 2000
8 The Mask 1994
9 Charlie's Angels: Full Throttle 2003
10 Vanilla Sky 2001

* Voice

TOP 10 **JENNIFER ANISTON MOVIES**

MOVIE / YEAR

1 Bruce Almighty 2003
2 Marley and Me 2008
3 The Break-up 2006
4 Horrible Bosses 2011
5 Just Go With It 2011
6 He's Just Not That Into You 2009
7 Along Came Polly 2004
8 The Bounty Hunter 2010
9 Rumor Has It 2005
10 Derailed 2005

◄ **Something about...**
Diaz shot to fame playing the much sought-after heroine in There's Something About Mary.

◄ **Woman's best friend**
Marley and Me was a huge Christmas Day box-office hit for Jennifer Aniston in 2008.

DIRECTORS

▲ Out of this world
1982's E.T. remains at the top of Steven Spielberg's most successful movies.

TOP 10 **MOVIES DIRECTED BY STEVEN SPIELBERG**

MOVIE / YEAR

1 E.T.: the Extra-Terrestrial 1982
2 Jurassic Park 1993
3 Indiana Jones and the Kingdom of the Crystal Skull 2008
4 Jaws 1975
5 Raiders of the Lost Ark 1981
6 War of the Worlds 2005
7 The Lost World: Jurassic Park 1997
8 Saving Private Ryan 1998
9 Indiana Jones and the Last Crusade 1989
10 Indiana Jones and the Temple of Doom 1984

TOP 10 **MOVIES DIRECTED BY CHRIS COLUMBUS**

MOVIE / YEAR

1 Harry Potter and the Sorcerer's Stone 2001
2 Home Alone 1990
3 Harry Potter and the Chamber of Secrets 2002
4 Mrs Doubtfire 1993
5 Home Alone 2: Lost in New York 1992
6 Stepmom 1998
7 Percy Jackson and the Olympians: The Lightning Thief 2010
8 Nine Months 1995
9 Bicentennial Man 1999
10 Adventures in Babysitting 1987

▶ Something to scream about
Columbus has directed some of the highest-grossing films ever, including two Harry Potter movies.

▶ How the Grinch Stole Christmas
Ron Howard directed the first Dr. Seuss movie to make it to the big screen in 2000.

TOP 10 **MOVIES DIRECTED BY RON HOWARD**

MOVIE / YEAR

1 How the Grinch Stole Christmas 2000
2 The Da Vinci Code 2006
3 Apollo 13 1995
4 A Beautiful Mind 2001
5 Ransom 1996
6 Angels and Demons 2009
7 Parenthood 1989
8 Backdraft 1991
9 Cocoon 1985
10 Splash 1984

TOP 10 DIRECTORS BY BIGGEST BUDGET FILMS

	DIRECTOR	MOVIE	ESTIMATED BUDGET ($)
1	Gore Verbinski	Pirates of the Caribbean: At World's End	300,000,000
2 =	Peter Jackson	The Hobbit: There and Back Again*	270,000,000
=	Peter Jackson	The Hobbit: An Unexpected Journey*	270,000,000
4	Nathan Greno	Tangled	260,000,000
5	Sam Raimi	Spider-Man 3	258,000,000
6 =	Gore Verbinski	Pirates of the Caribbean: On Stranger Tides	250,000,000
=	David Yates	Harry Potter and the Half-Blood Prince	250,000,000
=	Christopher Nolan	The Dark Knight Rises*	250,000,000
9	James Cameron	Avatar	237,000,000
10	Bryan Singer	Superman Returns	232,000,000

* Not yet released

▲ **An Unexpected Journey**
The two Hobbit *movies were filmed back to back, with a combined budget of $540,000,000.*

▶ *Fantastic fantasy*
Burton's Alice in Wonderland earned $1,024,299,904, making it the 9th highest-grossing movie of all time.

TOP 10 MOVIES DIRECTED BY TIM BURTON

MOVIE / YEAR

1 Alice in Wonderland 2010
2 Batman 1989
3 Charlie and the Chocolate Factory 2005
4 Planet of the Apes 2001
5 Batman Returns 1992
6 Sleepy Hollow 1999
7 Beetlejuice 1988
8 Big Fish 2003
9 Edward Scissorhands 1990
10 Tim Burton's Corpse Bride 2005

OSCAR-WINNERS

THE 10 LATEST BEST ACTRESS OSCAR WINNERS

YEAR* / ACTRESS / MOVIE

2012 Meryl Streep
The Iron Lady

2011 Natalie Portman
Black Swan

2010 Sandra Bullock
The Blind Side

2009 Kate Winslet
The Reader

2008 Marion Cotillard
La Vie en Rose

2007 Helen Mirren
The Queen

2006 Reese Witherspoon
Walk the Line

2005 Hilary Swank
Million Dollar Baby

2004 Charlize Theron
Monster

2003 Nicole Kidman
The Hours

* Of award ceremony

TOP 10 ACTORS AND ACTRESSES WITH THE MOST OSCAR NOMINATIONS*

	ACTOR/ACTRESS	SUPPORTING	WINS BEST	NOMINATIONS
1	Meryl Streep	1	2	17
2 =	Katharine Hepburn	0	4	12
=	Jack Nicholson	1	2	12
4 =	Bette Davis	0	2	10
=	Laurence Olivier	0	1	10
6 =	Paul Newman	0	1	9
=	Spencer Tracy	0	2	9
8 =	Marlon Brando	0	2	8
=	Jack Lemmon	1	1	8
=	Peter O'Toole	0	0	8
=	Al Pacino	0	1	8
=	Geraldine Page	0	1	8

* In all acting categories

▲ **Leading ladies**
Meryl Streep (left) as Margaret Thatcher in The Iron Lady *and 12-times Best Actress winner Katharine Hepburn (above).*

▶ **Jamie Foxx**
As well as being an Oscar-winning actor, Foxx has won several music awards, including a Grammy.

THE 10 LATEST BEST ACTOR OSCAR WINNERS

YEAR* / ACTOR / MOVIE

2012 Jean Dujardin
The Artist

2011 Colin Firth
The King's Speech

2010 Jeff Bridges
Crazy Heart

2009 Sean Pean
Milk

2008 Daniel Day-Lewis
There Will Be Blood

2007 Forest Whitaker
The Last King of Scotland

2006 Philip Seymour Hoffman
Capote

2005 Jamie Foxx
Ray

2004 Sean Penn
Mystic River

2003 Adrien Brody
The Pianist

* Of award ceremony

THE 10 **LATEST MOVIES TO WIN THE "BIG THREE"** *

	MOVIE	YEAR#
1	The Artist	2012
2	The King's Speech	2011
3	The Hurt Locker	2010
4	Slumdog Millionaire	2009
5	No Country for Old Men	2008
6	The Departed	2007
7	The Lord of the Rings: The Return of the King	2004
8	A Beautiful Mind	2002
9	American Beauty	2000
10	Forrest Gump	1995

* Best Picture, Director and Screenplay
\# Of award ceremony

▶ **The Artist**
The romantic drama was the first French film ever to scoop the Best Picture Oscar.

▼ **Ben-Hur**
The screen spectacular was adapted from the 1880 novel Ben-Hur: A Tale of the Christ.

TOP 10 **MOVIES TO WIN THE MOST OSCARS** *

	MOVIE	YEAR#	NOMINATIONS	AWARDS
1 =	Ben-Hur	1960	12	11
=	Titanic	1998	14	11
=	The Lord of the Rings: The Return of the King	2003	11	11
4	West Side Story	1961	11	10
5 =	Gigi	1958	9	9
=	The Last Emperor	1987	9	9
=	The English Patient	1996	12	9
8 =	Gone With the Wind	1939	13	8
=	From Here to Eternity	1953	13	8
=	On the Waterfront	1954	12	8
=	My Fair Lady	1964	12	8
=	Cabaret	1972	10	8
=	Gandhi	1982	11	8
=	Amadeus	1984	11	8
=	Slumdog Millionaire	2008	10	8

* Oscar® is a Registered Trade Mark
\# Of award ceremony

MOVIES NOMINATED FOR THE MOST OSCARS

Thirteen is not an unlucky number where Oscar nominations are concerned: eight movies have received that total. Only two others—*All About Eve* (1951) and *Titanic* (1998)—have received more, with 14 apiece. *Who's Afraid of Virginia Woolf?* (1967) was uniquely nominated in every eligible category: picture, actor, actress, supporting actor, supporting actress, director, adapted screenplay, art direction/set decoration (b&w), cinematography (b&w), sound, costume design (b&w), music score, and film editing.

Ten other films have won seven Oscars each: *Going My Way* (1944), *The Best years of Our Lives* (1946), *The Bridge on the River Kwai* (1957), *Lawrence of Arabia* (1962), *Patton* (1970), *The Sting* (1973), *Out of Africa* (1985), *Dances With Wolves* (1991), *Schindler's List* (1993), and *Shakespeare in Love* (1998).

TV WORLD

TOP 10 SATELLITE TV COUNTRIES

	COUNTRY	SATELLITE TV HOUSEHOLDS*
1	USA	40,281,100
2	Japan	20,730,500
3	Germany	16,750,100
4	Egypt	13,014,800
5	India	11,235,900
6	UK	10,330,100
7	Turkey	8,311,100
8	Italy	8,030,400
9	France	7,487,600
10	Algeria	5,642,200

* Latest year for which data available

Source: Euromonitor International

◄ **Rooftop array**
Satellite dishes pick up the mainly state-owned Egyptian television networks broadcasting around the Arab world.

TOP 10 TV AUDIENCES IN THE USA

	SHOW	BROADCAST	AUDIENCE
1	M*A*S*H Special	Feb 28, 1983	50,150,000
2	Dallas	Nov 21, 1980	41,470,000
3	Roots Part 8	Jan 30, 1977	36,380,000
4	Super Bowl XVI	Jan 24, 1982	40,020,000
5	Super Bowl XVII	Jan 30, 1983	40,480,000
6	XVII Winter Olympics	Feb 23, 1994	45,690,000
7	Super Bowl XX	Jan 26, 1986	41,490,000
8	Gone With the Wind Part 1	Nov 7, 1976	33,960,000
9	Gone With the Wind Part 2	Nov 8, 1976	33,750,000
10	Super Bowl XII	Jan 15, 1978	34,410,000

Source: Television Bureau of Advertising, 2010–11 (from Nielsen Company Research)

Historically, as more households acquired television sets, audiences generally increased, but the rise in channel choice and use of recording has checked this trend, and the high viewing figures of the past are unlikely ever to be attained again. The 2.5-hour feature-length "Goodbye, Farewell, and Amen" episode of *M*A*S*H* was the last in a series that had run for more than 10 years. An estimated 50.15 million households, or almost 106 million individual viewers, tuned in—making it the most-watched broadcast of all time.

FIRST TELEVISION COUNTRIES

Television first appeared in the UK in 1936, followed by the USA and the USSR in 1939. Initially the service was limited to a few cities, and outside of these areas TV was not available until some years later. Today there are still a few remote countries that have no TV service.

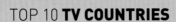

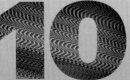

TOP 10 **TV COUNTRIES**

COUNTRY / TV HOUSEHOLDS*

1 China
384,288,600

2 USA
120,233,800

3 India
87,514,100

4 Indonesia
63,287,100

5 Brazil
54,853,200

6 Russia
51,323,500

7 Japan
50,578,900

8 Germany
39,326,500

9 Mexico
27,971,900

10 UK
27,409,500

* Households with color televisions

▲ Man power
Charlie Sheen and Jon Cryer
won their high-earning status
playing brothers in the sitcom
Two and a Half Men.

▶ Presidential alias
Joint highest-earning actress
Tina Fey playing vice-presidential
candidate Sarah Palin.

TOP 10 **HIGHEST-EARNING TV ACTORS**

	NAME	EARNINGS 2010–11 ($)
1	Charlie Sheen	40,000,000
2	Ray Romano	20,000,000
3	Steve Carell	15,000,000
4	Mark Harmon	13,000,000
5 =	Jon Cryer	11,000,000
=	Laurence Fishburne	11,000,000
7	Patrick Dempsey	10,000,000
8 =	Simon Baker	9,000,000
=	Hugh Laurie	9,000,000
=	Chris Meloni	9,000,000

Source: *Forbes*

TOP 10 **HIGHEST-EARNING TV ACTRESSES**

	NAME	EARNINGS 2010–11 ($)
1 =	Eva Longoria	13,000,000
=	Tina Fey	13,000,000
3 =	Marcia Cross	10,000,000
=	Mariska Hargitay	10,000,000
=	Marg Helgenberger	10,000,000
6 =	Terri Hatcher	9,000,000
=	Felicity Huffman	9,000,000
8 =	Courteney Cox	7,000,000
=	Ellen Pompeo	7,000,000
=	Julianna Margulies	7,000,000

Source: *Forbes*

TOP 10 **VIDEO GAMES**

	GAME	SALES, 2011
1	Star Wars: The Old Republic	1,682,326
2	Just Dance 3	1,352,008
3	Super Mario 3D Land	1,077,189
4	Mario Kart 7	1,033,254
5	Kinect Adventures!	1,010,053
6	Call of Duty: Modern Warfare 3 (X360)	866,231
7	Call of Duty: Modern Warfare 3 (PS3)	852,457
8	Mario & Sonic at the London 2012 Olympic Games	783,609
9	Mario Kart Wii	545,990
10	The Elder Scrolls V: Skyrim	513,330

Source: VGChartz

▲ *Video stars*
Call of Duty *(above)*
and Star Wars: The Old
Republic *(above right) are*
two of the most popular
video games available.

▼ *Super Mario*
Produced by Nintendo,
Mario is the bestselling
video-game franchise of
all time.

TOP 10 **GAMES CONSOLES**

	CONSOLE / RELEASE YEAR / UNITS
1	PlayStation 2 (2000) 155,800,000
2	Nintendo DS (2004) 149,000,000
3	Game Boy/ Game Boy Color (1989/98) 118,690,000
4	PlayStation (1994) 102,500,000
5	Wii (2006) 89,360,000
6	Game Boy Advance (2001) 81,510,000
7	PlayStation Portable (2004) 73,000,000
8	Nintendo Entertainment System (1983) 61,910,000
9	Xbox 360 (2005) 57,600,500
10	PlayStation 3 (1990) 55,500,000

TOP 10 **VIDEO-GAME FRANCHISES**

	FRANCHISE / FIRST GAME RELEASED	SALES
1	Mario (1980)	271,000,000
2	Pokémon (1996)	215,000,000
3	Wii (2006)	181,000,000
4	Tetris (1985)	175,000,000
5	The Sims (2000)	150,000,000
6	Grand Theft Auto (1997)	124,000,000
7	Call of Duty (2003)	122,000,000
8	= Final Fantasy (1987)	100,000,000
	= FIFA (1993)	100,000,000
	= Need for Speed (1994)	100,000,000

TOP 10 **PC GAMES**

	GAME	ESTIMATED SALES*
1	The Sims	16,000,000
2	The Sims 2	13,000,000
3	World of Warcraft	12,500,000#
4	Half-Life 2	12,000,000
5	= StarCraft	11,000,000
	= Battlefield 2	11,000,000
7	The Sims 3	10,000,000
8	Half-Life	9,300,000
9	Elder Scrolls V: Skyrim	7,000,000
10	Guild Wars	6,500,000

* Not including expansion packs
except *Guild Wars*
\# Based on subscription sales

▲ World of Warcraft
*The online fantasy
role-playing game
has a record-breaking
number of
subscribers.*

▶ The Sims 3
*Building on its
predecessors' success,
Sims 3 is one of the
bestselling computer
games of all time.*

▲ *Deathly drive*
*The two final instalments in the Harry Potter
series rank in the Top 3 bestselling DVDs.*

TOP 10 **DVD PLAYER-OWNING COUNTRIES**

	COUNTRY	DVD PLAYERS PER HOUSEHOLD*
1	United Arab Emirates	8.5
2	Belgium	2.8
3	Chile	2.7
4	Spain	2.6
5	Australia	2.2
6	Canada	1.9
7	UK	1.7
8	France	1.6
9	Japan	1.5
10	USA	1.4
	World	*0.6*

* 1998–2012

Source: Euromonitor International

TOP 10 **BESTSELLING MOVIES ON DVD, 2011**

	MOVIE	SALES
1	Harry Potter and the Deathly Hallows Part 1	6,913,160
2	Tangled	6,263,504
3	Harry Potter and the Deathly Hallows Part 2	5,792,158
4	Cars 2	4,533,033
5	Bridesmaids	3,591,569
6	Rio	3,392,882
7	Megamind	3,354,255
8	Despicable Me	2,739,750
9	Red	2,634,112
10	Transformers: Dark of the Moon	2,557,308

DOWNLOADS

LOADING...

TOP 10 **MOST DOWNLOADED iPHONE APPS (FREE)**

APP

1 Cut the Birds
2 101-in-1 Games!
3 Crime City
4 Magic LockScreen (+Todo)
5 Facebook Messenger
6 Flick Home Run!
7 Facebook
8 Flashlight
9 GlassPong
10 Family Feud and Friends

▲ *Angry Birds*
This strategy puzzle game—hugely successful on the iPhone—has been adapted for other smartphones.

TOP 10 **MOST DOWNLOADED iPHONE APPS (PAID)**

APP

1 Zombieville USA 2
2 Angry Birds
3 Angry Birds Seasons
4 Fruit Ninja
5 Camera+
6 Plants vs. Zombies
7 Modern Combat 3
8 Where's My Water?
9 Flashlight
10 WhatsApp Messenger

ONE IN EVERY 14 PEOPLE IN THE WORLD HAVE DOWNLOADED THE ANGRY BIRDS APP!

TOP 10 **BESTSELLING iPAD APPS***

▼ *Earth explorer*
Google Earth shows global satellite and aerial imagery on the iPad.

APP (PAID)	APP (FREE)
1 SoundHound	1 Pandora
2 StickWars	2 Google Mobile App
3 FlightTrack	3 Movies by Flixster
4 Backbreaker Football	4 Google Earth
5 Calorie Tracker	5 Yelp
6 BlocksClassic	6 Fandango Movies
7 iFart Mobile	7 Remote
8 GoodReader for iPad	8 iBooks
9 Cro-Mag Rally	9 Bible
10 Ambiance	10 Solitaire

* 2008–11

TOP 10 **MOST-DOWNLOADED US TV SHOWS WORLDWIDE**

	SHOW	DOWNLOADS	US VIEWERS
1	Lost	5,940,000	13,570,000
2	Heroes	5,480,000	5,300,000
3	Dexter	3,880,000	2,540,000
4	The Big Bang Theory	3,270,000	16,310,000
5	House	2,610,000	14,210,000
6	How I Met Your Mother	2,490,000	10,520,000
7	24	2,240,000	11,500,000
8	True Blood	1,920,000	5,440,000
9	Glee	1,700,000	13,660,000
10	Family Guy	1,620,000	7,730,000

This list of TV shows from the USA includes downloads from viewers outside the US, weeks or months ahead of the shows being scheduled in their own countries.

▶ *All at sea*
Multi award-winning drama Lost was downloaded by millions inside and outside the USA.

TOP 10 **MOST-PIRATED MOVIE DOWNLOADS**

MOVIE / YEAR OF RELEASE / ESTIMATED DOWNLOADS

1 Avatar (2009)
21,000,000

2 = The Dark Knight (2008)
19,000,000

= Transformers (2007)
19,000,000

4 Inception (2010)
18,000,000

5 The Hangover (2009)
17,000,000

6 Star Trek (2008)
16,000,000

7 Kick-Ass (2010)
15,000,000

8 = The Departed (2006)
14,000,000

= The Incredible Hulk (2008)
14,000,000

= Pirates of the Caribbean:
The World's End (2007)
14,000,000

▲ *Download downfall*
Inception's unique blend of action and sci-fi made it a massive download hit.

TOP 10 **INTERNET COUNTRIES**

	COUNTRY	% OF POPULATION	% OF WORLD TOTAL	INTERNET USERS
▶ 1	China	36.3	23.0	485,000,000
▶ 2	USA	78.2	11.6	245,000,000
▶ 3	India	8.4	4.7	100,000,000
▶ 4	Japan	78.4	4.7	99,182,000
▶ 5	Brazil	37.4	3.6	75,982,000
▶ 6	Germany	79.9	3.1	65,125,000
▶ 7	Russia	43.0	2.8	59,700,000
▶ 8	UK	82.0	2.4	51,442,100
▶ 9	France	69.5	2.1	45,262,000
▶ 10	Nigeria	28.3	2.1	43,982,200

Source: Internet World Stats

8

THE COMMERCIAL WORLD

Top: Twitter was used as a weapon for revolution in Egypt.
Above: The men who started Twitter—Biz Stone (left) and Evan Williams (right).

THE TWITTER PHENOMENON

Launched in July 2006, Twitter has become a global social networking phenomenon. The 140-character restriction has not limited its growth, which has been exponential: from 400,000 "tweets" per quarter in 2007 to 50 million a day three years later. A dictionary definition of "twitter" is "a short burst of inconsequential information." This appealed to the site's founders, though the microblogging site's role as a communications channel during the Arab Spring of 2011 proved anything but inconsequential. The same can be said of the company's commercial prospects—informed sources say that Twitter expects to have a billion users by the end of 2013, and that its worldwide profits will exceed a billion dollars.

TOP 10 COMPANIES WITH THE MOST EMPLOYEES

COMPANY / COUNTRY	INDUSTRY	EMPLOYEES
1 Wal-Mart Stores, USA	Retail	2,100,000
2 China National Petroleum, China	Oil and gas	1,674,541
3 State Grid, China	Electricity	1,564,000
4 Sinopec, China	Oil and gas	640,535
5 Hon Hai Precision Industries, China	Electronics	611,000
6 PetroChina, China	Oil and gas	552,698
7 China Telecommunications, China	Telecoms	493,919
8 Carrefour, France	Retail	475,976
9 Tesco, UK	Retail	472,094
10 Agricultural Bank of China, China	Banking	444,447

Source: *Financial Times FT 500 2011/Fortune Global 500 2011*

▲ **On the big stage** Giant companies such as Wal-Mart hold shareholders' meetings in huge sports arenas.

TOP 10 BEST-PAID JOBS IN THE USA

JOB	AVERAGE ANNUAL SALARY ($)
1 Surgeon	225,390
2 Anaesthesiologist	220,100
3 Medical consultant	210,000
4 Family and general practitioner	173,860
5 Chief executive	173,350
6 Dentist	158,770
7 Natural science manager	129,320
8 Lawyer	129,440
9 Petroleum engineer	127,970
10 Architect	125,900

Source: US Bureau of Labor Statistics

▲ **Growing out of poverty** Increased fruit production may contribute to growing prosperity in Zambia.

THE 10 COUNTRIES WITH THE HIGHEST UNEMPLOYMENT

COUNTRY / ESTIMATED LABOR FORCE UNEMPLOYED (%)*

1 Zimbabwe 97.0
2 Djibouti 59.0
3 Zambia 50.0
4 Senegal 48.0
5 Nepal 46.0
6 = Kenya 40.0
6 = Kosovo 40.0
8 Gaza Strip 37.8
9 Yemen 35.0
10 Afghanistan 35.0

USA 9.1

* Latest year for which data available
Source: CIA, World Factbook 2011

TOP 10 **OCCUPATIONS IN THE USA**

OCCUPATION / EMPLOYEES

1 Retail salespersons
4,155,190

2 Cashiers
3,354,170

3 Office clerks (general)
2,789,590

4 Food preparation
2,692,170

5 Registered nurses
2,655,020

6 Waiters and waitresses
2,244,480

7 Customer service representatives
2,146,120

8 Janitors and building cleaners
2,058,610

9 Drivers/sales workers and truck drivers
2,024,180

10 Secretaries and administrative assistants
1,841,020

Source: Bureau of Labor Statistics

► *Strength in numbers*
A large workforce has driven China's economic boom.

TOP 10 **COUNTRIES WITH THE LARGEST LABOR FORCES**

COUNTRY / LABOR FORCE*

As defined by the ILO, the "labor force" includes people aged 15–64 currently employed and those who are unemployed, but excludes unpaid groups such as students and retired people.

1 China
780,000,000

2 India
478,300,000

3 USA
154,900,000

4 Indonesia
116,500,000

5 Brazil
95,201,000

6 Russia
75,810,000

7 Bangladesh
72,500,000

8 Japan
65,930,000

9 Pakistan
55,880,000

10 Nigeria
47,330,000

* Latest available data
Source: World Bank

WITH 3,600 WORKERS, TUVALU HAS THE SMALLEST LABOR FORCE IN THE WORLD— BUT THIS STILL COMPRISES AROUND 35% OF ITS POPULATION!

◀ **Coke light**
The world's largest single-building illumination adorns the Coca-Cola HQ in Atlanta.

TOP 10 MOST-TRADED GOODS

CATEGORY / VALUE OF GOODS ($ BILLION) / SHARE (%)

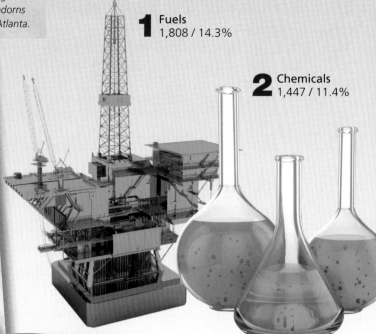

1 Fuels
1,808 / 14.3%

2 Chemicals
1,447 / 11.4%

3 Telecoms equipment
1,323 / 10.4%

4 Food
987 / 7.8%

5 Automotive products
847 / 6.7%

6 Mining products
455 / 4.3%

7 Iron and steel
326 / 2.6%

8 Clothing
316 / 2.5%

9 Textiles
211 / 1.7%

10 Other agriculture
182 / 1.4%

Source: World Trade Organization

TOP 10 MOST VALUABLE GLOBAL BRANDS

	BRAND NAME*	INDUSTRY	BRAND VALUE, 2011 ($)
1	Coca-Cola	Beverages	71,861,000,000
2	IBM	Technology	69,905,000,000
3	Microsoft	Technology	59,057,000,000
4	Google	Internet	55,317,000,000
5	General Electric	Diversified	42,808,000,000
6	McDonald's	Food retail	35,593,000,000
7	Intel	Technology	35,217,000,000
8	Apple	Technology	33,492,000,000
9	Disney	Leisure	29,018,000,000
10	Hewlett Packard	Electronics	28,479,000,000

* All US-owned

Source: Interbrand

TOP 10 BIGGEST PRICE INCREASES IN COMMODITIES

	COMMODITY	PRICE INCREASE* (%)			
1	Iron ore	292	6	Natural gas	205
2	Rubber	274	7	Coal	202
3	Crude petroleum	243	8	Nickel	198
4	Uranium	237	9	Lead	194
5	Copper	225	10	Tin	178

* 2000–10

Source: World Trade Organization

TOP 10 GLOBAL COMPANIES MAKING THE GREATEST PROFIT PER SECOND

COMPANY / COUNTRY	PROFIT ($) PER ANNUM	PER SECOND
1 Nestlé, Switzerland	36,651,900,000	1,162
2 Gazprom, Russia	31,671,800,000	1,004
3 Exxon Mobil, USA	30,460,000,000	966
4 Industrial and Commercial Bank of China, China	25,059,300,000	795
5 PetroChina, China	21,239,600,000	673
6 Petrobras, Brazil	21,198,200,000	672
7 China Construction Bank, China	20,460,100,000	649
8 Royal Dutch Shell, The Netherlands/UK	20,411,600,000	647
9 AT&T, USA	19,864,000,000	630
10 Chevron, USA	19,024,000,000	603

Source: *Financial Times Global 500*

▼ A bigger byte
In 10 years, Apple has gone from niche manufacturer to technology world leader.

TOP 10 ITEMS OF CONSUMER SPENDING IN THE USA

CATEGORY	ANNUAL EXPENDITURE PER HOUSEHOLD ($)
1 Housing	20,303
2 Transportation	10,123
3 Food	7,816
4 Personal insurance & pensions	7,611
5 Utilities fuels & public services	4,437
6 Healthcare	4,280
7 Entertainment	3,321
8 Apparel & services	2,075
9 Household furnishings	1,991
10 Education	1,468

Source: US Bureau of Labor Statistics

One of the biggest influences on the level of expenditure for any one particular household is the level of income, and there are some notable differences in expenditure patterns associated with different household incomes. Households with the lowest incomes spend a higher proportion of their total income on essentials such as food, fuel, light, and power than those with higher incomes.

TOP 10 GLOBAL COMPANIES BY MARKET VALUE

COMPANY / COUNTRY	SECTOR	MARKET VALUE ($)
1 Exxon Mobil, USA	Oil and gas	417,166,700,000
2 Petrochina, China	Oil and gas	326,199,200,000
3 Apple, USA	Computer equipment	321,072,100,000
4 Industrial and Commercial Bank of China, China	Banking	251,078,100,000
5 Petrobras, Brazil	Oil and gas	247,417,600,000
6 BHP Billiton, Australia/UK	Mining	247,079,500,000
7 China Construction Bank, China	Banking	232,608,600,000
8 Royal Dutch Shell, The Netherlands/UK	Oil and gas	228,128,700,000
9 Chevron, USA	Oil and gas	215,780,600,000
10 Microsoft, USA	Software	213,336,400,000

Source: *Financial Times Global 500*

RICHEST PEOPLE

THE 10 RICHEST MEN OF ALL TIME*

NAME / COUNTRY / DATES	$	PEAK WEALTH AS % OF GDP	2011 VALUE ($)
1 John D. Rockefeller (1839–1937)	1,400,000,000	1.54	232,339,800,000
2 Cornelius Vanderbilt (1794–1877)	105,000,000	1.15	173,500,500,000
3 John Jacob Astor (1763–1848)	20,000,000	0.93	140,309,100,000
4 Bill Gates (b. 1955)	101,000,000,000	0.92	138,800,400,000
5 Stephen Girard (1750–1831)	7,500,000	0.67	101,082,900,000
6 Andrew Carnegie (Scotland/USA, 1835–1919)	475,000,000	0.60	90,522,000,000
7 Alexander Turney Stewart (1803–76)	50,000,000	0.56	84,487,200,000
8 Frederick Weyerhäuser (1834–1914)	200,000,000	0.55	82,978,500,000
9 Jay Gould (1836–1892)	77,000,000	0.54	81,469,800,000
10 Stephen Van Rensselaer (1764–1839)	10,000,000	0.52	78,452,400,000

* Based on peak wealth as at death, or in case of Bill Gates, as at April 5, 1999; all US unless otherwise stated

▲ *John D. Rockefeller*
The oil baron donated large sums of money to medical science and other causes.

▼ *Men of fortune*
Buffet and Gates have given away substantial fortunes and have helped to redefine modern philanthropy.

TOP 10 RICHEST PEOPLE

NAME / COUNTRY / SOURCE / NET WORTH ($)

1 **Carlos Slim Helu,** Mexico
Communications
$74,000,000,000

2 **Bill Gates,** USA
Microsoft (software)
$56,000,000,000

3 **Warren Buffett,** USA
Berkshire Hathaway (investments)
$50,000,000,000

4 **Bernard Arnault,** France
LVMH (luxury goods)
$41,000,000,000

5 **Lawrence Ellison,** US.
Oracle (software)
$39,500,000,000

◀ *Carlos Slim Helu*
The Mexican tycoon's business interests include numerous telecoms companies.

◄ *Bon Jovi*
The leader of the enduringly popular rock band earned more than $200 million in 2011.

▲ *Millionaire Fair, Moscow*
200 luxury goods companies show their wares at this annual fair.

TOP 10 CITIES WITH THE MOST BILLIONAIRES

	CITY / COUNTRY	BILLIONAIRES
1	Moscow, Russia	79
2	New York, USA	59
3	London, UK	41
4	Hong Kong, China	40
5	Istanbul, Turkey	36
6	= Mumbai, India	21
	= São Paulo, Brazil	21
8	= Taipei, China	19
	= Los Angeles, USA	19
	= Beijing, China	19

Source: *Forbes* magazine, *The World's Billionaires 2011*

THE WORLD'S RICHEST WOMEN

Of the 50 wealthiest people on the planet, only six are women, and none of them are self-made, having all inherited their fortunes. The richest woman in the world is Wal-Mart heiress Christy Walton ($26.5 billion), with Liliane Bettencourt—whose fortune of $23.5 billion derives from l'Oreal—in 2nd place.

OPRAH WINFREY HAS AMASSED A LIFETIME FORTUNE OF $2.7 BILLION—MORE THAN JOHN D. ROCKEFELLER!

TOP 10 HIGHEST-EARNING CELEBRITIES

	CELEBRITY*	SOURCE	EARNINGS, 2010–11 ($)
1	Oprah Winfrey	Television	290,000,000
2	Tyler Perry	Film	130,000,000
3	Jon Bon Jovi	Music	125,000,000
4	Steven Spielberg	Film	107,000,000
5	Jerry Bruckheimer	Film	113,000,000
6	Elton John	Music	100,000,000
7	= Lady Gaga	Music	90,000,000
	= Simon Cowell	Television	90,000,000
9	Dr. Phil McGraw	Television	80,000,000
10	Leonardo DiCaprio	Film	77,000,000

* Individuals, excluding groups

Source: *Forbes* magazine, *The Celebrity 100*, 2011

6 **Lakshmi Mittal**, India/UK
Mittal Steel
$31,100,000,000

7 **Amancio Ortega**, Spain
Zara (clothing)
$31,000,000,000

8 **Eike Batista**, Brazil
OGX (mining, oil)
$30,000,000,000

9 **Mukesh Ambani**, India
Reliance Industries (petrochemicals)
$27,000,000,000

Source: *Forbes* magazine, *The World's Billionaires 2011*

10 **Christy Walton**, USA
Wal-Mart (retail)
$26,500,000,000

FOOD FAVORITES

TOP 10 VEGETABLE CONSUMERS

COUNTRY	AVERAGE CONSUMPTION PER CAPITA (LB)		COUNTRY	AVERAGE CONSUMPTION PER CAPITA (LB)
1 Greece	566.6		**6** Romania	423.3
2 South Korea	557.8		**7** Egypt	407.6
3 Turkey	556.0		**8** Bulgaria	383.6
4 China	480.4		**9** Belgium	345.2
5 Israel	424.6		**10** New Zealand	284.0

World average 209.9

Source (all lists): Euromonitor International

▲ **Fast food in the USA**
The leader of the free world, Barack Obama, orders a burger and fries.

TOP 10 FRUIT CONSUMERS

COUNTRY / ANNUAL CONSUMPTION PER CAPITA (LB)

1 Greece — 309.3
2 Argentina — 267.0
3 Denmark — 222.9
4 Thailand — 216.1
5 Israel — 209.9
6 Norway — 209.4
7 Mexico — 205.3
8 Turkey — 200.4

= 20 lb

9 = Canada — 177.9
= Italy — 177.9

World 111.8

TOP 10 FAST-FOOD COUNTRIES

COUNTRY / ANNUAL SPENDING PER CAPITA ($)

1 USA 291.7

2 Canada 196.3

3 Sweden 175.2

4 Australia 156.4

▲ Catch of the day
Raw tuna (chawm chee hwey) is a local favorite in South Korea.

TOP 10 FISH AND SEAFOOD CONSUMERS

COUNTRY	ANNUAL CONSUMPTION PER CAPITA (KG)
1 China	119.7
2 Malaysia	55.3
3 South Korea	49.3
4 Portugal	45.2
5 Japan	38.1
6 Norway	36.0
7 Philippines	32.3
8 Thailand	31.4
9 New Zealand	29.4
10 Singapore	24.3
World average	*14.7*

TOP 10 MEAT CONSUMERS

COUNTRY	ANNUAL CONSUMPTION PER CAPITA (LB)
1 Argentina	262.4
2 Portugal	233.4
3 Greece	228.8
4 Austria	228.6
5 Australia	225.5
6 New Zealand	215.8
7 Brazil	194.4
8 USA	179.7
9 Ireland	176.4
10 Canada	170.4
World average	*375.6*

TOP 10 CHEESE CONSUMERS

COUNTRY	ANNUAL CONSUMPTION PER CAPITA (LB)
1 France	37.7
2 Norway	36.8
3 Finland	35.3
4 Sweden	35.1
5 Italy	34.8
6 Belgium	34.0
7 Switzerland	33.7
8 The Netherlands	31.3
9 Greece	30.6
10 Denmark	29.3
World average	*4.6*

5
Finland
127.3

6
Ireland
124.9

7
France
116.1

8
New Zealand
100.0

9
Switzerland
95.3

World total 23.0

10
Norway
88.5

DRINK

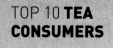

TOP 10 TEA CONSUMERS

	COUNTRY	CONSUMPTION PER CAPITA (CUPS)
1	Turkey	1,656
2	Morocco	1,113
3	Uzbekistan	982
4	Russia	840
5	Kazakhstan	830
6	Ireland	821
7	New Zealand	778
8	Iran	686
9	Egypt	679
10	UK	644
	World average	*183*

Source (all lists): Euromonitor International

◀ **Tea break in Morocco**
Green tea with mint leaves is popular throughout North Africa and is always served to guests.

THE AVERAGE PERSON IN THE UK DRINKS AS MUCH TEA AS 23 ITALIANS!

TOP 10 COFFEE CONSUMERS

	COUNTRY	CONSUMPTION PER CAPITA (CUPS)
1	Norway	2,364
2	The Netherlands	1,539
3	Iceland	1,459
4	Finland	1,206
5	Germany	1,054
6	Sweden	1,025
7	Denmark	863
8	Belgium	667
9	Brazil	660
10	Serbia	559

TOP 10 BOTTLED-WATER CONSUMERS

COUNTRY / CONSUMPTION PER CAPITA (LITERS)

World average 20.5

1	2	3	4	5	6	7	8	9	10
Mexico 143.4	Spain 115.2	France 101.0	Italy 99.1	Belgium 74.1	Turkey 71.5	USA 67.8	Portugal 64.5	Israel 61.1	Indonesia 58.1

TOP 10 COLA DRINK CONSUMERS

COUNTRY / CONSUMPTION PER CAPITA (LITRES)

#	Country	
1	Mexico	87.2
2	Chile	71.4
3	Norway	67.6
4	Argentina	65.2
5	USA	63.3
6	Belgium	60.3
7	Canada	49.6
8	Ireland	46.5
9	New Zealand	46.3
10	Australia	44.5
	World average	12.7

TOP 10 ALCOHOLIC DRINK CONSUMERS

COUNTRY / CONSUMPTION PER CAPITA (LITERS)

#	Country		#	Country	
1	Czech Republic	151.2	6	Australia	88.7
2	Germany	108.2	7	Poland	86.8
3	Austria	101.8	8	Finland	81.3
4	Ireland	101.0	9	Romania	77.8
5	Belgium	89.7	10	USA	77.3

World average 37.9

▼ **Festival spirit**
The traditional dirndl is generally worn by barmaids at German beer festivals.

▼ **Barrel tossing**
Enjoyed in the Czech Republic, barrel tossing involves throwing an empty half-barrel as far as possible.

TOP 10 OF EVERYTHING

TOP 10 BEER CONSUMERS

COUNTRY / COMSUMPTION PER CAPITA (LITERS)

#	Country	
1	Czech Republic	151.2
2	Germany	108.2
3	Austria	101.8
4	Ireland	101.0
5	Slovenia	98.0
6	Estonia	91.0
7	Luxembourg	90.7
8	Belgium	89.7
9	Australia	88.7
10	Poland	86.8

World average 27.5

RESOURCES & RESERVES

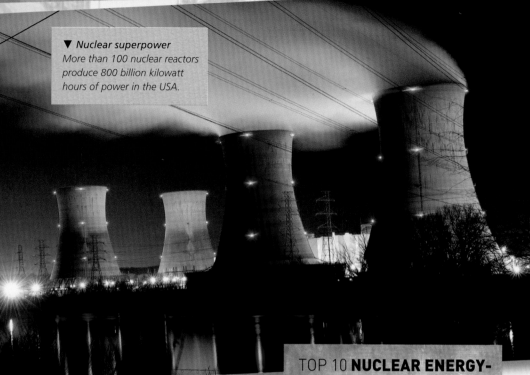

▼ Nuclear superpower
More than 100 nuclear reactors produce 800 billion kilowatt hours of power in the USA.

TOP 10 COUNTRIES WITH MOST NUCLEAR REACTORS

COUNTRY / REACTORS

1 USA 104

2 France 58

3 Japan 50

4 Russia 32

5 Republic of Korea 21

6 India 20

7 = UK 18

= Canada 18

9 = China 15

= Ukraine 15

There are some 433 nuclear power stations in operation in 30 countries around the world, with a further 65 under construction.

Source: International Atomic Energy Agency

TOP 10 NUCLEAR ENERGY-CONSUMING COUNTRIES

COUNTRY	ANNUAL CONSUMPTION*
1 USA	192,200,000,000
2 France	96,900,000,000
3 Japan	66,200,000,000
4 Russia	38,500,000,000
5 South Korea	33,400,000,000
6 Germany	31,800,000,000
7 Canada	20,300,000,000
8 Ukraine	20,200,000,000
9 China	16,700,000,000
10 UK	14,100,000,000

* Tons of oil equivalent

TOP 10 RENEWABLE POWER-CONSUMING COUNTRIES*

COUNTRY / ANNUAL CONSUMPTION#

1 USA
39,100,000,000

2 Germany
18,600,000,000

3 Spain
12,400,000,000

4 China
12,100,000,000

5 Brazil
7,900,000,000

6 Italy
5,600,000,000

7 Japan
5,100,000,000

8 India
5,000,000,000

9 UK
4,900,000,000

10 Sweden
4,300,000,000

* Includes geothermal, solar, wind, wood, and waste electric power
# Tons of oil equivalent

Source: BP Statistical Review of World Energy 2011

▶ Solar Germany
This German boat has a staggering 5,780 sq ft (537 sq m) of solar panels.

TOP 10 **COUNTRIES WITH THE GREATEST OIL RESERVES**

	COUNTRY	PROVEN RESERVES (TONS)	% OF WORLD TOTAL
1	Saudi Arabia	40,013,901,000	19.1
2	Venezuela	33,510,264,000	15.3
3	Iran	20,723,453,000	9.9
4	Iraq	17,085,825,000	8.3
5	Kuwait	15,432,358,000	7.3
6	United Arab Emirates	14,330,047,000	7.1
7	Russia	11,684,500,000	5.6
8	Libya	6,613,868,000	3.4
9	Kazakhstan	6,062,712,000	2.9
10 =	Canada	5,511,557,000	2.7
=	Nigeria	5,511,557,000	2.7

Source: *BP Statistical Review of World Energy 2011*

▲ **Russian oil**
Crew members face dangerous and harsh conditions when drilling for oil in the Arctic Sea.

TOP 10 **OIL-PRODUCING COUNTRIES**

COUNTRY / ANNUAL PRODUCTION (TONS) / % OF WORLD TOTAL

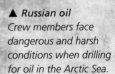

1 Russia
556,777,443
12.9%

2 Saudi Arabia
515,661,231
12.0%

3 USA
373,793,766
8.7%

4 Iran
223,989,658
5.2%

5 China
223,769,196
5.2%

6 Canada
179,456,281
4.2%

7 Mexico
161,268,145
3.7%

8 United Arab Emirates
144,182,319
3.3%

9 Venezuela
139,773,074
3.2%

10 Kuwait
135,033,136
3.1%

TOP 10 **MOST-PRODUCED METALS**

	METAL	ANNUAL PRODUCTION (TONS)
1	Steel	1,543,235,835
2	Iron	1,102,311,311
3	Aluminum	45,635,688
4	Chromium	24,250,849
5	Manganese	14,330,047
6	Zinc	13,227,736
7	Titanium	6,944,561
8	Lead	4,519,476
9	Nickel	1,708,583
10	Zirconium	1,311,750

Source: US Geological Survey

RENEWABLE ENERGY

TOP 10 COUNTRIES INVESTING IN RENEWABLE ENERGY

COUNTRY / INVESTMENT ($ MILLION)*

WHAT IS RENEWABLE?

Renewable energy comes from natural sources that are continually replenished. These include energy from water, rain, tides, wind, sunlight, geothermal sources, and biomass such as energy crops, rather than from fuels such as coal, oil, and natural gas that are non-renewable and cannot be replenished once stocks are depleted. Renewable energy is used to generate electricity, power vehicles, and provide heating, cooling, and light.

* Latest available year

Source: Bloomberg New Energy Finance, UNEP

1	2	3	4	5	6	7	8	10
China	Germany	USA	Italy	Brazil	Canada	Spain	= France	Czech Republic
49,800	41,000	29,600	13,800	6,900	5,200	4,900	4,000	3,600
							= India	
							4,000	

BIOMASS POWER

Biomass is carbon-, hydrogen- and oxygen-based, and is obtained from living organisms: that is, plants and plant-derived materials, residues from agriculture or forestry, and the organic component of municipal and industrial wastes. Biomass can be used for heating, for generating electricity, or can be converted into liquid fuels to meet transportation energy needs. Biomass is close to a carbon-neutral electric power generation option, as it absorbs carbon dioxide from the atmosphere during its growth and then emits an equal amount of carbon dioxide when it is processed to generate electricity.

HYDROELECTRIC POWER

Flowing water creates energy which can be turned into electricity. Many hydroelectric power plants use a dam on a river in which to store water. Water released from behind the dam flows through a turbine, spinning it, which then turns a generator to produce electricity. Electricity generated this way is known as hydroelectricity.

WIND POWER

Electricity from wind turbines is the fastest-growing energy technology and currently generates about 2.5% of worldwide usage. Wind turns the blades, which rotate a shaft connected to a generator that produces electricity. Large turbines can be as tall as a 20-story building with 200 ft (60 m) blades, and are able to generate enough electricity to supply about 600 homes. Wind is in abundant supply, easy to harness, and clean. Wind farms require a moderate capital outlay to install, but the ongoing costs are minimal. The disadvantages are that turbines can be unsightly and noisy, and the rotating blades can kill wildlife.

▲ *Powering the USA*
Nearly 3% of US energy comes from wind farms, a figure that has doubled in the last three years.

◄ *Geothermal energy*
This geothermal plant in Reykjavik, Iceland, uses underground reservoirs of hot steam and water to produce electricity and supply heat to buildings.

TOP 5 **WIND-POWER COUNTRIES**

COUNTRY	WIND-POWER CAPACITY (MW)*
1 China	44,733
2 USA	40,180
3 Germany	27,215
4 Spain	20,676
5 India	13,066

* Latest available year

Source: World Wind Energy Association

SOLAR POWER

Solar technologies harness the energy of the Sun to provide heat, light, hot water, and electricity. Different types of solar collectors are used to meet different energy needs. Passive solar building designs capture the Sun's heat to provide heating and light, while photovoltaic cells convert sunlight directly to electricity. Concentrating solar power systems focus sunlight with mirrors to create a high-intensity heat source, and flat-plate collectors absorb the heat of the Sun directly into water or other fluids to provide hot water or space heating. Solar technologies are not harmful to the environment, but solar cells and related equipment is expensive.

TOP 5 **COUNTRIES INVESTING IN SOLAR POWER**

COUNTRY	INVESTMENT ($ MILLION)
1 Germany	34,300
2 Italy	5,500
3 USA	4,500
4 Japan	3,300
5 France	2,700

* Latest available year

Source: Bloomberg New Energy Finance, UNEP

▶ *Solar field*
Germany has record amounts of energy from solar power.

ENVIRONMENT

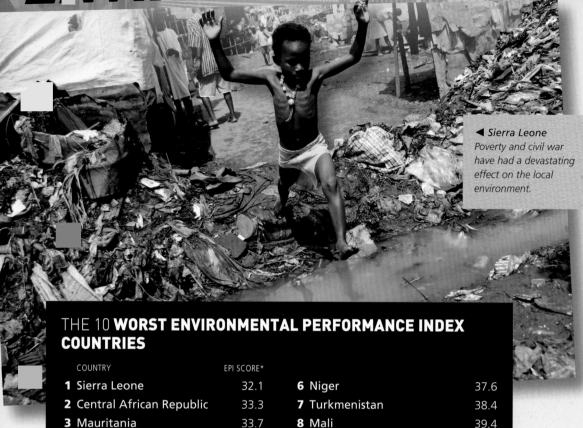

◄ *Sierra Leone*
Poverty and civil war have had a devastating effect on the local environment.

THE 10 WORST ENVIRONMENTAL PERFORMANCE INDEX COUNTRIES

COUNTRY	EPI SCORE*	COUNTRY	EPI SCORE*
1 Sierra Leone	32.1	6 Niger	37.6
2 Central African Republic	33.3	7 Turkmenistan	38.4
3 Mauritania	33.7	8 Mali	39.4
4 Angola	36.3	9 Haiti	39.5
5 Togo	36.4	10 Benin	39.6

* Environmental Performance Index score out of 100

Source: EPI

TOP 10 ENVIRONMENTAL PERFORMANCE INDEX COUNTRIES

COUNTRY / EPI SCORE*

1 Iceland
93.5

2 Switzerland
89.1

3 Costa Rica
86.4

4 Sweden
86.0

5 Norway
81.1

6 Mauritius
80.6

7 France
78.2

8 = Austria
78.1

= Cuba
78.1

10 Colombia
76.8

USA 63.5

* Environmental Performance Index score out of 100

Source: EPI 2010

TOP 10 GARBAGE PRODUCERS

COUNTRY / DOMESTIC WASTE PER CAPITA (LB/KG)

1 = Ireland
1,764 / 800

= Norway
1,764 / 800

3 USA
1,676 / 760

4 Denmark
1,631 / 740

5 Switzerland
1,543 / 700

6 Australia
1,518 / 689

7 Luxembourg
1,499 / 680

8 Netherlands
1,379 / 625

9 Spain
1,323 / 600

10 = Austria
1,290 / 585

= UK
1,290 / 585

The Environmental Performance Index (formerly Environmental Sustainability Index) is a measure of environmental health and ecosystem vitality based on an assessment of 16 indicators in each country. These include air quality, water resources, biodiversity and habitat, productive natural resources, and sustainable energy.

TOP 10 **COUNTRIES WITH THE BEST WATER QUALITY**

COUNTRY* / EPI SCORE#

1 Sweden
96.2

2 Canada
93.1

3 Japan
87.8

4 France
86.5

5 Russia
82.4

6 Italy
82.2

7 UK
81.6

8 Germany
78.6

9 USA
77.5

10 Australia
61.7

* Selected industrialized countries
# Environmental Performance Index score out of 100

Source: EPI

▶ *Clean Paris*
The French capital has low levels of pollution, making it a pleasant environment.

TOP 10 **CAPITAL CITIES WITH THE CLEANEST AIR**

	CITY / COUNTRY	PARTICULATE MATTER*
1	Minsk, Belarus	9
2 =	Paris, France	12
=	Stockholm, Sweden	12
=	Wellington, New Zealand	12
5	Cape Town, South Africa	15
6 =	St. Johns, Antigua and Barbuda	16
=	Kampala, Uganda	16
8 =	Luxembourg, Luxembourg	18
=	Ottawa, Canada	18
=	Caracas, Venezuela	18

* Micrograms per cubic metre

Source: The World Bank

TOP 10 **ECO-CITIES**

	CITY / COUNTRY	ECO-CITY INDEX
1	Calgary, Canada	145.7
2	Honolulu, USA	145.1
3 =	Ottawa, Canada	139.9
=	Helsinki, Finland	139.9
5	Wellington, New Zealand	138.9
6	Minneapolis, USA	137.8
7	Adelaide, Australia	137.5
8	Copenhagen, Denmark	137.4
9 =	Kobe, Japan	135.6
=	Oslo, Norway	135.6
=	Stockholm, Sweden	135.6

Source: Mercer Quality of Living Survey

Eco-friendly
▲ *Hawaii's capital, Honolulu, thrives on its eco-city status.*
▼ *The solar taxi in Stockholm is an eco-friendly way of traveling around the city.*

COMMUNICATIONS

◄ Street map
Google's Street View trike in Jerusalem. The 360° views caught on camera cover locations across the globe.

FACEBOOK IS VALUED AT AROUND $100 BILLION—MORE THAN 12 TIMES THE VALUE OF TWITTER!

TOP 10 SOCIAL NETWORKS

	NETWORK	REGISTERED USERS, 2011			
1	Facebook	600,000,000	6	Pengyou	131,000,000
2	Qzone	481,000,000	7	Bebo	117,000,000
3	Habbo	203,000,000	8	= MySpace	100,000,000
4	Twitter	190,000,000		= Tagged	100,000,000
5	Renren	170,000,000	10	LinkedIn	90,000,000

TOP 10 MOST-VISITED WEBSITES*

WEBSITE

1	Google (google.com)	6	Baidu.com
2	Facebook (facebook.com)	7	Blogger.com
3	YouTube (youtube.com)	8	Windows Live (live.com)
4	Yahoo! (yahoo.com)	9	Twitter (twitter.com)
5	Wikipedia (wikipedia.org)	10	qq.com

* Based on Alexa traffic rankings

Founded in 1996, California-based internet information company Alexa was acquired by Amazon.com in 1999. Its traffic rankings are widely regarded as the most accurate snapshot of the world's most-visited websites.

TOP 10 COUNTRIES ON FACEBOOK

COUNTRY / USERS*

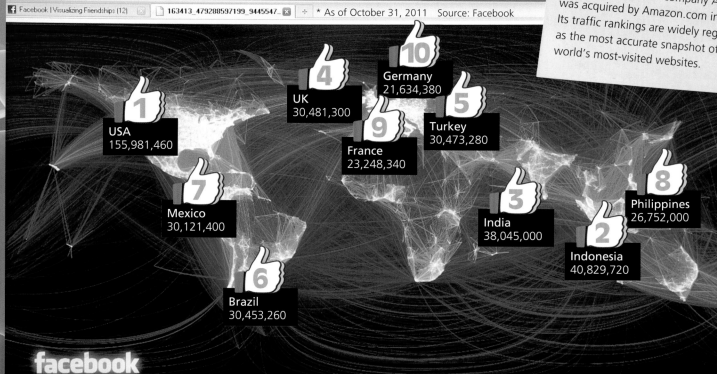

Facebook | Visualizing Friendships (12)   163413_479288597199_9445547_   ÷   * As of October 31, 2011   Source: Facebook

1 USA 155,981,460

4 UK 30,481,300

10 Germany 21,634,380

5 Turkey 30,473,280

9 France 23,248,340

7 Mexico 30,121,400

3 India 38,045,000

8 Philippines 26,752,000

2 Indonesia 40,829,720

6 Brazil 30,453,260

facebook

TOP 10 **MOST WATCHED YOUTUBE VIDEOS**

NAME / VIDEO TITLE	VIEWS*
1 Justin Bieber (Baby ft. Ludacris)	730,418,334
2 Jennifer Lopez (On the Floor ft. Pitbull)	530,830,689
3 Shakira (Waka Waka—this Time for Africa)	463,699,010
4 Lady Gaga (Bad Romance)	461,262,479
5 Eminem (Love the Way You Lie ft. Rihanna)	454,066,812
6 Charlie bit my Finger—again!	449,003,099
7 LMFAO (Party Rock Anthem)	425,699,701
8 Eminem (Not Afraid)	333,444,337
9 Justin Bieber (Never Say Never ft. Jaden Smith)	313,288,708
10 Michel Teló (Ai Se Eu Te Pego)	309,553,224

* As of April 2012

▲ *Young YouTuber*
Justin Bieber's videos on YouTube have made him a huge success worldwide.

◄ *Top Twitterers*
Celebrities such as Katy Perry (far left), Rihanna (left), and Barack Obama (below) all have Twitter accounts where they post frequent "Tweets" of their activities for their followers.

TOP 10 **MOST-FOLLOWED PEOPLE ON TWITTER**

NAME / SCREEN NAME	FOLLOWERS*
1 Lady Gaga (ladygaga)	24,070,361
2 Justin Bieber (justinbieber)	21,719,056
3 Katy Perry (katyperry)	19,469,700
4 Rihanna (rihanna)	18,732,036
5 Britney Spears (britneyspears)	16,565,195
6 Shakira (shakira)	15,968,363
7 Barack Obama (BarackObama)	15,276,778
8 Kim Kardashian (KimKardashian)	14,638,000
9 Taylor Swift (taylorswift13)	13,869,681
10 Nicki Minaj (NICKIMINAJ)	12,380,960

* As of April 2012

Source: twitaholic.com

9
ON THE MOVE

FERRUCCIO'S FAST CARS CLOCK UP 50 YEARS

According to automotive folklore, Ferruccio Lamborghini—who made his first fortune out of tractors—only moved into high-performance cars after rivals Ferrari failed to deal satisfactorily with a complaint. As befitted an aggrieved customer and a Taurean, he chose a fighting bull as the badge of the company he founded in 1963, which is still based in Sant'Agata Bolognese, northern Italy. Lamborghini marked its 25th anniversary with a special edition of the Lamborghini Countach, which is still considered by many to be the definitive supercar. For its 50th anniversary, industry insiders are anticipating something equally special—perhaps a variant of the sensational Sesto Elemento, a super-lightweight sports car that can hit 62 mph (100 km/h) in an astonishing 2.5 seconds.

Main image: Sesto Elemento. Inset: Lamborghini Countach

▲ The Red Devil
The red-bearded Jenatzy was nicknamed "le diable rouge."

THE FIRST HOLDERS OF THE LAND SPEED RECORD

The earliest officially recognized land speed records were set in France—and in electric cars. In December 1898, Count Gaston de Chassloup-Laubat completed a kilometer run in 57 seconds, recording an average speed of 39 mph (63.13 km/h). Over the succeeding months he fought a record-setting duel with the Belgian Camille Jenatzy, in which the latter had the last word; on April 29, 1899, he recorded an average speed of 65.7 mph (105 km/h) in *La Jamais Contente* (pictured), a feat not bettered for three years.

00657
mph (105.26 km/h)

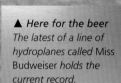

▲ Here for the beer
The latest of a line of hydroplanes called Miss Budweiser *holds the current record.*

The current world speed record holder Andy Green—the first to go supersonic—is an RAF fighter pilot and mathematics graduate.

▼ Rocket fuel
Gary Gabelich's Blue Flame was powered by a mixture of liquefied natural gas and hydrogen peroxide.

THE 10 LATEST HOLDERS OF THE LAND SPEED RECORD

DRIVER / CAR	DATE	SPEED MPH	KM/H
1 Andy Green (UK), ThrustSSC*	Oct 15, 1997	763.04	1,227.99
2 Richard Noble (UK), Thrust2*	Oct 4, 1983	633.47	1,019.47
3 Gary Gabelich (USA), The Blue Flame	Oct 23, 1970	622.41	995.85
4 Craig Breedlove (USA), Spirit of America—Sonic 1	Nov 15, 1965	600.60	960.96
5 Art Arfons (USA), Green Monster	Nov 7, 1965	576.55	922.48
6 Craig Breedlove (USA), Spirit of America—Sonic 1	Nov 2, 1965	555.48	888.76
7 Art Arfons (USA), Green Monster	Oct 27, 1964	536.71	858.73
8 Craig Breedlove (USA), Spirit of America	Oct 15, 1964	526.28	842.04
9 Craig Breedlove (USA), Spirit of America	Oct 13, 1964	468.72	749.95
10 Art Arfons (USA), Green Monster	Oct 5, 1964	434.02	694.43

* Location, Black Rock Desert, Nevada, USA; all other speeds were achieved at Bonneville Salt Flats, Utah, USA; speed averaged over a measured mile in two directions

07630
mph (1,227.99 km/h)

THE 10 **LATEST HOLDERS OF THE WATER SPEED RECORD**

DRIVER / BOAT / LOCATION	DATE	SPEED MPH	KM/H
1 Dave Villwock, Miss Budweiser, Lake Oroville, California, USA	Mar 13, 2004	220.493	354.849
2 Russ Wicks, Miss Freei, Lake Washington, Washington, USA	Jun 15, 2000	205.494	330.711
3 Roy Duby, Miss US1, Lake Guntersville, Alabama, USA	Apr 17, 1962	200.419	322.543
4 Bill Muncey, Miss Thriftaway, Lake Washington, Washington, USA	Feb 16, 1960	192.001	308.996
5 Jack Regas, Hawaii Kai III, Lake Washington, Washington, USA	Nov 30, 1957	187.627	301.956
6 Art Asbury, Miss Supertest II, Lake Ontario, Canada	Nov 1, 1957	184.540	296.988
7 Stanley Sayres, Slo-Mo-Shun IV, Lake Washington, Washington, USA	July 7, 1952	178.497	287.263
8 Stanley Sayres, Slo-Mo-Shun IV, Lake Washington, Washington, USA	Jun 26, 1950	160.323	258.015
9 Malcolm Campbell, Bluebird K4, Coniston Water, UK	Aug 19, 1939	141.740	228.108
10 Malcolm Campbell, Bluebird K3, Hallwiler See, Switzerland	Aug 17, 1938	130.910	210.679

02204 mph (354.849 km/h)

All these were propeller-driven craft, taking the average of two runs over a measured kilometer or mile course. Since the 1950s, jet-powered boats, which skim over the surface of the water, have achieved consistently faster speeds, with Ken Warby's *Spirit of Australia* setting the jet record of 317.58 mph (511.11 km/h) on October 8, 1978.

TOP 10 **FASTEST RAIL JOURNEYS**

JOURNEY*	TRAIN	DISTANCE MILES	KM	AVERAGE SPEED MPH	KM/H
1 Wuhan–Gangzhou North, China	CRH2	572.9	922.0	194.5	313.0
2 Lorraine–Champagne, France	TGV POS	104.1	167.6	173.5	279.3
3 Lyon St Exupéry–Aix-en-Provence, France	TGV Duple	179.9	289.6	163.6	263.3
4 Okayama–Hiroshima, Japan	Nozomi 1	90.0	144.9	158.9	255.7
5 Hiroshima–Kikoura, Japan	Nozomi Shinkansen	119.3	192.0	155.6	250.4
6 Paris-Lyon–Marseille St. Charles, France	TGV	466.0	750.0	155.3	250.0
7 Taichung–Zuoying, Taiwan	7 trains	111.5	179.5	152.0	244.7
8 Brussels, Belgium–Valence, France	Thalys Soleil	516.8	831.7	152.0	244.6
9 Beijing South–Tianjin, China	CRH	73.0	117.0	149.1	240.0
10 Frankfurt–Siegburg/Bonn, Germany	ICE 10	89.04	143.3	144.4	232.4

* Conventional trains between stations, where average speed is known

▼ *China express*
China's high-speed rail network is the longest in the world.

01945 mph (313.00 km/h)

ON THE ROAD

◄ *Made in Japan*
Japanese car manufacture has reduced slightly in recent years, partly due to competition from China.

TOP 10 COUNTRIES PRODUCING THE MOST VEHICLES

	COUNTRY	CARS	COMMERCIAL VEHICLES	TOTAL*
1	China	13,897,083	4,367,584	18,264,667
2	Japan	8,307,382	1,318,558	9,625,940
3	USA	2,731,105	5,030,335	7,761,440
4	Germany	5,552,409	353,576	5,905,985
5	South Korea	3,866,206	405,735	4,271,941
6	Brazil	2,828,273	820,085	3,648,358
7	India	2,814,584	722,199	3,536,783
8	Spain	1,913,513	474,387	2,387,900
9	Mexico	1,390,163	954,961	2,345,124
10	Canada	968,860	1,102,166	2,071,026
	Top 10 total	*44,269,578*	*15,549,586*	*59,819,164*
	World total	*58,478,810*	*19,378,895*	*77,857,705*

* Latest year for which data available

Source: International Organization of Motor Vehicle Manufacturers

TOP 10 COUNTRIES DRIVING ON THE LEFT

	COUNTRY	TOTAL VEHICLES REGISTERED*			
1	Japan	74,252,134	6	Malaysia	7,857,500
2	UK	34,974,500	7	Indonesia	7,350,000
3	Australia	13,410,000	8	South Africa	7,180,000
4	India	12,950,000	9	New Zealand	2,760,000
5	Thailand	9,500,000	10	Ireland	2,051,000

* Latest year for which data available

Source: *Ward's Motor Vehicle Facts & Figures*

TOP 10 BESTSELLING CARS OF ALL TIME

	MANUFACTURER / MODEL	YEARS IN PRODUCTION	APPROX. SALES*
1	Toyota Corolla	1966–	37,000,000
2	Volkswagen Golf	1974–	27,190,000
3	Volkswagen Beetle	1937–2003#	21,529,464
4	Ford Escort/Orion	1968–2003	20,000,000
5	Ford Model T	1908–27	16,536,075
6	Honda Civic	1972–	16,500,000
7	Nissan Sunny/Sentra/Pulsar	1966–	16,000,000
8	Volkswagen Passat	1973–	15,000,000
9	Lada Riva	1980–†	13,500,000
10	Chevrolet Impala/Caprice	1958–	13,000,000

* To 2010 unless otherwise indicated
\# Produced in Mexico 1978–2003
† Still manufactured in Ukraine and Egypt

▼ *Long-running bestseller*
The Volkswagen Beetle has been on the road since 1938. Right: This early advertising poster encouraged the people of Germany to save 5 marks a week to buy a Beetle.

▶ *Shanghai-ways*
China has a long-term road-building plan to create a national system of highways.

THE TOTAL OF ROAD NETWORKS IS EQUIVALENT TO OVER 800 TIMES THE CIRCUMFERENCE OF THE EARTH!

TOP 10 **COUNTRIES WITH THE LONGEST ROAD NETWORKS**

	COUNTRY	TOTAL ROAD NETWORK MILES	KM
1	USA	4,042,767	6,506,204
2	China	2,398,989	3,860,800
3	India	2,063,207	3,320,410
4	Brazil	1,088,560	1,751,868
5	Japan	747,992	1,203,777
6	Canada	647,655	1,042,300
7	Russia	610,186	982,000
8	France	591,048	951,200
9	Australia	508,502	818,356
10	Spain	423,339	681,298

Source: CIA, *The World Factbook 2011*

TOP 10 **MOTOR VEHICLE-OWNING COUNTRIES**

	COUNTRY	CARS	COMMERCIAL VEHICLES	TOTAL*
1	USA	135,222,259	113,478,738	248,700,997
2	Japan	57,623,753	16,505,195	74,128,948
3	Germany	41,183,594	2,837,021	44,020,615
4	Italy	35,680,098	4,687,968	40,368,066
5	China	13,758,000	26,336,000	40,094,000
6	France	30,550,000	6,297,000	36,847,000
7	UK	31,225,329	4,164,465	35,389,794
8	Russia	28,300,000	5,805,000	34,105,000
9	Spain	21,760,174	5,414,322	27,174,496
10	Brazil	20,430,000	5,166,000	25,596,000
	Top 10	*415,733,207*	*190,691,709*	*606,424,916*
	World	*645,286,033*	*266,236,158*	*911,522,191*

* Latest year for which data available

Source: *Ward's Motor Vehicle Facts & Figures*

TOP 10 **COUNTRIES WITH MOST PEOPLE PER CAR**

	COUNTRY	CARS	PEOPLE PER CAR*
1	Myanmar	8,200	5,777.3
2	Bangladesh	37,750	4,027.4
3	Central African Republic	1,950	2,244.6
4	Tanzania	23,000	1,712.3
5	Mali	9,500	1,262.6
6	Afghanistan	29,000	1,099.7
7	Ethiopia	73,100	1,093.5
8	Malawi	12,650	1,075.3
9	Sudan	39,500	996.9
10	Côte d'Ivoire	21,500	918.5
	USA	135,222,259	2.2
	World average	645,286,033	9.9

* latest year for which data available

Source: *Ward's Motor Vehicle Facts & Figures*

▶ *Hitching a lift*
There are fewer cars per head of population in Myanmar than in any other country.

GIANTS OF THE SEA

◄ *Sister ships*
Although built to the same specification, Allure of the Seas *is fractionally bigger than its sister ship,* Oasis of the Seas.

TOP 10 **BIGGEST PASSENGER SHIPS**

	SHIP	IN SERVICE	LENGTH FT	LENGTH M	TONNAGE*
1	= Allure of the Seas	2010	1,187	360	225,282
	= Oasis of the Seas	2009	1,187	360	225,282
3	Norwegian Epic	2010	1,081	329	155,873
4	= Freedom of the Seas	2006	1,112	339	154,407
	= Liberty of the Seas	2007	1,112	339	154,407
	= Independence of the Seas	2008	1,112	339	154,407
7	= Queen Mary 2	2004	1,132	345	151,400
	= Navigator of the Seas	2003	1,020	311	138,279
	= Mariner of the Seas	2004	1,020	311	138,279
10	= Adventure of the Seas	2001	1,020	311	138,279

* Ranked by gross tonnage

TOP 10 **LARGEST MOTOR YACHTS**

	NAME / LAUNCH YEAR	LENGTH FT	LENGTH M
1	Eclipse, 2010	536	163.5
2	Dubai, 2007	525	162.0
3	Al Said, 2007	509	155.0
4	= Prince Abulaziz, 1984	482	147.0
	= M147, 2011	482	147.0
	= Topaz, 2012	482	147.0
7	El Horriya, 1865	479	146.0
8	Swift 141, 2001	463	141.0
9	Al Salamah, 2000	457	139.3
10	Rising Sun, 2004	453	138.0

New Kingdom 5KR—currently under construction—at 551 ft (168 m) will trump Abramovich's *Eclipse.* Along with over 20 luxurious guest cabins and space to accommodate 70 crew members, it is equipped with a mini-submarine capable of diving to 160 ft (50 m), three launch boats, two helicopter pads, two swimming pools, and high-tech security such as a missile-detection defense system.

► Eclipse
The largest private yacht belongs to Russian oligarch Roman Abramovich.

TOP 10 LARGEST SAILING VESSELS

SHIP* / COUNTRY BUILT / YEAR	LENGTH FT	M	TONNAGE#
1 Club Med 2 (France) 1992	636	194	14,983
2 Wind Surf (France) 1990	617	187	14,745
3 = Wind Star (France) 1986	440	134	5,350
= Wind Spirit (France) 1998	440	134	5,350
5 Royal Clipper (Poland) 2000	439	134	5,000
6 Esmerelda (Spain) 1953	371	113	3,673
7 Sedov (Germany) 1921	385	117	3,432
8 Kruzenshtern (Germany) 1926	376	114	3,141
9 Juan Sebastián Elcano (Spain) 1927	370	113	2,983
10 Amerigo Vespucci (Italy) 1930	331	101	2,686

* Sailing vessel, sailing today
\# Ranked by gross tonnage

▶ **Royal Clipper**
The Polish square rigger combines traditional sailing with state-of the-art systems.

TOP 10 LONGEST SHIPS

SHIP*	TYPE	LAUNCHED	LENGTH FT	M
1 Emma Mærsk#	Container ship	2006	1,300	397
2 Nai Superba#	Supertanker	2002	1,253	382
3 Allure of the Seas	Cruise ship	2010	1,187	360
4 = Mozah	LNG carrier	2008	1,131	345
= Vale Brazil#	Bulk cargo ship	2008	1,131	345
6 USS Enterprise	Aircraft carrier	1961	1,123	342
7 Brasil Maru	Ore carrier	2007	1,115	340
8 USS Iowa#	Battleship	1942	887	271
9 Club Med 2	Sailing ship	1992	636	194
10 Eclipse	Motor yacht	2010	536	164

* Longest example of each type in operation
\# More than one vessel of same length in class

TOP 10 BUSIEST PORTS

PORT / COUNTRY	CARGO (TONS)
1 Shanghai, China	557,455,365
2 Singapore, Singapore	520,621,632
3 Rotterdam, Netherlands	426,547,078
4 Tianjin, China	420,101,864
5 Ningbo, China	409,552,744
6 Guangzhou, China	401,241,317
7 Qingdao, China	302,368,402
8 Qinhuangdao, China	268,798,613
9 Hong Kong, China	267,825,272
10 Busan, South Korea	249,322,977
Top 10 total	3,823,835,26

Source: American Association of Port Authorities

◀ **Container port**
Shanghai is one of China's most important gateways for foreign trading.

ON TRACK

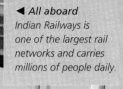

THE 10 FIRST COUNTRIES WITH RAILROADS

COUNTRY / FIRST RAILROAD ESTABLISHED

1 UK
Sep 27, 1825

2 France
Nov 7, 1829

3 USA
May 24, 1830

4 Ireland
Dec 17, 1834

5 Belgium
May 5, 1835

6 Germany
Dec 7, 1835

7 Canada
Jul 21, 1836

8 Russia
Oct 30, 1837

9 Austria
Jan 6, 1838

10 The Netherlands
Sep 24, 1839

Although there were earlier horse-drawn railways, the Stockton & Darlington Railway inaugurated the world's first steam service. In their early years, some of those listed here offered only limited services over short distances, but their opening dates mark the accepted beginning of each country's railroad system.

◄ **All aboard**
Indian Railways is one of the largest rail networks and carries millions of people daily.

THE INDIAN RAIL NETWORK CARRIES MORE THAN 30 MILLION PASSENGERS DAILY—EQUIVALENT TO THE POPULATION OF CANADA!

TOP 10 BUSIEST RAIL NETWORKS

LOCATION	PASSENGER/ KM PER ANNUM*		LOCATION	PASSENGER/ KM PER ANNUM*
1 China	722,800,000,000		6 Germany	74,730,000,000
2 India	696,000,000,000		7 Ukraine	53,230,000,000
3 Japan	254,000,000,000		8 UK	46,760,000,000
4 Russia	173,000,000,000		9 Italy	46,440,000,000
5 France	78,460,000,000		10 Egypt	40,840,000,000

* Number of passengers multiplied by distance carried; totals include national and local services where applicable

Source: UIC Railisa Database

TOP 10 LONGEST RAIL NETWORKS

LOCATION	TOTAL RAIL LENGTH MILES	KM
1 USA	139,67	224,7929
2 Russia	54,156	87,157
3 China	53,437	86,000
4 India	39,751	63,974
5 Canada	28,926	46,552
6 Germany	26,085	41,981
7 Australia	23,888	38,445
8 Argentina	22,969	36,966
9 France	18,417	29,640
10 Brazil	17,732	28,538

Source: CIA, *The World Factbook 2011*

▲ **Freight heavyweight**
The USA has the world's largest rail network, used for both freight and passenger travel.

THE 10 **FIRST UNDERGROUND RAILROAD SYSTEMS**

CITY / FIRST LINE ESTABLISHED*

(1) London, UK
Jan 10, 1863

(2) Budapest, Hungary
May 2, 1896

(3) Glasgow, UK
Dec 14, 1896

(4) Boston, USA
Sep 1, 1897

(5) Paris, France
Jul 19, 1900

(6) Berlin, Germany
Feb 15, 1902

(7) New York, USA
Oct 27, 1904

(8) Philadelphia, USA
Mar 4, 1907

(9) Hamburg, Germany
Feb 15, 1912

(10) Buenos Aires, Argentina
Dec 1, 1913

* Excluding those where overground part preceded underground, such as the Chicago "L"

Source: World Metro Database

◀ *London tube*
The Metropolitan line, built 1860–63, was the first underground passenger railway.

TOP 10 **BUSIEST UNDERGROUND RAILROAD SYSTEMS**

UNDERGROUND SYSTEM	ESTIMATED DAILY USERS
1 Tokyo, Japan	8,700,000
2 Moscow, Russia	6,500,000
3 Seoul, South Korea	5,600,000
4 New York, USA	4,330,000
5 Paris, France	4,000,500
6 Beijing, China	3,990,000
7 Mexico City, Mexico	3,880,000
8 Hong Kong, China	3,620,000
9 Shanghai, China	3,560,000
10 London, UK	2,900,000

Source: World Metro Database, 2011

TOP 10 **LONGEST UNDERGROUND RALROAD NETWORKS**

CITY / OPENED	STATIONS	TOTAL TRACK LENGTH MILES	TOTAL TRACK LENGTH KM
1 Shanghai, China, 1995	279	263	423
2 London, UK, 1863	270	250	402
3 New York, USA,1904	468	229	368
4 Beijing, China, 1969	196	209	337
5 Seoul, South Korea,1974	293	196	316
6 Tokyo, Japan, 1927	290	190	304
7 Moscow, Russia, 1935	182	188	302
8 Madrid, Spain, 1919	282	178	286
9 Gungzhou, China, 1999	146	144	232
10 Paris, France, 1900	381	134	215

Source: World Metro Database, 2011

▶ *Commuter crush*
Tokyo is home to the world's busiest modern metro system, designed to carry commuters from the suburbs across the city.

TOP FLIGHT

▲ Airbus 340-600
One of the world's longest commercial aircraft, the Airbus can carry up to 419 passengers.

TOP 10 LONGEST AIRCRAFT

| | | | LENGTH | |
AIRCRAFT	FT	IN		M
1 Ekranoplan KM Caspian Sea Monster	348	0		106.1
2 Antonov An-225 Cossack	275	7		84.0
3 Lockheed C-5 Galaxy	247	10		75.5
4 Airbus A340-600	246	11		75.3
5 Boeing 777-300ER	242	4		73.9
6 Lun Ekranoplan	240	0		73.2
7 Airbus A380F	239	3		72.9
8 Boeing 747	231	10		70.7
9 Antonov An-124 Condor	226	9		69.1
10 H-4 Hercules ("Spruce Goose")	218	6		66.6

▼ Sea Monster
The Soviet Ekranoplan was a huge military craft designed to travel close to the water at high speed.

TOP 10 AIRLINES WITH THE MOST DISTANCE FLOWN

AIRLINE / DISTANCE FLOWN (MILES)*

1 Delta Air Lines 141,045,047

2 American Airlines 125,443,038

3 United Airlines 102,316,223

4 Emirates 89,266,185

5 Lufthansa 80,573,824

6 Continental Airlines 79,623,126

7 Southwest Airlines 78,032,416

8 Air France 77,778,896

9 China Southern Airlines 68,689,478

10 British Airways 65,588,215

TOP 10 AIRLINES WITH THE MOST PASSENGERS

AIRLINE	PASSENGERS CARRIED*
1 Delta Air Lines	111,159,000
2 Southwest Airlines	106,228,000
3 American Airlines	86,129,000
4 China Southern Airlines	76,078,000
5 Ryanair	71,229,000
6 Lufthansa	56,693,000
7 United Airlines	54,015,000
8 US Airways	51,814,000
9 China Eastern Airlines	50,336,000
10 Air France	47,029,000

* Latest year for which figures available; total of international and domestic passengers on scheduled flights

* Latest year for which data available; total of international and domestic scheduled flights

Source: International Air Transport Association

▶ *Terminal travelers*
Designed by Sir Norman Foster, Beijing's Terminal 3 has made the airport one of the world's largest and busiest.

TOP 10 **BUSIEST AIRPORTS**

AIRPORT / COUNTRY	PASSENGERS (2010)	CODE
1 Atlanta, USA	89,331,622	ATL
2 Beijing, China	73,948,113	PEK
3 Chicago, USA	66,774,738	ORD
4 London, UK	65,884,143	LHR
5 Tokyo, Japan	64,211,074	HND
6 Los Angeles, USA	59,070,127	LAX
7 Paris, France	58,167,062	CDG
8 Dallas/Fort Worth, USA	56,906,610	DFW
9 Frankfurt, Germany	53,009,221	FRA
10 Denver, USA	52,209,277	DEN

Source: Airports Council International

▲ *Panda Express*
FedEx's specially branded aircraft transports pandas around the world.

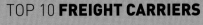

TOP 10 **COUNTRIES WITH THE MOST AIRPORTS**

COUNTRY	AIRPORTS
1 USA	5,194
2 Brazil	726
3 Russia	593
4 Canada	514
5 China	442
6 Germany	330
7 Australia	326
8 UK	306
9 France	297
10 Mexico	250

Source: CIA, *The World Factbook 2011*

TOP 10 **FREIGHT CARRIERS**

AIRLINE / COUNTRY	FREIGHT TONS/KM*
1 Federal Express, USA	15,743,000,000
2 UPS Airlines, USA	10,194,000,000
3 Cathay Pacific Airways, Hong Kong, China	9,587,000,000
4 Korean Air Lines, South Korea	9,542,000,000
5 Emirates, United Arab Emirates	7,913,000,000
6 Lufthansa, Germany	7,428,000,000
7 Singapore Airlines, Singapore	7,001,000,000
8 China Airlines, Taiwan	6,410,000,000
9 EVA Air, Taiwan	5,166,000,000
10 Cargolux, Luxembourg	4,901,000,000

* Total weight of cargo multiplied by distance carried

FIRST TO FLY

TOP **10** FEATURE

THE 10 **FIRST PEOPLE TO PILOT HEAVIER-THAN-AIR AIRCRAFT**

PILOT / DATES / COUNTRY / LOCATION	AIRCRAFT	APPROX. DISTANCE (FT)	DATE*
1 Orville Wright (1871–1948, USA) Kitty Hawk, North Carolina, USA	Wright Flyer I	121	Dec 17, 1903
2 Wilbur Wright (1867–1912, USA) Kitty Hawk, North Carolina, USA	Wright Flyer I	174	Dec 17, 1903
3 Jacob Christian Hansen Ellehammer (1871–1946, Denmark) Lindholm, Denmark	Ellehammer	138	Sep 12, 1906
4 Alberto Santos-Dumont (1873–1932, Brazil) Bagatelle, Paris, France	No. 14-bis	197	Oct 23, 1906
5 Charles Voisin (1882–1912, France) Bagatelle, Paris, France	Voisin Delagrange I	197	Mar 30, 1907
6 Robert Esnault-Pelterie (1881–1957, France) Buc, France	REP No.1	328	Oct 10, 1907
7 Henri Farman (1874–1958, UK, later France) Issy les Moulineaux, Paris, France	Voisin-Farman I-bis	2,336	Oct 26, 1907
8 Ferdinand Léon Delagrange (1873–1910, France) Issy les Moulineaux, Paris, France	Voisin-Delagrange I	328	Nov 5, 1907
9 Comte Henri de La Vaulx (1870–1930, France) St Cyr, France	Antoinette	230	Nov 19, 1907
10 Alfred de Pischoff (1882–1922, Hungary) Issy les Moulineaux, Paris, France	Anzani	164–328	Dec 12, 1907

* Of first flight only

▼ *Anglo-French*
Of British parentage, Henri Farman did not take French citizenship until 1937.

▼ The Wright Brothers aircraft Kitty Hawk—the first to fly!

▼ *All-round airman*
The Brazilian Santos-Dumont designed and flew both airships and fixed-wing planes.

While most of the fliers listed flew on numerous subsequent occasions and broke their first-time records, most other "flights" of the 1906–08 period were uncontrolled or no more than short hops of a few seconds' duration, such as those of Hungarian Trajan Vuia in 1907–08, Horatio Phillips—who claimed to have flown 500 ft (152 m) at Norbury, England, in 1907—and Danish Jabob Christian Ellehammer, who hopped 578 ft (176 m) on January 14, 1908, and is credited with the first ever hop-flight in Germany, at Kiel on June 28, 1908. Meanwhile, the Wrights were so far in advance of their competitors that they were flying under full control for more than an hour and over distances of 50 miles (80 km). French aviator Thérèse Peltier became the first female air passenger when she accompanied Léon Delagrange in a Voisin flight of 656 ft (200 m) in Italy on July 8, 1908.

EXHAUST VALVE 4 OFF:-

79

TRANSATLANTIC FEATS

The first transatlantic flight took place on May 16–27, 1919, when Albert Cushing Read and a crew of five crossed the Atlantic in the US Navy Curtiss seaplane in a series of hops, refueling at sea. British pilot John Alcock and navigator Arthur Whitten Brown achieved the first nonstop flight, ditching in Derrygimla bog after their epic 16-hour 28-minute journey from Newfoundland to Galway on June 14–15, 1919. In early July of that same year, George Herbert Scott and a crew of 30 (including the first transatlantic air stowaway, William Ballantyne) made the first east-west crossing. The first airship to do so, when the R-34 returned to Pulham, UK, on July 13, it was also the first to complete a double crossing.

LINDBERGH ALONE

The most famous transatlantic flight of all was that of Charles Lindbergh. He was actually the 92nd individual to fly the Atlantic, but he was the first to cross solo. Lindbergh's journey took place on May 20–21, 1927 from Long Island, New York to Paris, France, in the *Spirit of St. Louis*, a single-engined Ryan monoplane. The total distance covered was 3,610 miles (5,810 km) in a time of 33 hours and 29.5 minutes.

▼ This photo was taken one hour into the historic flight.

▼ **The old and the new**
The Graf Zeppelin's 1931 flight to the Middle East crossed 14 countries and took 97 hours.

THE 5 FIRST ROUND-THE-WORLD FLIGHTS

PILOT(S) / AIRCRAFT / ROUTE (START/END LOCATION)	TOTAL DISTANCE MILES	KM	DATES
1 Lt. Lowell H. Smith/Lt. Leslie P. Arnold (USA) Douglas World Cruiser Chicago Seattle / Washington, USA	26,345	42,398	Apr 6–Sep 28, 1924
2 Lt. Erik H. Nelson/Lt. John Harding Jr. (USA) Douglas World Cruiser New Orleans Seattle / Washington, USA	27,553	44,342	Apr 6–Sep 28, 1924
3 Dr. Hugo Eckener, Ernst Lehmann, and crew (Germany) Airship Graf Zeppelin Lakehurst / New Jersey, USA	20,373	37,787	Apr 8–29, 1929
4 Wiley Post and Harold Gatty (US) Lockheed Vega Winne Mae Roosevelt Field / Long Island, New York, USA	15,474	24,903	Jun 23–Jul 1, 1931
5 Wolfgang von Gronau, Ghert von Roth, Franz Hack, Fritz Albrecht (Germany), Dornier seaplane, Grönland-Wal D-2053 List, Germany	27,240	44,000	Jul 22–Nov 23, 1932

▶ **Strength in numbers**
Two of the four planes used in Lowell Smith's round-the-world run did not make it, but no crew were lost.

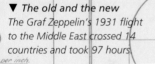

TRANSPORT DISASTERS

THE 10 WORST MOTOR VEHICLE AND ROAD DISASTERS

LOCATION / DATE / INCIDENT	NO. KILLED
Afghanistan, Nov 3, 1982	>2,000

Following a collision with a Soviet army truck, a petrol tanker exploded in the 1.7-mile (2.7-km) Salang Tunnel. Some authorities have put the death toll from the explosion, fire, and fumes as high as 3,000.

Colombia, Aug 7, 1956	1,200

Seven army ammunition trucks exploded at night in the centre of Cali, destroying eight city blocks, including a barracks where 500 soldiers were sleeping.

Dem. Rep. of Congo, Jul 2, 2010	230

A fuel tanker overturned and exploded, unleashing a fireball that devastated the town of Sange.

Spain, Jul 11, 1978	217

A liquid gas tanker exploded in Los Alfaques, a camping site at San Carlos de la Rapita.

Thailand, Feb 15, 1991	171

A dynamite truck exploded in Phang Nga.

Nigeria, Nov 5, 2000	150–200

A gas tanker collided with a line of parked cars on the Ile-Ife-Ibadan Expressway, exploding and burning many to death. Some 96 bodies were recovered, but some estimates put the final toll as high as 200.

Nepal, Nov 26, 1974	148

Hindu pilgrims were killed when a suspension bridge over the River Mahakali collapsed.

Egypt, Aug 9, 1973	127

A bus drove into an irrigation canal.

Togo, Dec 6, 1965	>125

Two trucks collided with dancers during a festival at Sotouboua.

Kenya, Feb 1, 2009	113

A gas tanker overturned near Molo and burst into flames as locals attempted to remove fuel.

THE 10 WORST RAIL DISASTERS

LOCATION / DATE / INCIDENT	NO. KILLED
Telwatta, Sri Lanka, Dec 26, 2004	<2,000

The *Queen of the Sea* train was struck by the Indian Ocean tsunami. The resulting devastation made it impossible to determine the precise number of casualties on the train, a figure of 1,700 to 2,000 being officially quoted.

Bagmati River, India, Jun 6, 1981	c. 800

Carriages of the train plunged off a bridge when the driver braked, apparently to avoid hitting a sacred cow. Although the official death toll was said to have been 268, many authorities have claimed that the train was so massively overcrowded that the actual figure was in excess of 800.

Chelyabinsk, Russia, Jun 3, 1989	<800

Two passenger trains, laden with holidaymakers heading to and from Black Sea resorts, were destroyed when liquid gas from a nearby pipeline exploded.

Guadalajara, Mexico, Jan 18, 1915	>600

A train derailed on a steep incline, but political strife in the country meant that full details of the disaster were suppressed.

Modane, France, Dec 12, 1917	543

A troop-carrying train ran out of control and was derailed. It has been claimed that it was so overcrowded that as many as 800 may have died.

Balvano, Italy, Mar 2, 1944	521

A heavily laden train stalled in the Armi Tunnel, and many passengers were asphyxiated. Like the disaster at Torre, wartime secrecy prevented full details from being published.

Torre, Spain, Jan 3, 1944	>500

A double collision and fire in a tunnel resulted in many deaths —some authorities have put the total as high as 800.

Awash, Ethiopia, Jan 13, 1985	428

A derailment hurled a train laden with some 1,000 passengers into a ravine.

Cireau, Romania, Jan 7, 1917	374

An overcrowded passenger train crashed into a military train and was derailed.

Reqa al-Gharbiya, Egypt, Feb 20, 2002	373

A fire on the Cairo-Luxor train engulfed the carriages. The driver was unaware and continued while passengers were burned or leapt from the train to their deaths.

▲ **Road and rail wrecks**
Left: Carnage at the Los Alfaques campsite. Right: Remarkably, the train's guard survived the Telwatta disaster.

◀ Abandon ship
Left: The Titanic has
become a byword for
disaster. Right: The
General Slocum disaster.

THE 10 WORST PEACETIME MARINE DISASTERS

SHIP / LOCATION / DATE / INCIDENT	NO. KILLED
1 MV Doña Paz Tabias Strait, Philippines, Dec 20, 1987 The ferry *Doña Paz* was struck by oil tanker *MT Vector*. The official death toll was 1,749, but the *Doña Paz* was overcrowded, and some sources claim a total of 4,341.	>4,000
2 SS Kiangya Off Shanghai, China, Dec 4, 1948 The overloaded passenger steamship *Kiangya*, carrying Chinese refugees, is believed to have struck a Japanese mine. An estimated 700–1,000 survivors were rescued by other vessels.	2,750–3,920
3 MV Le Joola Off The Gambia, Sep 26, 2002 The overcrowded Senegalese ferry capsized in a storm.	>1,863
4 Tek Sing Gaspar Strait, Indonesia, Feb 6, 1822 The large Chinese junk laden with migrant Chinese workers ran aground and sunk.	1,600
5 Sultana Mississippi River, USA, Apr 27, 1865 A boiler on the Mississippi paddleboat *Sultana* exploded and the vessel sank. As it occurred soon after the assassination of President Abraham Lincoln, it received little press coverage.	1,547
6 RMS Titanic North Atlantic, Apr 15, 1912 The most famous marine disaster of all, the *Titanic*, the world's largest liner, sank on its maiden voyage after striking an iceberg.	1,517
7 Toya Maru Tsugaru Strait, Japan, Sep 26, 1954 The Japanese ferry between Hokkaido and Honshu sank in a typhoon, with an estimated 150 rescued.	1,159
8 SS General Slocum New York, USA, Jun 15, 1904 The excursion steamship caught fire in the East River, New York, with many victims burned or drowned.	1,021
9 MS al-Salam Boccaccio 98 Red Sea, Feb 3, 2006 The Egyptian car ferry sank following a fire on board.	1,018
10 RMS Empress of Ireland Saint Lawrence River, Canada, May 29, 1914 The Royal Mail ship was struck by Norwegian collier SS *Storstad*, resulting in Canada's worst-ever marine disaster.	1,012

THE 10 WORST BRIDGE COLLAPSES

BRIDGE / LOCATION / DATE / INCIDENT*	NO. KILLED
1 Angers, France, Apr 16, 1850 The bridge began to vibrate and collapsed as 478 soldiers marched across it.	226
2 Tangiwai, New Zealand, Dec 24, 1953 Volcanic lava engulfed the bridge over the Walouru River as a passenger train crossed; some victims were carried 30 miles (48 km) by the force of the flow.	151
3 Makahali, Nepal, Nov 26, 1974 A suspension bridge over a river collapsed in the Baitadi district.	140
4 Liziyida, China, Jul 9, 1981 The bridge was destroyed by a mudflow, resulting in a train derailment.	130
5 Munnar, India, Nov 8, 1984 A rope bridge collapsed over a swollen stream; the victims were mostly schoolchildren.	125
6 Hyatt Regency Skywalks, USA, Jul 17, 1981 The collapse of two aerial footbridges occurred during a dance at the hotel.	114
7 Mahububnagar, India, Sep 2, 1956 A narrow-gauge train fell into the river when the bridge collapsed.	112
8 Colgante, Naga City, Philippines, Sep 16, 1972 Many pilgrims jumped into the river as the wooden bridge collapsed.	100
9 Ashtabula, Ohio, USA, Dec 29, 1876 The bridge collapsed in heavy snow, causing a train to plunge into the valley where it caught fire.	92
10 Yarmouth, UK, May 2, 1845 As a crowd of people on the bridge watched a performer in the river below, their weight caused its suspension chains to snap.	79

* Those where the collapse caused the disaster, excluding those where a ship, train, or other impact resulted in the collapse

10
SPORT

CHANGING THE COURSE OF GOLF

One hundred years ago—on a cold and miserable September day in 1913—a little-known American, Francis Ouimet, changed the course of golf history. He defeated the might of the British challenge to win the US Open by five strokes in an 18-hole play-off against Harry Vardon, the world's greatest player at the time. Ouimet's victory was remarkable: not only was he just 20 years old at the time, but he was also an amateur golfer. His victory was the first by an American golfer in the 16 years of the US Open, and his win heralded the start of US domination of the world of professional golf. Ouimet was honored in 1951 as the first American to be named captain of the royal and ancient golf club of St. Andrews.

US champions: Francis Ouimet and Tiger Woods.

OLYMPIC GAMES

THE 10 LATEST VENUES FOR THE SUMMER OLYMPICS

YEAR / VENUE / COUNTRY

2012
London / England

2008
Beijing / China

2004
Athens / Greece

2000
Sydney / Australia

1996
Atlanta / USA

1992
Barcelona / Spain

1988
Seoul / South Korea

1984
Los Angeles / USA

1980
Moscow / USSR

1976
Montreal / Canada

◄ *London 2012*
Located in Stratford, the Olympic Stadium was built in just under four years.

THE 10 SPORTS TO HAVE BEEN CONTESTED AT THE MOST SUMMER OLYMPICS*

	SPORT	YEARS	NO. OF TIMES CONTESTED
1	= Swimming	1896–2012	27
	= Cycling	1896–2012	27
	= Gymnastics	1896–2012	27
	= Athletics	1896–2012	27
	= Fencing	1896–2012	27
6	= Rowing	1900–2012	26
	= Wrestling	1896, 1904–2012	26
8	= Soccer	1900–28, 1936–2012	25
	= Sailing	1900, 1908–2012	25
	= Shooting	1896–1900, 1908–24, 1932–2012	25

* Including all Olympics 1896–2012 but excluding the unofficial Intercalated Games of 1906

THE 10 SUMMER OLYMPICS WITH THE FEWEST COUNTRIES WINNING GOLD MEDALS

	VENUE / COUNTRY	YEAR	COUNTRIES WINNING GOLD
1	St. Louis, USA	1904	9*
2	Athens, Greece	1896	11*
3	= Paris, France	1900	14*
	= London, England	1908	14*
5	= Antwerp, Belgium	1920	15
	= Stockholm, Sweden	1912	15*
7	= Los Angeles, USA	1932	19
	= Paris, France	1924	19
9	Berlin, Germany	1936	21
10	= London, England	1948	23
	= Rome, Italy	1960	23

* Some gold medals won by mixed teams

Athens, 1896
Fourteen countries were represented at the first Modern Olympics in 1896; 11 of them won gold.

241 ATHLETES COMPETED IN THE 1896 OLYMPICS; IN 2012 THERE WERE MORE THAN 10,000!

◄ **Aiming for gold**
Ole Einar Bjørndalen
has won 22
Olympic and World
Championship golds.

TOP 10 **MOST WINTER OLYMPIC MEDALS***

	ATHLETE / COUNTRY / MALE/FEMALE	SPORT	YEARS	G	S	B	TOTAL
					MEDALS		
1	Bjørn Dæhli, Norway (M)	Cross-country skiing	1992–98	8	4	0	12
2	Ole Einar Bjørndalen, Norway (M)	Biathlon	1998–2010	6	4	1	11
3	Reisa Smetanina, USSR/Russia (F)	Cross-country skiing	1976–92	4	5	1	10
4 =	Lyubov Yegorova, Russia (F)	Cross-country skiing	1992–94	6	3	0	9
=	Claudia Pechstein, Germany (F)	Speed skating	1992–2006	5	2	2	9
=	Sixten Jernberg, Sweden (M)	Cross-country skiing	1956–64	4	3	2	9
=	Ursula Disl, Germany (F)	Biathlon	1992–2006	2	4	3	9
8 =	Ricco Gross, Germany (M)	Biathlon	1992–2006	4	3	1	8
=	Galina Kulakova, USSR (F)	Cross-country skiing	1972–80	4	2	2	8
=	Kjetil André Aamodt, Norway (M)	Alpine Skiing	1992–2006	4	2	2	8
=	Sven Fischer, Germany (M)	Biathlon	1994–2006	4	2	2	8
=	Karin Enke, East Germany (F)	Speed Skating	1980–88	3	4	1	8
=	Gunda Niemann-Stimemann Germany (F)	Speed Skating	1992–98	3	4	1	8

* Up to and including the 2010 Vancouver Games

TOP 10 **MEDAL-WINNING COUNTRIES AT THE WINTER OLYMPICS**

	COUNTRY	GOLD	SILVER	BRONZE	TOTAL
1	Norway	107	106	90	303
2	USA	87	95	71	253
3	Austria	55	70	76	201
4	USSR*	78	57	59	194
5	Germany#	71	73	48	192
6	Finland	41	58	56	155
7	Canada	52	45	48	145
8	Sweden	48	33	48	129
9	Switzerland	43	37	46	126
10	East Germany	39	36	35	110

* USSR totals for the period 1956–88
# Germany totals for the periods 1928–36, 1952 and 1992–2010

This list is up to and including the 2010 Vancouver
Games and includes medals won at figure skating
and hockey that were included in the
Summer Olympics prior to the
inauguration of the Winter
Games in 1924.

THE 10 **LATEST VENUES FOR THE WINTER OLYMPICS**

YEAR	VENUE / COUNTRY
2010	Vancouver / Canada
2006	Turin / Italy
2002	Salt Lake City / USA
1998	Nagano / Japan
1994	Lillehammer / Norway
1992	Albertville / France
1988	Calgary / Canada
1984	Sarajevo / Yugoslavia*
1980	Lake Placid / USA
1976	Innsbruck / Austria

* Now Bosnia and Herzegovina

► **USA 2010**
The USA topped
the medal table
at Vancouver
2010, winning
37 medals.

The first Winter Olympics were
held at Chamonix in France
between January 25 and
February 5, 1924, when just
16 nations competed. At
Vancouver in 2010, a total of
82 nations took part. The USA
has hosted the Winter Games
a record four times (1932,
1960, 1980, and 2002).

LONDON 2012

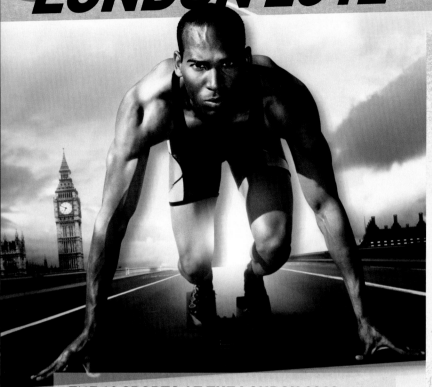

THE 10 SPORTS AT THE LONDON 2012 OLYMPICS WITH THE MOST MEDAL EVENTS

	SPORT	EVENTS
1	Athletics	47
2	Aquatics Swimming, diving, water polo, synchronized swimming	46
3 =	Cycling BMX, mountain bike, road racing, track racing	18
=	Gymnastics Artistic, rhythmic, trampoline	18
=	Wrestling Freestyle, Greco-Roman	18
6	Canoeing	16
7 =	Shooting	15
=	Weightlifting	15
9 =	Judo	14
=	Rowing	14

THE 10 SPORTS AT THE LONDON 2012 OLYMPICS LASTING THE MOST DAYS

	SPORTS	DATES CONTESTED	DAYS
1 =	Basketball	Jul 28–Aug 12	16
=	Boxing	Jul 28–Aug 12	16
=	Handball	Jul 28–Aug 12	16
=	Swimming	Jul 28–Aug 12	16
=	Volleyball	Jul 28–Aug 12	16
6	Gymnastics	Jul 28–Aug 7; Aug 9–12	15
7 =	Cycling	Jul 28–29; Aug 1–12	14
=	Field hockey	Jul 29–Aug 11	14
=	Sailing	Jul 29–Aug 11	14
10	Soccer	Jul 25–26; Jul 28–29; Jul 31–Aug 1; Aug 3–4; Aug 6–7; Aug 9–11	13

OLYMPICS ONLINE

This book was being printed as the London 2012 Olympic Games were taking place. To find out if any Top 10s had changed by the the close of the Games, visit the *Top 10 of Everything* website on:

http://www.octopusbooks.co.uk/top10

TOP 10 MEDAL-WINNING NATIONS AT THE 1948 LONDON OLYMPICS

	COUNTRY	GOLD	SILVER	BRONZE	TOTAL*
1	USA	38	27	19	84
2	Sweden	16	11	17	44
3	France	10	6	13	29
4 =	Hungary	10	5	12	27
=	Italy	8	11	8	27
6	Great Britain	3	14	6	23
7 =	Finland	8	7	5	20
=	Switzerland	5	10	5	20
=	Denmark	5	7	8	20
10	The Netherlands	5	2	9	16

* Not including medals presented for the art contests

► *London 1948* 100,000 copies of the Walter Herz-designed poster for the 1948 Games were printed.

OLYMPIC GAMES

29 JULY 1948 14 AUGUST LONDON

THE 10 MOST EXPENSIVE SPORTS TO WATCH AT THE LONDON 2012 OLYMPICS*

	SPORT	PRICE*
1	Athletics	£725
2	=Beach volleyball	£450
	=Diving	£450
	=Gymnastics (artistic)	£450
	=Swimming	£450
6	Basketball	£425
7	Boxing	£395
8	Cycling (track)	£325
9	Equestrian (dressage & show jumping)	£275
10	Tennis	£225

* Based on the most expensive tickets per sport

▲ Tom Daley
Many young British athletes were favorites to win medals in 2012, none more so than diver Tom Daley.

AROUND 40 TIMES AS MANY WOMEN COMPETED IN LONDON 2012 AS THEY DID IN THE 1948 LONDON OLYMPICS!

▼ On the beach
The beach volleyball competition at London 2012 took place in Horse Guards Parade.

THE 10 LARGEST VENUES FOR THE 2012 OLYMPIC GAMES

	STADIUM	LOCATION	USED FOR	CAPACITY*
1	Wembley Stadium	London	Soccer	90,000
2	Olympic Stadium	London	Athletics/opening and closing ceremonies	80,000
3	Old Trafford	Manchester	Soccer	75,957
4	Millennium Stadium	Cardiff	Soccer	74,500
5	St. James' Park	Newcastle upon Tyne	Soccer	52,409
6	Hampden Park	Glasgow	Soccer	52,103
7	City of Coventry Stadium	Coventry	Soccer	32,609
8	=All England Club	Wimbledon	Lawn tennis	30,000
	=Dorney Lake	Dorney, Bucks	Canoeing/rowing	30,000
10	Greenwich Park	London	Equestrian	23,000

* Based on 2011 capacity

▼ Past and present
Both the old and new Wembley Stadiums have now hosted Olympic events.

TOP 10 FEATURE

SPORTING FIRSTS

10 MAJOR SPORTING FIRSTS

1 **The first world champion**
The first recorded world champion in any sport was a Frenchman called Clergé, who won the world Real Tennis championship in around 1740.

▲ **Changing game**
The early Wimbledon championships were a far cry from the modern game.

3 **The first Wimbledon championships**
The first Wimbledon championships were held July 9–19, 1877. Only men competed that year; women made their debut in 1884. The inaugural men's champion was Spencer Gore, who beat fellow Brit William Marshall in just 48 minutes.

2 **The first organized golf club**
The Honourable Company of Edinburgh Golfers, the oldest organized golf club in the world, was formed on March 7, 1744. Now based at Muirfield, its original home was at Leith Links and they drew up the rules of the game for its first competition, the Silver Club, won by John Rattray.

4 **The first boxing world heavyweight title fight**
On September 7, 1892, James J. Corbett beat John L. Sullivan with a 21st-round knockout to become the first world heavyweight champion under Queensberry Rules. There are other claims to being the first world heavyweight title with gloves, but this is widely accepted as the first one.

▲ **Champion and loser**
Corbett (right) with Sullivan, the man he beat to become the first heavyweight champ.

▼ **Athens, 1896**
Just 241 athletes from 14 nations took part in the first Modern Olympics.

5 **The first Modern Olympic Games**
The first Modern Olympic Games were held at Athens, Greece, on April 6–15, 1896, revived after more than 1,500 years thanks to the determined efforts of Frenchman Pierre de Coubertin. American James Connolly was the first Modern Olympic champion when he won the triple jump (then known as the hop, step, and jump).

6 **The first baseball World Series**
On October 1, 1903, at Huntington Avenue Baseball Grounds in Boston, Massachusetts, 16,242 fans saw the first in the best-of-nine series in the inaugural World Series. Boston Americans (now the Red Sox) clinched the series by beating Pittsburgh Pirates 5-3. The Americans came from 3-1 down to win the last four games and take the series on October 13.

▲ *Ferenc Szisz*
Winner of the 1906 French GP.

7 The first Grand Prix

The first motor racing Grand Prix was the French Grand Prix at Le Mans on June 26–27, 1906. The race was won by Hungarian Ferenc Szisz, driving a Renault AK 90CV at an average speed of 63 mph (101 km/h). Thirty-two cars started the race, but just 11 finished. Some sources incorrectly cite the 1901 Circuit du Sud-Ouest at Pau, France, as the first Grand Prix race.

▼ *Historic firsts*
Posters depicting the first Winter Olympics in 1924 and the inaugural FIFA World Cup in 1930.

8 The first Winter Olympics

The first Winter Olympics took place at Chamonix, France, between January 25 and February 5, 1924. There were 258 athletes (247 men and 11 women) who competed in 16 events. The first gold medalist was Charles Jewtraw (USA) in the 500 meters speed-skating competition on January 26, 1924.

9 The first soccer World Cup

The first FIFA World Cup took place in Uruguay on July 13–30, 1930. France's Lucien Laurent scored the first World Cup goal in a 4-1 win over Mexico. Uruguay beat Argentina 4-2 in the first Final.

10 The first Super Bowl

On January 15, 1967, Green Bay Packers beat Kansas City Chiefs 35-10 to win the first Super Bowl. Green Bay's reserve receiver, Max McGee, scored the first touchdown in Super Bowl history with a 37-yard touchdown reception. In 1967 the game was known as the AFL-NFL World Championship Game—the name Super Bowl was not officially adopted until Super Bowl III.

THE FOUR-MINUTE MILE

On May 6, 1954, Roger Bannister became the first man to break the 4-minute barrier for the mile, doing so in 3 minutes and 59.4 seconds at Iffley Road, Oxford, UK.

FIRST TOUR DE FRANCE

The first Tour de France started in Paris on July 1, 1903 with a 291-mile (468-km) stage to Lyon. The race finished at Paris two and a half weeks later, with Frenchman Maurice Garin the winner in a time of 94 hours, 33 minutes, and 14 seconds for the 1,509-mile (2,429-km) race over six stages.

BASKETBALL 100

On March 2, 1962, Wilt Chamberlain became the first —and so far the only—player to score 100 points in an NBA game. He achieved the feat in the Philadelphia Warriors 169-147 win over New York Knicks, in what was the highest-scoring game in NBA history at the time.

TENNIS GRAND SLAM

Donald Budge (USA) was the first person to win all four Grand Slam events (Wimbledon, Australian, French, and US Opens) in a single year when he won the US Open on September 24, 1938. Only four other players have completed the Grand Slam: Rod Laver (Australia, twice), Maureen Connolly (USA), Margaret Court (Australia), and Steffi Graf (Germany).

LYON - MEDITERRANEE

VAINQUEURS DU CONCOURS DE LA VIIIᵐᵉ OLYMPIADE
CHAMONIX MONT-BLANC
25 Janvier-5 Février 1924

URUGUAY

SOLER Y CA

CAMPEONATO MUNDIAL DE FOOTBALL
1930

ATHLETICS

TOP 10 MEDAL-WINNING COUNTRIES AT THE 2011 IAAF WORLD CHAMPIONSHIPS

	COUNTRY	GOLD	SILVER	BRONZE	TOTAL
1	USA	12	8	5	25
2	Russia	9	4	6	19
3	Kenya	7	6	4	17
4	Jamaica	4	4	1	9
5 =	Germany	3	3	1	7
=	Great Britain	2	4	1	7
7	Ethiopia	1	0	4	5
8 =	China	1	2	1	4
=	South Africa	0	2	2	4
=	Cuba	0	1	3	4
=	France	0	1	3	4

TOP 10 LEADING MEDALISTS IN THE IAAF WORLD CHAMPIONSHIPS*

	ATHLETE / COUNTRY	YEARS	GOLD	SILVER	BRONZE	TOTAL
1	Merlene Ottey, Jamaica	1983–97	3	4	7	14
2 =	Carl Lewis, USA	1983–93	8	1	1	10
=	Allyson Felix, USA	2005–11	8	1	1	10
4 =	Jearl Miles Clark, USA	1993–2003	4	3	2	9
=	Veronica Campbell-Brown, Jamaica	2005–11	2	7	0	9
6 =	Michael Johnson, USA	1991–99	8	0	0	8
=	Gail Devers, USA	1993–2001	5	3	0	8
=	Gwen Torrence, USA	1991–95	3	4	1	8
9 =	Usain Bolt, Jamaica	2007–11	5	2	0	7
=	Haile Gebrselassie, Ethiopia	1993–2003	4	2	1	7
=	Yuliya Pechonkina, Russia (née Nosova)	2001–07	2	3	2	7
=	Lorraine Graham, Jamaica	1997–2005	1	3	3	7

* Up to and including the 2011 Championships

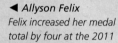

◄ **Allyson Felix**
Felix increased her medal total by four at the 2011 Championships.

► **Usain Bolt**
Bolt may increase his medal haul at the 2013 World Championships.

The first World Championship was held at Helsinki, Finland, in 1983, and then every four years until 1991. Since 1993 the Championships have been held every two years, with the next event being in Moscow in 2013.

► **New York Marathon**
A world record 46,795 finished the 2011 New York Marathon.

The World Marathon Majors consists of the world's five great marathons of Berlin (BER), Boston (BOS), Chicago (CHI), London (LON), and New York (NY), as well as the World Championships (WC) and Olympic Games marathons (OG) when held. Since 2006, these races have formed a competition, with the world's leading marathon runners being awarded points accordingly for finishing in the first five in any of the seven marathons that are regarded as "majors."

TOP 10 **MOST WINS IN THE WORLD MARATHON MAJORS RACES**

	RUNNER / COUNTRY	YEARS	BER	BOS	CHI	LON	NY	OG	WC	TOTAL*
1	Greta Waitz, Norway	1978–88	0	0	0	2	9	0	1	12
2	=Rosa Mota, Portugal	1983–91	0	3	2	1	0	1	1	8
	=Ingrid Kristiansen, Norway	1984–89	0	2	1	4	1	0	0	8
	=Catherine Ndereba, Kenya	2000–07	0	4	2	0	0	0	2	8
	=Paula Radcliffe, UK	2002–08	0	0	1	3	3	0	1	8
	=Bill Rodgers, US	1975–80	0	4	0	0	4	0	0	8
7	=Uta Pippig, Germany	1990–96	3	3	0	0	1	0	0	7
	=Clarence DeMar, US	1911–30	0	7	0	0	0	0	0	7
9	=Joyce Chepchumba, Kenya	1997–2002	0	0	2	2	1	0	0	5
	=Robert Kipkoech Cheruiyot, Kenya	2003–08	0	4	1	0	0	0	0	5
	=Khalid Khannouchi, Morocco/US	1997–2002	0	0	4	1	0	0	0	5
	=Martin Lel, Kenya	2003–08	0	0	0	3	2	0	0	5

* As of January 1, 2012

THE 10 **OLDEST MEN'S OUTDOOR IAAF WORLD RECORDS***

	EVENT	ATHLETE / COUNTRY	TIME/ DISTANCE	SET AT	DATE
1	Discus throw	Jürgen Schult, East Germany East Germany	74.08 m	Neubrandenburg,	Jun 6, 1986
2	Hammer throw	Yurih Sedykh, USSR	86.74 m	Stuttgart, W. Germany	Aug 30, 1986
3	Shot put	Randy Barnes, USA	23.12 m	Westwood, USA	May 20, 1990
4	Long jump	Mike Powell, USA	8.95 m	Tokyo, Japan	Aug 30, 1991
5	400-m hurdles	Kevin Young, USA	46.78 s	Barcelona, Spain	Aug 6, 1992
6	High jump	Javier Sotomayor, Cuba	2.45 m	Salamanca, Spain	Jul 27, 1993
7	4 x 400-m relay	USA	2m 54.29 s	Stuttgart, Germany	Aug 22, 1993
8	Pole vault	Sergey Bubka, Ukraine	6.14 m	Sestriere, Italy	Jul 31, 1994
9	Triple jump	Jonathan Edwards, UK	18.29 m	Gothenburg, Sweden	Aug 7, 1995
10	Javelin throw	Jan Zelezny, Czech Republic	98.48 m	Jena, Germany	May 25, 1996

* In recognized Olympic events; as of January 1, 2012

Source: IAAF

► **Mike Powell**
In 1991, Mike Powell broke Bob Beamon's "unbeatable" world long-jump record after 23 years.

211

CRICKET

TOP 10 MOST RUNS IN THE 2011 ICC WORLD CUP

BATSMAN / COUNTRY	INNINGS	RUNS
1 Tillakaratne Dilshan, Sri Lanka	9	500
2 Sachin Tendulkar, India	9	482
3 Kumar Sangakkara, Sri Lanka	8	465
4 Jonathan Trott, England	7	422
5 Upul Tharanga, Sri Lanka	9	395
6 Gautam Gambhir, India	9	393
7 Virender Sehwag, India	8	380
8 Yuvraj Singh, India	8	362
9 AB de Villiers, South Africa	5	353
10 Andrew Strauss, England	7	334

▼ *Tillakaratne Dilshan*
Dilshan's highest score in the 2011 World Cup was 144 not out against Zimbabwe.

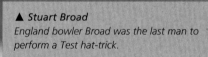

▲ *Stuart Broad*
England bowler Broad was the last man to perform a Test hat-trick.

THE 10 LAST MEN TO PERFORM A TEST MATCH HAT-TRICK*

PLAYER / COUNTRY V. OPPONENTS / VENUE	DATE
1 Stuart Broad, England v. India Nottingham	Jul 30, 2011
2 Peter Siddle, Australia v. England Brisbane	Nov 25, 2010
3 Ryan Sidebottom, England v. New Zealand Hamilton	Mar 8, 2008
4 Irfan Pathan, India v. Pakistan Karachi	Jan 20, 2006
5 James Franklin, New Zealand v. Bangladesh Dhaka	Oct 20, 2004
6 Matthew Hoggard, England v. West Indies Barbados	Apr 3, 2004
7 Andy Blignaut, Zimbabwe v. Bangladesh Harare	Feb 22, 2004
8 Alok Kapali, Bangladesh v. Pakistan Peshawar	Aug 29, 2003
9 Jermaine Lawson, West Indies v. Australia Bridgetown	May 2/5, 2003
10 Mohammad Sami, Pakistan v. Sri Lanka Lahore	Mar 8, 2002

* As of March 16, 2012

TOP 10 MOST CENTURIES IN TEST AND ONE-DAY INTERNATIONALS*

	PLAYER / TEAM(S)	YEARS	TEST	ODI	TOTAL
1	Sachin Tendulkar, India	1989–2012	51	49	100
2	Ricky Ponting, Australia/ICC	1995–2012	41	30	71
3	Jacques Kallis, Africa/ICC/South Africa	1995–2012	42	17	59
4	Brian Lara, ICC/West Indies	1990–2007	34	19	53
5	Rahul Dravid, Asia/ICC/India	1996–2011	36	12	48
6	Mahela Jayawardene, Asia/Sri Lanka	1997–2011	29	15	44
7	Sanath Jayasuriya, Asia/Sri Lanka	1989–2011	14	28	42
8	Kumar Sangakkara, Asia/ICC/Sri Lanka	2000–2012	28	13	41
9	Matthew Hayden, Australia/ICC	1993–2009	30	10	40
10	Mohammad Yousuf, Asia/Pakistan	1998–2010	24	15	39

* As of March 16, 2012

HIGHEST FIRST-CLASS PARTNERSHIPS

On the opening day of the first Test with South Africa at Colombo, on July 27, 2006, the Sri Lankan batsmen Kumar Sangakkara and Mahela Jayawardene came together with their team on 14-2. Two days and 157 overs later they had pushed their total to 638-3, with a world-record stand of 624 when Sangakkara was dismissed for 287. Jayawardene went on to make 374, the 4th-highest innings in Test cricket.

TOP 10 MOST WICKETS IN A WORLD CUP CAREER

	BOWLER / COUNTRY	YEARS	WICKETS
1	Glenn McGrath, Australia	1996–2007	71
2	Muttiah Muralitharan, Sri Lanka	1996–2011	68
3	Wasim Akram, Pakistan	1987–2003	55
4	Chaminda Vaas, Sri Lanka	1996–2007	49
5	= Zaheer Khan, India	2003–11	44
	= Javagal Srinath, India	1992–2003	44
7	Allan Donald, South Africa	1992–2003	38
8	Jacob Oram, New Zealand	2003–11	36
9	Brett Lee, Australia	2003–11	35
10	= Brad Hogg, Australia	2003–07	34
	= Imran Khan, Pakistan	1975–92	34
	= Shaun Tait, Australia	2007–11	34

◄ Sachin Tendulka In November 2011 Tendulkar became the first man to score 15,000 Test runs.

BASEBALL

TOP 10 MOST CAREER RUNS BATTED IN*

	PLAYER	YEARS	RBI
1	Hank Aaron	1954–76	2,297
2	Babe Ruth	1914–35	2,213
3	Cap Anson	1871–97	2,075
4	Barry Bonds	1986–2007	1,996
5	Lou Gehrig	1923–39	1,995
6	Stan Musial	1941–63	1,951
7	Ty Cobb	1905–28	1,938
8	Jimmie Foxx	1925–45	1,922
9	Eddie Murray	1977–97	1,917
10	Willie Mays	1951–73	1,903

* In major league baseball regular-season games up to and including 2011

▶ **Baseball Babe**
Probably the greatest and best-known baseball player of all time, Babe Ruth.

MOST HOME RUNS
Only three men have hit 700 career home runs—Babe Ruth, Hank Aaron, and record holder Barry Bonds with 762.

TOP 10 MOST GAMES PLAYED IN MAJOR LEAGUE BASEBALL WITHOUT APPEARING IN THE WORLD SERIES

	PLAYER	YEARS	GAMES*
1	Rafael Palmeiro	1986–2005	2,831
2	Ken Griffey	1989–2010	2,671
3	Andre Dawson	1976–96	2,627
4	Ernie Banks	1953–71	2,528
5	Julio Franco	1982–2007	2,527
6	Billy Williams	1959–76	2,488
7	Rod Carew	1967–85	2,469
8	Luke Appling	1930–50	2,422
9	Mickey Vernon	1939–60	2,409
10	Buddy Bell	1972–89	2,405

* Regular-season games up to and including 2011

TOP 10 BATTERS WITH THE MOST STRIKEOUTS IN A SEASON*

	PLAYER	TEAM	YEAR	STRIKEOUTS
1	Mark Reynolds	Arizona Diamondbacks	2009	223
2	Mark Reynolds	Arizona Diamondbacks	2010	211
3 =	Mark Reynolds	Arizona Diamondbacks	2008	204
=	Drew Stubbs	Cincinnati Reds	2011	204
5 =	Adam Dunn	Washington Nationals	2010	199
=	Ryan Howard	Philadelphia Phillies	2007	199
=	Ryan Howard	Philadelphia Phillies	2008	199
8	Jack Cust	Oakland Athletics	2008	197
9	Mark Reynolds	Baltimore Orioles	2011	196
10	Adam Dunn	Cincinnati Reds	2004	195

* In major league baseball regular-season games to end of 2011 season

◀ **Mark Reynolds**
In his first three seasons, Reynolds was the National League strikeout leader.

► *Cuba*
Cuba won three of the five Baseball Olympic Games titles between 1992 and 2008.

The first baseball World Cup (then known as the Amateur World Series) was held in 1938 and consisted of just two entrants, Great Britain and the United States. Britain won the first match at the Wavertree Stadium, Liverpool 3-0. The event is now held every two years.

TOP 10 MOST WINS IN THE BASEBALL WORLD CUP*

	COUNTRY	MEN	WOMEN	TOTAL
1	Cuba	25	0	25
2	USA	4	2	6
3	Venezuela	3	0	3
4	= Colombia	2	0	2
	= Japan	0	2	2
6	= Dominican Republic	1	0	1
	= The Netherlands	1	0	1
	= Puerto Rico	1	0	1
	= South Korea	1	0	1
	= UK	1	0	1

* Men's competition 1938–2011; women's competition 2004–10   Source: IBAF

TOP 10 MOST WORLD SERIES WINS*

	TEAM	FIRST	WINS LAST	TOTAL
1	New York Yankees	1923	2009	27
2	St. Louis Cardinals	1926	2011	11
3	Oakland Athletics (5 titles as Philadelphia Athletics)	1910	1989	9
4	Boston Red Sox	1903	2007	7
5	= Los Angeles Dodgers (1 title as Brooklyn Dodgers)	1955	1988	6
	= San Francisco Giants (5 titles as New York Giants)	1905	2010	6
7	= Pittsburgh Pirates	1909	1979	5
	= Cincinnati Reds	1919	1990	5
9	Detroit Tigers	1935	1984	4
10	= Baltimore Orioles	1966	1983	3
	= Minnesota Twins (1 title as Washington Senators)	1924	1991	3
	= Atlanta Braves (1 title as Boston Braves, 1 as Milwaukee Braves)	1914	1995	3
	= Chicago White Sox	1906	2005	3

* Up to and including the 2011 World Series

▲ *New York Yankees*
The Yankees uniform— with its famous badge— is worn by people all over the world.

BASKETBALL

TOP 10 BIGGEST CAPACITY ARENAS IN THE NBA*

	TEAM	HOME ARENA	CAPACITY
1	Detroit Pistons	The Palace of Auburn Hills	22,076
2	Chicago Bulls	United Center	21,711
3	Philadelphia 76ers	Wells Fargo Center	21,600
4	Cleveland Cavaliers	Quicken Loans Arena	20,562
5	Minnesota Timberwolves	Target Center	20,500
6	Washington Wizards	Verizon Center	20,173
7	Portland Trail Blazers	Rose Garden Arena	19,980
8	Utah Jazz	EnergySolutions Arena	19,911
9	Toronto Raptors	Air Canada Center	19,800
10	New York Knicks	Madison Square Garden (IV)	19,763

* At the start of the 2011–12 season

◄ Don Nelson
Don Nelson overtook Lenny Wilkens' all-time most record wins on April 7, 2010.

TOP 10 NBA COACHES WITH THE MOST WINS*

	COACH	YEARS	GAMES	WINS
1	Don Nelson	1976–2010	2,398	1,335
2	Lenny Wilkens	1969–2005	2,487	1,332
3	Jerry Sloan	1979–2011	2,024	1,221
4	Pat Riley	1981–2008	1,904	1,210
5	Phil Jackson	1989–2011	1,640	1,155
6	Larry Brown#	1976–2011	2,002	1,098
7	George Karl	1984–2011	1,739	1,036
8	Rick Adelman	1988–2011	1,561	945
9	Bill Fitch	1970–98	2,050	944
10	Red Auerbach	1946–66	1,417	938

* Regular season wins up to the end of the 2010–11 season
# Larry Brown also won 229 games in the ABA (1972–76)

◄ Karl Malone
Karl Malone spent most of his 19-year career with Utah Jazz.

TOP 10 MOST POINTS IN AN NBA CAREER*

	PLAYER	YEARS	GAMES	POINTS
1	Kareem Abdul-Jabbar	1969–89	1,560	38,387
2	Karl Malone	1985–2004	1,476	36,928
3	Michael Jordan	1984–2003	1,072	32,292
4	Wilt Chamberlain	1959–73	1,045	31,419
5	Shaquille O'Neal	1992–2011	1,287	28,596
6	Kobe Bryant	1996–2011	1,103	27,868
7	Moses Malone	1976–95	1,329	27,409
8	Elvin Hayes	1968–84	1,303	27,313
9	Hakeem Olajuwon	1984–2002	1,238	26,946
10	Oscar Robertson	1960–74	1,040	26,710

* Regular season games up to and including the 2010–11 season
Source: NBA

Kareem Abdul-Jabbar broke Wilt Chamberlain's 11-year record on April 5, 1984, when he scored his 22nd point for LA Lakers in their 129–115 victory over Utah Jazz at the Thomas and Mack Center, Las Vegas—the temporary home of the Jazz.

TOP 10 **MOST ASSISTS IN AN NBA CAREER***

PLAYER / YEARS / GAMES / ASSISTS

1
John Stockton
1984–2003
1,504 / 15,806

2
Jason Kidd
1994–2011
1,267 / 11,578

3
Mark Jackson
1987–2004
1,296 / 10,334

4
Magic Johnson
1979–96
906 / 10,141

5
Oscar Robertson
1960–74
1,040 / 9,887

6
Steve Nash
1996–2011
1,090 / 9,252

7
Isiah Thomas
1981–94
979 / 9,061

8
Gary Payton
1990–2007
1,335 / 8,966

9
Rod Strickland
1988–2005
1,094 / 7,987

10
Maurice Cheeks
1978–93
1,101 / 7,392

* Regular season games up to the end of the 2010–11 season

The NBA was founded in June 1946 as the Basketball Association of America, and changed its name to the National Basketball Association in 1949 following the merger between the BAA and the rival National Basketball League (NBL). Another rival, the ABA (American Basketball Association) was formed in 1967 and merged with the NBA in 1976.

▲ **Boston Celtics**
The Boston Celtics, with 5,085, have played more games than any other NBA team.

TOP 10 **NBA TEAMS WITH THE MOST WINS***

	TEAM	LEAGUE(S)	FROM	TO	PLAYED	WON
1	Los Angeles Lakers	NBA/BAA	1949	2011	4,975	3,084
2	Boston Celtics	NBA/BAA	1947	2011	5,085	3,028
3	Philadelphia 76ers	NBA	1950	2011	4,910	2,610
4	New York Knicks	NBA/BAA	1947	2011	5,081	2,525
5	Detroit Pistons	NBA/BAA	1949	2011	4,974	2,457
6	Atlanta Hawks	NBA	1950	2011	4,912	2,420
7	Golden State Warriors	NBA/BAA	1947	2011	5,080	2,329
8	Sacramento Kings	NBA/BAA	1949	2011	4,975	2,324
9	San Antonio Spurs#	NBA/ABA	1968	2011	3,582	2,092
10	Phoenix Suns	NBA	1969	2011	3,494	1,954

* In regular season games up to the end of the 2010–11 season
# Known as Dallas Chaparrals and then Texas Chaparrals until 1973

THE 10 LAST WORLD HEAVYWEIGHT BOXING TITLE FIGHTS TO END IN THE FIRST ROUND*

	BOXER# / COUNTRY / OPPONENT / COUNTRY	DURATION (MIN:SEC)	DATE
1	Vitali Klitschko, Ukraine v. Odlanier Solis, Cuba	2:59	Mar 19, 2011
2	Lamon Brewster v. Andrew Golota, Poland	0:52	May 21, 2005
3	Herbie Hide, UK v. Damon Reed	0:52	Apr 18, 1998
4	Lennox Lewis, UK v. Andrew Golota, Poland	1:35	Oct 4, 1997
5	Mike Tyson v. Bruce Seldon	1:49	Sep 7, 1996
6	Michael Bentt v. Tommy Morrison	1:33	Oct 29, 1993
7	Riddick Bowe v. Michael Dokes	2:19	Feb 6, 1993
8	Mike Tyson v. Carl Williams	1:33	Jul 21, 1989
9	Mike Tyson v. Michael Spinks	1:31	Jun 21, 1988
10	James Smith v. Tim Witherspoon	2:12	Dec 12, 1986

* In bouts as recognized by the four main bodies: WBA, WBC, IBF, and WBO;
as of January 1, 2012
All boxers from the USA unless otherwise stated

◄ **Knockout**
Lamon Brewster knocked out Andrew Golota in a record-equaling 52 seconds in 2005.

THE 10 LIGHTEST BOXERS TO WIN THE WORLD HEAVYWEIGHT TITLE*

	WINNER# / COUNTRY / OPPONENT / COUNTRY	DATE	WEIGHT (LB)
1	Bob Fitzsimmons, UK v. James J. Corbett	Mar 17, 1897	167
2	James J. Corbett v. John L. Sullivan	Sep 7, 1892	178
3	Tommy Burns, Canada v. Marvin Hart	Feb 3, 1906	180
4	Ezzard Charles v. Jersey Joe Walcott	Jun 22, 1949	181³/₄
5	Floyd Patterson v. Archie Moore	Nov 30, 1956	182¹/₄
6	Rocky Marciano v. Jersey Joe Walcott	Sep 23, 1952	184
7	Jack Dempsey v. Jess Willard	Jul 4, 1919	187
8	Max Schmelling, Germany v. Jack Sharkey	Jun 12, 1930	188
9	Gene Tunney v. Jack Dempsey	Sep 23, 1926	189
10 =	Marvin Hart v. Jack Root, Austria	Jul 3, 1905	190
=	Floyd Patterson† v. Ingemar Johansson, Sweden	Jun 20, 1960	190

* Weight on first winning or regaining the title
# All boxers from the USA unless otherwise stated
† Patterson became the first man to regain his title

◄ **Jim Corbett**
The Irish-American heavyweight was affectionately known as "Gentleman Jim."

BOB FITZSIMMONS WEIGHED ABOUT HALF THAT OF HEAVIEST-EVER CHAMPION NIKOLAI VALUEV!

TOP 10 LONGEST WWE WORLD HEAVYWEIGHT TITLE REIGNS*

	WRESTLER	NO. OF REIGNS	FROM	TO	DAYS
1	Triple H	5	Sep 2, 2002	Apr 3, 2005	616
2	Batista	4	Apr 3, 2005	Nov 3, 2008	507
3	Edge	7	May 8, 2007	Feb 15, 2011	409
4	The Undertaker	3	Apr 1, 2007	Feb 21, 2010	207
5	CM Punk	3	Jun 30, 2008	Oct 4, 2009	160
6 =	Chris Benoit	1	Mar 14, 2004	Aug 15, 2004	154
=	Kane	1	Jul 18, 2010	Dec 19, 2010	154
8	Rey Mysterio	2	Apr 2, 2006	Jul 18, 2010	140
9	Randy Orton	3	Aug 15, 2004	Sep 28, 2011	138
10	King Booker	1	Jul 23, 2006	Nov 26, 2006	126

* Based on aggregate number of days as champion; as of January 1, 2012

▲ Batista
Batista won six different world titles and also the 2005 Royal Rumble.

TOP 10 MOST MEDALS WON AT THE TAEKWONDO WORLD CHAMPIONSHIPS*

	REGION	GOLD	SILVER	BRONZE	TOTAL
1	South Korea	152	27	28	207
2	Spain	22	22	57	101
3	USA	13	19	47	79
4	Chinese Taipei#	13	23	36	73
5	Turkey	10	18	30	58
6	Mexico	3	24	29	56
7	West Germany/ Germany	4	12	30	46
8	Iran	10	14	18	42
9	France	5	10	12	27
10	China	10	8	8	26

* Up to and including 2011
# Commonly known as Taiwan

▼ Taekwondo
The USA has twice hosted the World Taekwondo Championships, in 1977 and 1993.

TOP 10 LONGEST TIMES SPENT IN THE RING IN A SINGLE ROYAL RUMBLE*

	WRESTLER	YEAR	TIME HR:MIN:SEC
1	Rey Mysterio	2006	1:02.12
2	Chris Benoit	2004	1:01.30
3	Bob Backlund	1993	1:01.10
4	Triple H	2006	1:00.09
5	Ric Flair	1992	59.36
6 =	Steve Austin	1999	56.38
=	Vince McMahon	1999	56.38
8	Kane	2001	54.49
9	Rick Martel	1991	52.17
10	The Rock	1998	51.32

* Up to and including 2012

The first Royal Rumble took place on January 24, 1988 and was won by Jim Duggan. It is a "last man standing" contest, with around 30 wrestlers entering the ring at regular intervals based on what number entry they have drawn. A wrestler is eliminated if he is thrown over the top rope by another wrestler who has both feet on the canvas at the time.

HOCKEY

TOP 10 MOST GAMES PLAYED IN THE NHL*

PLAYER / YEARS / GAMES

1 Gordie Howe
1946–80
1,767

2 Mark Messier
1979–2004
1,756

3 Ron Francis
1981–2004
1,731

4 Mark Recchi
1988–2011
1,652

5 Chris Chelios
1983–2010
1,651

6 Dave Andreychuk
1982–2006
1,639

7 Scott Stevens
1982–2004
1,635

8 Larry Murphy
1980–2001
1,615

9 Ray Bourque
1979–2001
1,612

10 Alex Delvecchio
1950–74
1,549

* Regular season only, up to the end of the 2010–11 season

Source: NHL

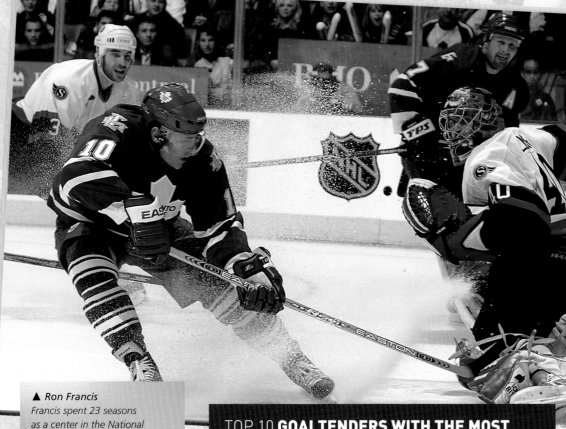

▲ Ron Francis
Francis spent 23 seasons as a center in the National Hockey League.

MOST GOALS IN A SEASON

Wayne Gretzky scored a record 92 goals in 1981–82. Two seasons later he topped the league with 87 goals, still the 2nd-highest total for a season.

TOP 10 GOALTENDERS WITH THE MOST WINS IN THE NHL*

	GOALIE	YEARS	MATCHES	WINS
1	Martin Brodeur	1991–2011	1,132	625
2	Patrick Roy	1984–2003	1,029	551
3	Ed Belfour	1988–2007	963	484
4	Curtis Joseph	1989–2009	943	454
5	Terry Sawchuk	1949–70	971	447
6	Jacques Plante	1952–75	837	437
7	Tony Esposito	1968–84	886	423
8	Glenn Hall	1952–71	906	407
9	Grant Fuhr	1981–2000	868	403
10	Chris Osgood	1993–2011	744	401

* Regular season only; up to the end of the 2010–11 season

◀ Martin Brodeur
Brodeur spent his entire NHL career with the New Jersey Devils.

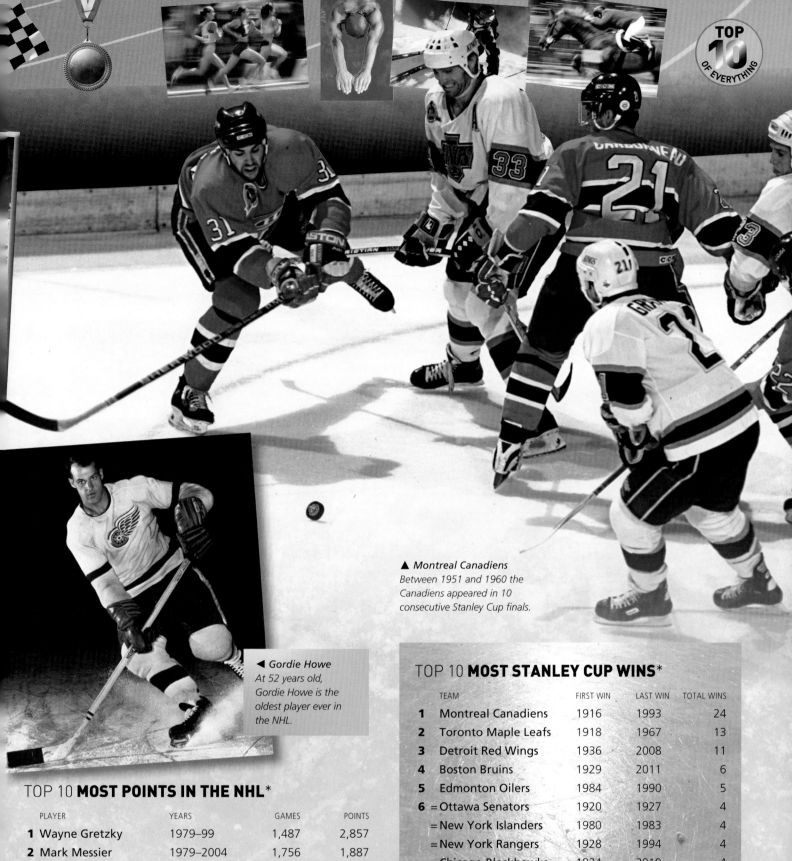

▲ **Montreal Canadiens**
Between 1951 and 1960 the Canadiens appeared in 10 consecutive Stanley Cup finals.

◀ **Gordie Howe**
At 52 years old, Gordie Howe is the oldest player ever in the NHL.

TOP 10 **MOST STANLEY CUP WINS***

	TEAM	FIRST WIN	LAST WIN	TOTAL WINS
1	Montreal Canadiens	1916	1993	24
2	Toronto Maple Leafs	1918	1967	13
3	Detroit Red Wings	1936	2008	11
4	Boston Bruins	1929	2011	6
5	Edmonton Oilers	1984	1990	5
6 =	Ottawa Senators	1920	1927	4
=	New York Islanders	1980	1983	4
=	New York Rangers	1928	1994	4
=	Chicago Blackhawks	1934	2010	4
10 =	New Jersey Devils	1995	2003	3
=	Pittsburgh Penguins	1991	2009	3

* Since the abolition of the challenge match format in 1915; up to and including 2011

Source: NHL

TOP 10 **MOST POINTS IN THE NHL***

	PLAYER	YEARS	GAMES	POINTS
1	Wayne Gretzky	1979–99	1,487	2,857
2	Mark Messier	1979–2004	1,756	1,887
3	Gordie Howe	1946–80	1,767	1,850
4	Ron Francis	1981–2004	1,731	1,798
5	Marcel Dionne	1971–89	1,348	1,771
6	Steve Yzerman	1983–2006	1,514	1,755
7	Mario Lemieux	1984–2006	915	1,723
8	Joe Sakic	1988–2009	1,378	1,641
9	Jaromir Jagr	1990–2008	1,273	1,599
10	Phil Esposito	1963–81	1,282	1,590

* Regular season only; up to the end of the 2010–11 season

Source: NHL

SOCCER

▶ Edwin van der Sar
Van der Sar played for Ajax, Juventus, Fulham, and Manchester United.

TOP 10 MOST APPEARANCES IN THE EUROPEAN CHAMPIONSHIP*

	PLAYER / COUNTRY	YEARS	MATCHES
1	= Edwin van der Sar, The Netherlands	1996, 2000, 2004, 2008	16
	= Lilian Thuram, France	1996, 2000, 2004, 2008	16
3	= Luis Figo, Portugal	1996, 2000, 2004	14
	= Zinedine Zidane, France	1996, 2000, 2004	14
	= Karel Poborsky, Czech Republic	1996, 2000, 2004	14
	= Nuno Gomes#, Portugal	2000, 2004, 2008	14
7	= Dennis Bergkamp, The Netherlands	1992, 1996, 2000	13
	= Paolo Maldini, Italy	1988, 1996, 2000	13
	= Peter Schmeichel, Denmark	1988, 1992, 1996, 2000	13
	= Laurent Blanc, France	1992, 1996, 2000	13
	= Jürgen Klinsmann, West Germany/Germany	1988, 1992, 1996	13
	= Didier Deschamps, France	1992, 1996, 2000	13
	= Phillip Cocu, The Netherlands	1996, 2000, 2004	13
	= Thomas Hässler, Germany	1992, 1996, 2000	13
	= Alessandro del Piero, Italy	1996, 2000, 2004, 2008	13

* In all tournaments up to and including 2008
# Active international player who could add to his total in 2012

TOP 10 NATIONS IN THE COPA AMÉRICA*

	COUNTRY	WINNERS	RUNNERS-UP	3RD	4TH	POINTS
1	Argentina	14	12	4	2	102
2	Uruguay	15	6	9	5	101
3	Brazil	8	11	7	3	82
4	Paraguay	2	6	7	6	46
5	Chile	0	4	5	10	32
6	Peru	2	0	7	5	27
7	Colombia	1	1	3	2	15
8	Mexico	0	2	3	0	12
9	Bolivia	1	1	0	2	9
10	= Ecuador	0	0	0	2	2
	= Honduras	0	0	1	0	2

* Based on 4 points for winning the tournament, 3 for being runners-up, 2 for coming 3rd, and 1 for finishing 4th; up to and including 2011

▶ Argentina
Argentina has also won the World Cup and the Olympic soccer title.

MOST DOMESTIC LEAGUE TITLES

Up to the start of the 2011–12 season, Glasgow Celtic and Rangers had won 96 Scottish titles between them, with Rangers' total of 54 being a world record for any domestic league. They were the inaugural Scottish champions in 1891 (shared with Dumbarton). The last time Rangers or Celtic did not win the title was in 1984–85, when Aberdeen were champions.

► *Fernando Torres*
Fernando's transfer deals to Liverpool and Chelsea cost more than $100 million.

▼ *Egypt*
Egypt celebrating one of their seven African Nations Cup wins.

TOP 10 **TRANSFERS WORLDWIDE***

	PLAYER / COUNTRY	FROM	TO	YEAR	FEE ($)
1	Cristiano Ronaldo, Portugal	Manchester United	Real Madrid	2009	115,950,000
2	Zlatan Ibrahimovic, Sweden	Inter Milan	Barcelona	2009	88,975,000#
3	Kaká, Brazil	AC Milan	Real Madrid	2009	81,163,000
4	Fernando Torres, Spain	Liverpool	Chelsea	2011	77,500,000
5	Zinedine Zidane, France	Juventus	Real Madrid	2001	71,200,000
6	Luis Figo, Portugal	Barcelona	Real Madrid	2000	60,500,000
8	Hernán Crespo, Argentina	Parma	Lazio	2000	57,750,000
7	Javier Pastore, Argentina	Palermo	Paris Saint-Germain	2011	54,350,000
9 =	Sergio Agüero, Argentina	Atlético Madrid	Manchester City	2011	54,250,000
=	Andy Carroll, England	Newcastle United	Liverpool	2011	54,250,000
=	Radamel Falcao, Colombia	Porto	Atlético Madrid	2011	54,250,000

* As of February 2, 2012
# The Ibrahimovic deal involved a reported cash payment of $67 million plus Samuel Eto'o

In June 2009, Kaká held the world transfer record for just over two weeks, when he was surpassed by Cristiano Ronaldo. The record transfer fee paid for a goalkeeper is the approximately $53 million that Juventus paid Parma for Gianluigi Buffon in 1981.

TOP 10 **MOST WINS IN THE AFRICAN NATIONS CUP***

	COUNTRY	YEARS	WINS
1	Egypt	1957/59/86/98/2006/08/10	7
2 =	Ghana	1963/65/78/82	4
=	Cameroon	1984/88/2000/02	4
4 =	Zaire#	1968/74	2
=	Nigeria	1980/94	2
6 =	Ethiopia	1962	1
=	Sudan	1970	1
=	Congo	1972	1
=	Morocco	1976	1
=	Algeria	1990	1
=	Ivory Coast	1992	1
=	South Africa	1996	1
=	Tunisia	2004	1

* Up to and including 2012
# Now the Democratic Republic of Congo

The African Nations Cup was first contested in 1957 and is the principal international tournament organized by the CAF (Confederation of African Football). Since 1968 it has been held every two years.

FOOTBALL

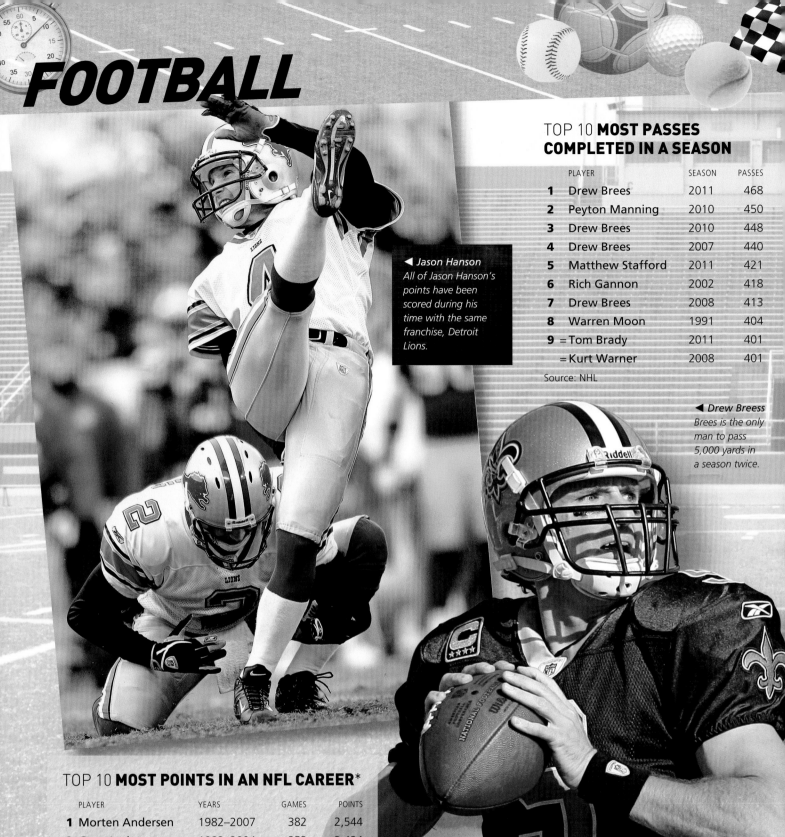

◀ **Jason Hanson**
All of Jason Hanson's points have been scored during his time with the same franchise, Detroit Lions.

TOP 10 **MOST PASSES COMPLETED IN A SEASON**

	PLAYER	SEASON	PASSES
1	Drew Brees	2011	468
2	Peyton Manning	2010	450
3	Drew Brees	2010	448
4	Drew Brees	2007	440
5	Matthew Stafford	2011	421
6	Rich Gannon	2002	418
7	Drew Brees	2008	413
8	Warren Moon	1991	404
9	= Tom Brady	2011	401
	= Kurt Warner	2008	401

Source: NHL

◀ **Drew Breess**
Brees is the only man to pass 5,000 yards in a season twice.

TOP 10 **MOST POINTS IN AN NFL CAREER***

	PLAYER	YEARS	GAMES	POINTS
1	Morten Andersen	1982–2007	382	2,544
2	Gary Anderson	1982–2004	353	2,434
3	John Carney	1988–2010	302	2,062
4	Jason Hanson	1992–2011	312	2,016
5	Matt Stover	1991–2009	297	2,004
6	George Blanda	1949–75	340	2,002
7	Jason Elam	1993–2009	263	1,983
8	John Kasay	1991–2011	302	1,970
9	Adam Vinatieri	1996–2011	243	1,752
10	Norm Johnson	1982–99	273	1,736

* In a regular season

Source: NFL

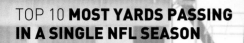

TOP 10 MOST YARDS PASSING IN A SINGLE NFL SEASON

PLAYER / YEAR / YARDS

1 Drew Brees 2011
5,476

2 Tom Brady 2011
5,235

3 Dan Marino 1984
5,084

4 Drew Brees 2008
5,069

5 Matthew Stafford 2011
5,038

6 Eli Manning 2011
4,933

7 Kurt Warner 2001
4,830

8 Tom Brady 2007
4,806

9 Dan Fouts 1981
4,802

10 Matt Schaub 2009
4,770

Source: NFL

TOP 10 MOST SUPER BOWL WINS*

	TEAM	YEARS	WINS
1	Pittsburgh Steelers	1975–76, 1979–80, 2006, 2009	6
2	=San Francisco 49ers	1982, 1985, 1989–90, 1995	5
	=Dallas Cowboys	1972, 1978, 1993–94, 1996	5
4	=Green Bay Packers	1967–68, 1997, 2011	4
	=New York Giants	1987, 1991, 2008, 2012	4
6	=Oakland/ Los Angeles Raiders	1977, 1981, 1984	3
	=Washington Redskins	1983, 1988, 1992	3
	=New England Patriots	2002, 2004–05	3
9	=Miami Dolphins	1973–74	2
	=Denver Broncos	1998–99	2
	=Baltimore/ Indianapolis Colts	1971, 2007	2

* Up to and including 2012

▲ **Men of steel**
The Pittsburgh Steelers have appeared in a record-equaling eight Super Bowls, winning six.

TOP 10 MOST ROSE BOWL GAME WINS*

	COLLEGE	YEARS	WINS
1	Southern California	1923–2009	24
2	=Washington#	1924–2001	8
	=Michigan	1902–98	8
4	Ohio State	1950–2010	7
5	Stanford#	1927–72	6
6	=UCLA	1966–86	5
	=Alabama#	1926–46	5
8	=Wisconsin	1994–2000	3
	=Michigan State	1954–88	3
	=Illinois	1947–64	3
	=California#	1921–38	3

* Up to and including January 2, 2012
# Totals include one shared win

RUGBY

▶ *England vs. Italy*
Chris Ashton scoring England's 8th try against Italy at Twickenham in 2011.

TOP 10 **HIGHEST-SCORING SIX NATIONS MATCHES***

	WINNER	SCORE	OPPONENTS	SCORE	VENUE	YEAR	TOTAL POINTS
1	England	80	Italy	23	Twickenham	2001	103
2	England	60	Wales	26	Twickenham	1998	86
3	France	53	Italy	27	Rome	2003	80
4	Wales	43	France	35	Stade de France	2001	78
5	Ireland	51	Italy	24	Rome	2007	75
6	France	43	Ireland	31	Stade de France	2006	74
7 =	Ireland	60	Italy	13	Lansdowne Road	2000	73
=	France	42	Italy	31	Stade de France	2000	73
9	England	59	Italy	13	Twickenham	2011	72
10	England	59	Italy	12	Rome	2000	71

* In all tournaments 1883–2012

TOP 10 **MOST IRB WORLD CUP MATCHES***

	PLAYER	COUNTRY	YEARS	MATCHES
1	Jason Leonard	England	1991–2003	22
2	George Gregan	Australia	1995–2007	20
3 =	Mike Catt	England	1995–2007	19
=	Jonny Wilkinson	England	1999–2011	19
5 =	Martin Johnson	England	1995–2003	18
=	Brian Lima	Samoa	1991–2007	18
=	Raphaël Ibanez	France	1999–2007	18
=	Mario Ledesama Arocena	Argentina	1999–2011	18
=	Lewis Moody	England	2003–11	18
10 =	Sean Fitzpatrick	New Zealand	1987–95	17
=	Lawrence Dallaglio	England	1999–2007	17
=	Aurélien Rougerie	France	2003–11	17
=	Jean-Baptiste Poux	France	2003–11	17
=	Brian O'Driscoll	Ireland	1999–2011	17
=	John Smit	South Africa	2003–11	17
=	Felipe Contepomi	Argentina	1999–2011	17

* In the final stages of the IRB World Cup 1987–2011

Source: IRB

TOP 10 **MOST APPEARANCES IN THE ENGAGE SUPER LEAGUE***

	PLAYER / YEARS / CLUBS	APPEARANCES
1	Keith Senior, 1996–2011 Sheffield, Leeds	413
2	Keiron Cunningham, 1996–2010, St. Helens	381
3	Lee Gilmour, 1997–2011 Wigan, Bradford, St. Helens, Huddersfield	364
4	Danny Orr, 1997–2011 Castleford, Wigan, Harlequins	358
5	Paul Wellens, 1998–2011 St. Helens	355
6	Kevin Sinfield, 1997–2011 Leeds	350
7	Stuart Fielden, 1998–2011 Bradford, Wigan	348
8	Paul Deacon, 1997–2011 Oldham, Bradford, Wigan	346
9	Les Briers, 1997–2011 St. Helens, Warrington	342
10	Jamie Peacock, 1999–2011 Bradford, Leeds	333

* In all Super League games 1996–2011

Source: *Gillette Rugby League Yearbook*

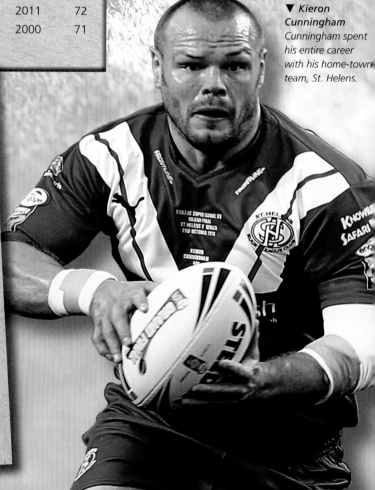

▼ *Kieron Cunningham*
Cunningham spent his entire career with his home-town team, St. Helens.

TOP 10 **POINTS SCORERS IN THE 2011 IRB WORLD CUP**

	PLAYER / COUNTRY	MATCHES	POINTS
1	Morné Steyn, South Africa	5	62
2	James O'Connor, Australia	6	52
3	Kurt Morath, Tonga	4	45
4	Ronan O'Gara, Ireland	5	44
5	Piri Weepu, New Zealand	7	41
6	Dimitri Yachvili, France	7	39
7	Morgan Parra, France	7	37
8	Colin Slade, New Zealand	5	36
9	James Arlidge, Japan	3	34
10 =	Vincent Clerc, France	7	30
=	Chris Ashton, England	5	30

▲ *Dan Carter*
Carter is regarded as one of the game's greatest-ever fly-halves.

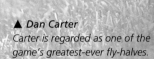
▼ *James O'Connor*
O'Connor kicked 8 points in Australia's bronze final win over Wales in 2011.

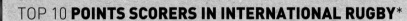

TOP 10 **POINTS SCORERS IN INTERNATIONAL RUGBY***

	PLAYER	COUNTRY	YEARS	TESTS	POINTS
1	Dan Carter	New Zealand	2003–11	85	1,250
2	Jonny Wilkinson	England/Lions	1998–2011	97	1,246
3	Neil Jenkins	Wales/Lions	1991–2003	91	1,090
4	Ronan O'Gara	Ireland/Lions	2000–12	123	1,075
5	Diego Dominguez	Argentina/Italy	1989–2003	76	1,010
6	Stephen Jones	Wales/Lions	1998–2010	110	970
7	Andrew Mehrtens	New Zealand	1995–2004	70	967
8	Michael Lynagh	Australia	1984–95	72	911
9	Percy Montgomery	South Africa	1997–2008	102	893
10	Matthew Burke	Australia	1993–2004	81	878

* As of the end of the 2012 Six Nations Championship

THE 10 **BIGGEST SUPER LEAGUE GROUNDS***

	GROUND	CLUB	CAPACITY
1	Odsal Stadium	Bradford Bulls	27,491
2	KC Stadium	Hull FC	25,404
3	DW Stadium	Wigan Warriors	25,138
4	Galpharm Stadium	Huddersfield Giants	24,500
5	Headingley Carnegie Stadium	Leeds Rhinos	22,000
6	Langtree Park	St. Helens	18,000
7	Halliwell Jones Stadium	Warrington Wolves	15,500
8	Twickenham Stoop	London Broncos	14,816
9	Stobart Stadium	Widnes Vikings	13,500
10	Stade Gilbert Brutus	Catalans Dragons	13,000

* Based on ground capacities of teams in Engage Super League XVII in 2012

TENNIS

TOP 10 MOST WEEKS SPENT AT NO. 1 ON THE WTA RANKINGS

PLAYER / COUNTRY	FIRST DATE AT NO.1	LAST DATE AT NO.1	TOTAL WEEKS
1 Steffi Graf, Germany	Aug 17, 1987	Mar 30, 1997	377
2 Martina Navratilova, Czechoslovakia/USA	Jul 10, 1978	Aug 16, 1987	332
3 Chris Evert, USA	Nov 3, 1975	Nov 24, 1985	260
4 Martina Hingis, Switzerland	Mar 31, 1997	Oct 14, 2001	209
5 Monica Seles, Yugoslavia/USA	Mar 11, 1991	Nov 24, 1996	178
6 Serena Williams, USA	Jul 8, 2002	Oct 10, 2010	123
7 Justine Henin, Belgium	Oct 20, 2003	May 18, 2008	117
8 Lindsay Davenport, USA	Oct 12, 1998	Jan 29, 2006	98
9 Caroline Wozniacki, Denmark	Oct 11, 2010	Jan 2, 2012	64
10 Amélie Mauresmo, France	Sep 13, 2004	Nov 12, 2006	39

* As of January 2, 2012

Source: WTA

▲ Caroline Wozniacki
Caroline Wozniacki started 2012 as world No. 1.

▼ Ivo Karlovic
At 6 ft 10 in, Ivo Karlovic is the tallest player on the ATP Tour.

MOST WINS IN THE DAVIS CUP

Italy's Nicola Pietrangeli holds the record for the most wins in the Davis Cup, with 120 between 1954 and 1972. His 78 singles and 42 doubles wins are also both records. The only other man to win 100 matches is Romania's Ilie Nastase, who won 109 between 1966 and 1985. Fred Perry, with 45 wins, is the most successful British player.

TOP 10 FASTEST TENNIS SERVES*

	PLAYER / COUNTRY / YEAR / EVENT / VENUE	SPEED MPH	KM/H
1	Ivo Karlovic, Croatia 2011 Davis Cup, Zagreb	156.0	251.1
2	Andy Roddick, USA 2004 Davis Cup, Charleston	155.0	249.4
3	Roscoe Tanner, USA 1978 ATP World Tour, Palm Springs	153.0	246.2
4	Joachim Johansson, Sweden 2004 Davis Cup, Adelaide	152.0	244.6
5	Milos Raonic, Canada 2011 ATP World Tour 500, Memphis	150.0	241.4
6	John Isner, USA 2011 ATP World Masters 1000, Cincinnati	149.9	241.2
7	Taylor Dent, USA 2006 ABN/AMRO World Tennis Tournament, Rotterdam	149.8	241.1
8	Ernests Gulbis, Latvia 2007 St. Petersburg Open, St.Petersburg	149.3	240.3
9	Greg Rusedski, UK 1998 ATP Super 9, Indian Wells	149.0	239.8
10 =	Gaël Monfils, France 2007 Legg Mason Tennis Classic, Washington	146.0	235.0
=	Dusan Vemic, Serbia 2008 Countrywide Classic, Los Angeles	146.0	235.0

* Fastest known serve per player

TOP 10 MOST GRAND SLAM TITLES (MEN)*

	PLAYER#	YEARS	SINGLES	DOUBLES	MIXED	TOTAL
1	Roy Emerson	1959–71	12	16	0	28
2	John Newcombe	1964–76	7	17	1	25
3	= Frank Sedgman	1948–52	5	9	8	22
	= Todd Woodbridge	1990–2004	0	16	6	22
5	Bill Tilden, USA	1913–30	10	6	5	21
6	Rod Laver	1959–71	11	6	3	20
7	= John Bromwich	1938–50	2	13	4	19
	= Neale Fraser	1956–62	3	11	5	19
9	= Jean Borotra, France	1924–36	4	9	5	18
	= Ken Rosewall	1953–72	8	9	1	18
	= Fred Stolle	1961–69	2	10	6	18
	= Bob Bryan, USA	2003–11	0	11	7	18

* Up to and including 2011
# All players from Australia unless
otherwise stated

▼ *John Newcombe*
Nine of John Newcombe's 25 titles were at Wimbledon.

◀ *Rafael Nadal*
Rafa Nadal is the second Mallorcan— after Carlos Moya— to top the rankings.

THE 10 LAST MEN TO TOP THE ATP RANKINGS*

PLAYER / COUNTRY / DATE REACHED NO. 1

1 **Novak Djokovic**, Serbia
Jul 4, 2011

2 **Rafael Nadal**, Spain
Jun 7, 2010

3 **Roger Federer**, Switzerland
Jul 6, 2009

4 **Rafael Nadal**, Spain
Aug 18, 2008

5 **Roger Federer**, Switzerland
Feb 2, 2004

6 **Andy Roddick**, USA
Nov 3, 2003

7 **Juan Carlos Ferrero**, Spain
Sep 8, 2003

8 **Andre Agassi**, USA
Jun 16, 2003

9 **Lleyton Hewitt**, Australia
May 12, 2003

10 **Andre Agassi**, USA
Apr 28, 2003

* As of January 1, 2012

Source: ATP

GOLF

TOP 10 MOST WOMEN'S MAJORS*

	PLAYER#	YEARS	A	B	C	D	E	F	G	TOTAL
1	Patty Berg	1937–58	–	–	1	–	–	7	7	15
2	Mickey Wright	1958–66	–	4	4	–	–	2	3	13
3	Louise Suggs	1946–59	–	1	2	–	–	4	4	11
4 =	Babe Zaharias	1940–54	–	–	3	–	–	3	4	10
=	Annika Sörenstam, Sweden	1995–2006	3	3	3	1	–	–	–	10
6	Betsy Rawls	1951–69	–	2	4	–	–	–	2	8
7 =	Juli Inkster	1984–2002	2	2	2	–	1	–	–	7
=	Karrie Webb, Australia	1999–2006	2	1	2	1	1	–	–	7
9 =	Kathy Whitworth	1965–75	–	3	–	–	–	2	1	6
=	Pat Bradley	1980–86	1	1	1	–	3	–	–	6
=	Patty Sheehan	1983–96	1	3	2	–	–	–	–	6
=	Betsy King	1987–97	3	1	2	–	–	–	–	6

* As recognized by the Ladies Professional Golf Association (LPGA), up to and including 2011
# All golfers from the USA unless otherwise stated

A = Kraft Nabisco Championship (previously Nabisco Dinah Shore, Nabisco Championship) 1983–2011
B = LPGA Championship 1955–2011 C = US Women's Open 1946–2011
D = Women's British Open 2001–11 E = du Maurier Classic 1979–2000
F = Titleholders Championship 1937–42, 1946–66, 1972 G = Western Open 1930–67

▲ **Annika Sörenstam**
Sweden's Annika Sörenstam is the top non-American golfer, with 10 Majors.

TOP 10 MOST MEN'S MAJORS*

	PLAYER#	YEARS	US MASTERS	US OPEN	BRITISH OPEN	US PGA	TOTAL
1	Jack Nicklaus	1962–86	6	4	3	5	18
2	Tiger Woods	1997–2008	4	3	3	4	14
3	Walter Hagen	1914–29	0	2	4	5	11
4 =	Ben Hogan	1946–53	2	4	1	2	9
=	Gary Player, South Africa	1959–78	3	1	3	2	9
6	Tom Watson	1975–83	2	1	5	0	8
7 =	Harry Vardon, England	1896–1914	0	1	6	0	7
=	Gene Sarazen	1922–35	1	2	1	3	7
=	Bobby Jones	1923–30	0	4	3	0	7
=	Sam Snead	1942–54	3	0	1	3	7
=	Arnold Palmer	1958–64	4	1	2	0	7

* Professional majors only, up to and including 2011
# All golfers from the USA unless otherwise stated

▶ **Ben Hogan**
Hogan survived a near-fatal accident in 1949 to win six more Majors.

THE 10 **LOWEST FOUR-ROUND TOTALS IN A MAJOR***

	PLAYER / COUNTRY	YEAR / TOURNAMENT	AVERAGE SCORE PER ROUND	SCORE
1	David Toms, USA	2001 PGA Championship	66.25	265
2	Phil Mickelson, USA#	2001 PGA Championship	66.5	266
3 =	Greg Norman, Australia	1993 British Open	66.75	267
=	Steve Elkington, Australia	1995 PGA Championship	66.75	267
=	Colin Montgomerie, UK#	1995 PGA Championship	66.75	267
6 =	Tom Watson, USA	1977 British Open	67	268
=	Nick Price, Zimbabwe	1994 British Open	67	268
=	Steve Lowery, USA#	2001 PGA Championship	67	268
=	Rory McIlroy, UK	2011 USA Open	67	268
10 =	Jack Nicklaus, USA#	1977 British Open	67.25	269
=	Nick Faldo, UK#	1993 British Open	67.25	269
=	Jesper Parnevik, Sweden#	1994 British Open	67.25	269
=	Nick Price, Zimbabwe	1994 PGA Championship	67.25	269
=	Ernie Els, South Africa#	1995 PGA Championship	67.25	269
=	Jeff Maggert, USA#	1995 PGA Championship	67.25	269
=	Davis Love III, USA	1997 PGA Championship	67.25	269
=	Tiger Woods, USA	2000 British Open	67.25	269

* Up to and including 2011
\# Player did not win the tournament

▲ *Rory McIlroy*
After winning the Honda Classic in March 2012, McIlroy became world No. 1.

◄ *Tiger Woods*
Tiger Woods is third behind Sam Snead and Jack Nicklaus on the PGA Tour wins list.

TOP 10 **BIGGEST WINNING MARGINS IN A MEN'S MAJOR**

	PLAYER / COUNTRY	YEAR / TOURNAMENT	WINNING MARGIN
1	Tiger Woods, USA	2000 US Open	15
2	Tom Morris Sr, UK	1862 British Open	13
3 =	Tom Morris Jr, UK	1870 British Open	12
=	Tiger Woods, USA	1997 US Masters	12
5	Willie Smith, USA	1899 US Open	11
6 =	Jim Barnes, USA	1921 US Open	9
=	Jack Nicklaus, USA	1965 US Masters	9
8 =	James Braid, UK	1908 British Open	8
=	Ray Floyd, USA	1976 US Masters	8
=	J. H. Taylor, UK	1900 British Open	8
=	J. H. Taylor, UK	1913 British Open	8
=	Tiger Woods, USA	2000 British Open	8
=	Rory McIlroy, UK	2011 US Open	8

The biggest winning margin in the other Major, the US PGA Championship, was in 1980 when Jack Nicklaus won by seven strokes from Andy Bean at Oak Hill. The biggest winning margin in a women's major is 14 strokes by Louise Suggs (USA) in winning the 1949 US Open.

ON FOUR WHEELS

TOP 10 MOST RALLY WORLD CHAMPIONSHIP RACE WINS*

DRIVER / COUNTRY	YEARS	WINS
1 Sébastien Loeb, France	2002–11	67
2 Marcus Gronholm, Finland	2000–07	30
3 Carlos Sainz, Spain	1990–2004	26
4 Colin McRae, UK	1993–2002	25
5 Tommi Mäkinen, Finland	1994–2002	24
6 Juhan Kankkunen, Finland	1985–99	23
7 Didier Auriol, France	1988–2001	20
8 Markku Alén, Finland	1975–88	19
9 Hannu Mikkola, Finland	1974–87	18
10 Masimo Biasion, Italy	1986–93	17

* To the end of the 2011 season

▶ *Carlos Sainz*
Spain's Carlos Sainz was World Rally Champion in 1990 and 1992.

TOP 10 SPRINT CUP CAREER MONEY WINNERS*

DRIVER#	YEARS	WINNINGS ($)
1 Jeff Gordon	1992–2011	121,991,611
2 Jimmie Johnson	2001–11	108,576,192
3 Tony Stewart	1999–2011	94,846,560
4 Mark Martin	1981–2011	84,690,128
5 Matt Kenseth	1998–2011	79,325,994
6 Jeff Burton	1993–2011	77,367,756
7 Bobby Labonte	1991–2011	72,650,075
8 Kevin Harvick	2001–11	72,015,671
9 Kurt Busch	2000–11	68,624,703
10 Dale Earnhardt, Jr.	1999–2011	67,628,650

* As of the end of the 2011 Sprint Cup series
# All drivers from the USA

Source: NASCAR

TOP 10 MOST FORMULA ONE GRAND PRIX RACES WITHOUT A WIN*

DRIVER / COUNTRY	YEARS	STARTS
1 Andrea de Cesaris, Italy	1980–94	208
2 Nick Heidfeld, Germany	2000–11	183
3 Martin Brundle, UK	1984–96	158
4 Derek Warwick, UK	1981–93	147
5 Jean-Pierre Jarier, France	1973–83	134
6 Eddie Cheever, USA	1978–89	132
7 Pierluigi Martini, Italy	1985–95	119
8 = Philippe Alliot, France	1984–94	109
= Mika Salo, Finland	1994–2002	109
10 Jos Verstappen, The Netherlands	1994–2003	108

* As of the end of the 2011 season

▲ *Sprinting ahead*
Jimmie Johnson is the only man to win five consecutive NASCAR championships.

◀ *Vettel at Monza*
Sebastian Vettel leading at Monza,
home to the Italian GP 61 times.

TOP 10 COUNTRIES HOSTING THE MOST FORMULA ONE WORLD CHAMPIONSHIP RACES

	COUNTRY	RACE / TIMES STAGED	TOTAL RACES*
1	Italy	Italian GP, 62 San Marino GP, 26 Pescara GP, 1	89
2	Germany	German GP, 58 European GP, 12 Luxembourg GP, 2	72
3	UK	British GP, 62 European GP, 3	65
4	USA	United States GP, 33 Indianapolis 500, 11 United States GP West, 8 Detroit GP, 7 Caesars Palace GP, 2 Dallas GP, 1	62
5	France	French GP, 58 Swiss GP, 1	59
6	Monaco	Monaco GP, 58	58
7	Belgium	Belgian GP, 56	56
8	Spain	Spanish GP, 41 European GP, 6	47
9	Canada	Canadian GP, 42	42
10	Brazil	Brazilian GP, 39	39

* As of the end of the 2011 season

Morocco (1958) and India (2011) are the
only countries to have staged just one GP.

TOP 10 MOST LAPS LED IN THE INDIANAPOLIS 500*

	DRIVER*	YEARS	TOTAL LAPS LED
1	Al Unser	1970–93	644
2	Ralph DePalma	1911–21	612
3	Mario Andretti	1966–93	556
4	A J Foyt	1961–82	555
5	Wilbur Shaw	1932–41	508
6	Emerson Fittipaldi	1985–94	505
7	Parnelli Jones	1961–67	492
8	Bill Vukovich	1952–55	485
9	Bobby Unser	1968–81	440
10	Michael Andretti	1986–2007	431

* Up to and including 2011
\# All drivers from the USA except Fittipaldi (Brazil)

Source: Indianapolis Motor Speedway

TOP 10 MOST INDIANAPOLIS 500 STARTS*

	DRIVER#	YEARS	STARTS
1	A. J. Foyt	1958–92	35
2	Mario Andretti	1965–94	29
3	Al Unser	1965–93	27
4	= Johnny Rutherford	1963–88	24
	= Gordon Johncock	1965–92	24
6	George Snider	1965–87	22
7	Gary Bettenhausen	1968–93	21
8	= Bobby Unser	1963–81	19
	= Al Unser Jr	1983–2007	19
10	= Lloyd Ruby	1960–77	18
	= Roger McCluskey	1961–79	18
	= Tom Sneva	1974–92	18

* Up to and including 2011
\# All drivers from the USA

Source: Indianapolis Motor Speedway

▼ *The big three*
The names Foyt, Unser, and Andretti are
synonymous with Indy car racing.

TOP 10 MEDAL-WINNING COUNTRIES AT THE UCI BMX WORLD CHAMPIONSHIPS*

	COUNTRY	GOLD	SILVER	BRONZE	TOTAL
1	USA	24	22	23	69
2	France	21	27	18	66
3 =	Australia	11	4	7	22
=	The Netherlands	5	7	10	22
5	Argentina	5	8	6	19
6	UK	7	4	6	17
7	Colombia	6	2	2	10
8	New Zealand	3	3	3	9
9	Czech Republic	0	4	4	8
10	Latvia	4	1	1	6

* Based on number of medals won in all events (men and women) 1996–2011

Source: Union Cycliste Internationale

▲ USA BMXers
USA BMX is the world's largest BMX sanctioned organization.

TOP 10 MOST STAGE WINS IN THE TOUR DE FRANCE*

	RIDER / COUNTRY	YEARS	STAGE WINS
1	Eddy Merckx, Belgium	1969–75	34
2	Bernard Hinault, France	1978–86	28
3	André Leducq, France	1927–38	25
4 =	André Darrigade, France	1953–64	22
=	Lance Armstrong, USA	1993–2005	22
6 =	Nicolas Frantz, Luxembourg	1924–29	20
=	Mark Cavendish, UK	2008–11	20
8	François Faber, Luxembourg	1908–14	19
9	Jean Alavoine, France	1909–23	17
10 =	Charles Pelissier, France	1929–35	16
=	René Le Greves, France	1933–39	16
=	Jacques Anquetil, France	1957–64	16

* Individual stage wins, 1903–2011

► Mark Cavendish
Britain's Mark Cavendish won five stages in the 2011 Tour, when he became the first British rider to win the coveted green jersey (maillot vert) for being the winner of the race's points competition.

TOP 10 **MOST INDIVIDUAL WORLD SPEEDWAY TITLES**

	RIDER / COUNTRY	YEARS	WINS*
1 =	Ivan Mauger, New Zealand	1968–70, 1972, 1977, 1979	6
=	Tony Rickardsson, Sweden	1994, 1998–99, 2001–02, 2005	6
3 =	Barry Briggs, New Zealand	1957–58, 1964–66	5
=	Ove Fundin, Sweden	1956, 1960–61, 1963, 1967	5
5	Hans Nielsen, Denmark	1986–87, 1989, 1995	4
6 =	Ole Olsen, Denmark	1971, 1975, 1978	3
=	Erik Gundersen, Denmark	1984–85, 1988	3
=	Nicki Pedersen, Denmark	2003, 2007–08	3
=	Jason Crump, Australia	2004, 2006, 2009	3
10 =	Jack Young, Australia	1951–52	2
=	Freddie Williams, UK	1950, 1953	2
=	Ronnie Moore, New Zealand	1954, 1959	2
=	Peter Craven, UK	1955, 1962	2
=	Bruce Penhall, USA	1981–82	2

* Up to and including 2011

▲ *Crump leads the pack*
Although born in Bristol, England, Jason Crump rides for Australia.

TOP 10 **MOST MOTOR CYCLING GRAND PRIX WORLD TITLES***

	RIDER / COUNTRY	YEARS	MOTOGP/ 500CC	350CC	MOTO2/ 250CC	125CC	50/80CC	TOTAL
1	Giacomo Agostini, Italy	1966–75	8	7	0	0	0	15
2	Angel Nieto, Spain	1969–84	0	0	0	7	6	13
3 =	Carlo Ubbiali, Italy	1951–60	0	0	3	6	0	9
=	Mike Hailwood, UK	1961–67	4	2	3	0	0	9
=	Valentino Rossi, Italy	1997–2009	7	0	1	1	0	9
6 =	John Surtees, UK	1956–60	4	3	0	0	0	7
=	Phil Read, UK	1964–74	2	0	4	1	0	7
8 =	Geoff Duke, UK	1951–55	4	2	0	0	0	6
=	Jim Redman, Southern Rhodesia	1962–65	0	4	2	0	0	6
10 =	Anton Mang, West Germany	1980–87	0	2	3	0	0	5
=	Mick Doohan, Australia	1994–98	5	0	0	0	0	5

* In all solo classes, 1949–2011

The first world championship was held at Wembley, London, in 1936, and was won by Australia's Lionel Van Praag. From 1936 to 1994, the champion was decided after a single night's racing following a series of qualifying events throughout the year. Since 1995 the championship has consisted of a season-long series of Grand Prix events, with the world champion being the rider who accrues the most points.

TOP 10 **MOST MOTOR CYCLING GRAND PRIX RACE WINS***

	RIDER / COUNTRY	YEARS	WINS
1	Giacomo Agostini, Italy	1965–76	122
2	Valentino Rossi, Italy	1996–2010	105
3	Angel Nieto, Spain	1969–85	90
4	Mike Hailwood, UK	1959–67	76
5	Mick Doohan, Australia	1990–98	54
6	Phil Read, UK	1961–75	52
7	Jim Redman, Southern Rhodesia	1961–66	45
8 =	Anton Mang, Germany	1976–88	42
=	Max Biaggi, Italy	1992–2004	42
10	Casey Stoner, Australia	2003–11	40

* Solo classes only; up to and including 2011

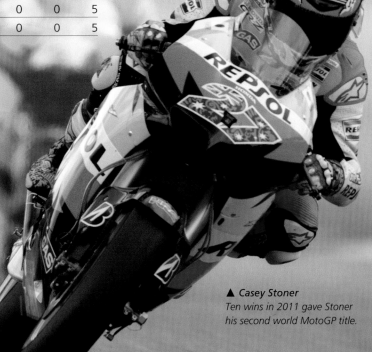

▲ *Casey Stoner*
Ten wins in 2011 gave Stoner his second world MotoGP title.

▲ **Ghostzapper**
In setting a Classic record time in 2004, Ghostzapper provided jockey Javier Castellano with his first Breeders' Cup win and a second win for trainer Robert J. Frankel.

▶ **Royal gold**
Zara Phillips and her father Mark have both won Eventing world gold medals.

THE 10 FASTEST WINNING TIMES OF THE BREEDERS' CUP CLASSIC

	HORSE	YEAR	JOCKEY	TIME MIN:SECS
1	Ghostzapper	2004	Javier Castellano	1:59.02
2	Skip Away	1997	Mike E. Smith	1:59.16
3	Raven's Pass	2008	Frankie Dettori	1:59.27
4	Cat Thief	1999	Pat Day	1:59.52
5	Cigar	1995	Jerry Bailey	1:59.58
6	Pleasantly Perfect	2003	Alex Solis	1:59.88
7 =	A.P. Indy	1992	Ed Delahoussaye	2:00.20
=	Sunday Silence	1989	Chris McCarron	2:00.20
9	Zenyatta	2009	Mike E. Smith	2:00.32
10	Skywalker	1986	Laffit Pincay, Jr.	2:00.40

Source: Breeders' Cup

TOP 10 MEDAL-WINNING COUNTRIES AT THE EVENTING WORLD CHAMPIONSHIPS

	COUNTRY	GOLD	SILVER	BRONZE	TOTAL*
1	UK	9	8	4	21
2	USA	4	2	7	13
3 =	New Zealand	5	2	2	9
=	Germany	2	3	4	9
5	France	1	5	0	6
6 =	Ireland	1	1	1	3
=	Australia	0	1	2	3
8 =	Argentina	1	1	0	2
=	Canada	1	1	0	2
10 =	Finland	0	0	1	1
=	Sweden	0	0	1	1

* Up to and including 2010

TOP 10 **LEADING JOCKEYS IN US TRIPLE CROWN RACES***

	JOCKEY#	YEARS	K	P	B	TOTAL
1	Eddie Arcaro	1938–57	5	6	6	17
2	Bill Shoemaker	1955–86	4	2	5	11
3	= Earl Sande	1921–30	3	1	5	9
	= Bill Hartack	1956–69	5	3	1	9
	= Pat Day	1985–2000	1	5	3	9
5	= Jim McLaughlin	1881–88	1	1	6	8
	= Gary Stevens	1988–2001	3	2	3	8
8	= Charley Kurtsinger	1931–37	2	2	2	6
	= Ron Turcotte, Canada	1965–73	2	2	2	6
	= Angel Cordero Jr., Puerto Rico	1974–85	3	2	1	6
	= Chris McCarron	1986–97	2	2	2	6
	= Jerry Bailey	1991–2003	2	2	2	6
	= Kent Desormeaux	1998–2009	3	2	1	6

* Up to and including 2011 # All jockeys from the USA unless otherwise stated

The Triple Crown races are: Kentucky Derby run at Churchill Downs, Louisville, the Preakness Stakes, run at Pimlico, Maryland and the Belmont Stakes, at Belmont Park, New York.

▼ *Leap to victory*
In 2009, Mon Mome became the fourth French-bred horse to win the Grand National.

TOP 10 **LONGEST PRICED WINNERS OF THE AINTREE GRAND NATIONAL***

	HORSE	YEAR	PRICE
1	= Tipperary Tim	1928	100-1
	= Gregalch	1929	100-1
	= Caughoo	1947	100-1
	= Foinavon	1967	100-1
	= Mon Mome	2009	100-1
6	= Rubio	1908	66-1
	= Russian Hero	1949	66-1
	= Ayala	1963	66-1
9	= Forbra	1932	50-1
	= Sheila's Cottage	1948	50-1
	= Anglo	1966	50-1
	= Last Suspect	1985	50-1

* Up to and including the 2011 race

The shortest priced winner was Poethlyn, at 11-4 in the 1919 Grand National. Poethlyn won the race the previous year when it was held at Gatwick due to World War I, and is uniquely the only horse to win the race at two different courses.

WATER SPORTS

TOP 10 FASTEST TIMES FOR SWIMMING THE ENGLISH CHANNEL

SWIMMER / COUNTRY / DATE	TIME HRS:MINS
1 Petar Stoychev, Bulgaria Aug 24, 2007	6:57.50
2 Christof Wandratsch, Germany Aug 1, 2005	7:03.52
3 Yuriy Kudinov, Russia Aug 24, 2007	7:05.42
4 Rostislav Vitek, Czech Republic Aug 14, 2009	7:16.25
5 Chad Hundaby, USA Sep 27, 1994	7:17.00
6 Christof Wandratsch, Germany Aug 20, 2003	7:20.00
7 Petar Stoychev, Bulgaria Aug 25, 2006	7:21.08
8 David Meca, Spain Aug 29, 2005	7:22.00
9 Yvetta Hlavacova*, Czech Republic Aug 5, 2006	7:25.15
10 Penny Lee Dean, USA Jul 29, 1978	7:40.00

* Fastest woman to swim the Channel

THE 10 LAST YACHT CLUBS TO SUCCESSFULLY DEFEND THE AMERICA'S CUP

YEAR	VENUE / BOAT	DEFENDING CLUB
2007	**Valencia**, Spain Alinghi	Société Nautique de Genève, Switzerland
2000	**Auckland**, New Zealand Black Magic	Royal New Zealand Yacht Squadron
1992	**San Diego**, USA America	San Diego Yacht Club, USA
1988	**San Diego**, USA Stars & Stripes 88	San Diego Yacht Club, USA
1980	**Newport**, Rhode Island, USA Freedom	New York Yacht Club, USA
1977	**Newport**, Rhode Island, USA Courageous	New York Yacht Club, USA
1974	**Newport**, Rhode Island, USA Courageous	New York Yacht Club, USA
1970	**Newport**, Rhode Island, USA Intrepid	New York Yacht Club, USA
1967	**Newport**, Rhode Island, USA Intrepid	New York Yacht Club, USA
1964	**Newport**, Rhode Island, USA Constellation	New York Yacht Club, USA

The first attempt to swim the Channel was made by 24-year-old J. B. Johnson in 1872, but he failed after just over an hour. He inspired Captain Matthew Webb to attempt it in early August 1875 but he too was thwarted. However, on August 25, he arrived in Calais as the first man to swim the Channel, in just under 22 hours.

TOP 10 WORLD AQUATICS CHAMPIONSHIPS WITH THE MOST COMPETITORS

	YEAR	VENUE	COMPETITORS
1	2009	Rome, Italy	2,438
2	2011	Shanghai, China	2,220
3	2007	Melbourne, Australia	2,158
4	2003	Barcelona, Spain	2,015
5	2005	Montreal, Canada	1,784
6	2001	Fukuoka, Japan	1,498
7	1994	Rome, Italy	1,400
8	1998	Perth, Australia	1,371
9	1991	Perth, Australia	1,142
10	1986	Madrid, Spain	1,119

Source: FINA

◄ Rome, 2009
A remarkable 43 world records were broken at the 2009 championships.

CHINA LED THE 2011 AQUATICS MEDAL TABLE, WITH A TOTAL OF 36—EXACTLY TWICE AS MANY AS THIRD-PLACED RUSSIA.

TOP 10 MOST WORLD AQUATICS CHAMPIONSHIP GOLD MEDALS*

	SWIMMER / COUNTRY	YEARS	IND.	RELAY	TOTAL
1	Michael Phelps, USA	2001–11	15	11	26
2	Ryan Lochte, USA	2005–11	7	5	12
3	Ian Thorpe, Australia	1998–2003	6	5	11
4 =	Grant Hackett, Australia	1998–2005	7	3	10
=	Aaron Peirsol, USA	2001–09	7	3	10
6 =	Kornelia Ender, East Germany	1973–75	4	4	8
=	Libby Trickett (née Lenton), Australia	2005–07	4	4	8
8 =	Jim Montgomery, USA	1973–78	2	5	7
=	Kristin Otto, East Germany	1982–86	3	4	7
=	Jenny Thompson, USA	1991–2003	3	4	7
=	Michael Klim, Australia	1998–2007	2	5	7
=	Leisel Jones, Australia	2001–07	4	3	7
=	Katie Hoff, USA	2005–11	4	3	7

* In individual and relay long course events up to and including 2011

▲ Yang Sun
Yang broke swimming's longest-standing record at the 2011 championships in Shanghai.

TOP 10 FASTEST TIMES FOR THE 1500-METRES FREESTYLE*

	SWIMMER / COUNTRY	VENUE	YEAR / CHAMPIONSHIP	TIME MINS:SECS
1	Yang Sun, China	Shanghai, China	2011 World Championships	14:34.14
2	Grant Hackett, Australia	Fukuoka, Japan	2001 World Championships	14:34.56
3	Yang Sun, China	Guangzhou, China	2010 Asian Games	14:35.43
4	Oussama Mellouli, Tunisia	Rome, Italy	2009 World Championships	14:37.28
5	Oussama Mellouli, Tunisia	Pescara, Italy	2009 Mediterranean Games	14:38.01
6	Grant Hackett, Australia	Beijing, China	2008 Olympic Games	14:38.91
7	Ryan Cochrane, Canada	Beijing, China	2008 Olympic Games	14:40.84
8	Yuriy Prilukov, Russia	Beijing, China	2008 Olympic Games	14:41.13
9	Ryan Cochrane, Canada	Rome Italy	2009 World Championships	14:41.37
10	Grant Hackett, Australia	Montreal, Canada	2005 World Championships	14:42.58

* As of January 1, 2012
Source: FINA

Brian Goodell (USA) almost broke the 15-minute barrier for the 1500-m freestyle at the 1976 Olympics. Four years later, Vladimir Salnikov (USSR) did break swimming's equivalent of the four-minute mile.

► Michelle Kwan
Michelle Kwan's total of five World and Olympic titles puts her level with two great American male skaters: Hayes Alan Jenkins and Scott Hamilton.

TOP 10 MOST WOMEN'S OLYMPIC AND WORLD FIGURE-SKATING TITLES*

	SKATER / COUNTRY	YEARS	O	WC	TOTAL
1	Sonja Henie, Norway	1927–36	3	10	13
2	= Herma Szabo, Austria	1922–26	1	5	6
	= Carol Heiss, USA	1956–60	1	5	6
	= Katarina Witt, East Germany	1984–88	2	4	6
5	Michelle Kwan, USA	1996–2003	0	5	5
6	= Lily Kronberger, Hungary	1908–11	0	4	4
	= Sjoukje Dijkstra, The Netherlands	1962–64	1	3	4
	= Peggy Fleming, USA	1966–68	1	3	4
9	= Opika von Méray Horváth, Hungary	1912–14	0	3	3
	= Barbara Ann Scott, Canada	1947–48	1	2	3
	= Anett Pötzsch, East Germany	1978-80	1	2	3
	= Madge Syers, UK	1907–08	1	2	3
	= Kristi Yamaguchi, USA	1991–92	1	2	3
	= Tenley Albright, USA	1953–56	1	2	3

* Individual event, up to and including 2012

► Curling for Canada
Canada is by far the world's leading men's and women's curling nation.

TOP 10 MOST ALPINE SKIING WORLD CUP RACE WINS IN A SINGLE DISCIPLINE*

	SKIER / COUNTRY	DISCIPLINE	YEARS	WINS
1	Ingemar Stenmark, Sweden	Men's giant slalom	1973–89	46
2	Ingemar Stenmark, Sweden	Men's slalom	1973–89	40
3	Annemarie Moser-Pröll, Austria	Women's downhill	1969–80	36
4	Alberto Tomba, Italy	Men's slalom	1986–98	35
5	Vreni Schneider, Switzerland	Women's slalom	1984–95	34
6	Marlies Schild, Austria	Women's slalom	2001–12	33
7	Lindsey Vonn, USA	Women's downhill	2001–12	26
8	Franz Klammer, Austria	Men's downhill	1972–85	25
9	= Hermann Maier, Austria	Men's Super G	1996–2009	24
	= Renate Götschl, Austria	Women's downhill	1993–2009	24

* To the end of the 2011–12 season

Source: FIS

TOP 10 NATIONS IN THE CURLING WORLD CHAMPIONSHIPS*

	COUNTRY	GOLD	SILVER	BRONZE	TOTAL
1	Canada	48	14	14	76
2	Scotland	6	23	12	41
3	Sweden	13	12	14	39
4	Norway	5	8	16	29
5	Switzerland	8	8	12	28
6	USA	5	10	12	27
7	Germany	2	8	8	18
8	Denmark	1	2	7	10
9	China	1	1	2	4
10	Finland	0	1	2	3

* Based on total medals won in men, women and mixed championships up to 2011

TOP 10 OLYMPIC SNOWBOARDING COUNTRIES

	COUNTRY	GOLD	SILVER	BRONZE	TOTAL
1	USA	7	5	7	19
2	Switzerland	5	1	3	9
3	France	2	3	3	8
4	Canada	3	1	1	5
5	Austria	0	1	3	4
6	=Germany	1	2	0	3
	=Norway	0	2	1	3
8	=Finland	0	1	1	2
	=Italy	0	1	1	2
10	=Australia	1	0	0	1
	=The Netherlands	1	0	0	1
	=Russia	0	1	0	1
	=Slovakia	0	1	0	1
	=Sweden	0	1	0	1

Source: FIS

▲ *Gold for Germany*
Nicola Thost won Germany's only snowboarding Olympic gold in 1998.

TOP 10 COUNTRIES IN THE NORDIC SKIING WORLD CHAMPIONSHIPS*

	COUNTRY	GOLD	SILVER	BRONZE	TOTAL
1	Norway	107	89	89	285
2	Finland	62	69	62	193
3	Sweden	41	33	40	114
4	USSR	36	32	24	92
5	Germany#	19	33	20	72
6	Russia	21	22	25	68
7	Austria	20	14	22	56
8	Italy	10	19	22	51
9	East Germany	12	15	11	38
10	Czechoslovakia	7	12	11	30

* Up to and including the 2011 World Championships in Oslo
# Including West Germany

The first Nordic World Championships were part of the 1924 Winter Olympics in Chamonix, and the first separate Championships were held the following year at Johannisbad, Czechoslovakia. Originally for men only, women first competed at Falun, Sweden in 1954. The Championships are now held every two years.

► *Norway*
Norway has dominated Nordic skiing at both the World Championships and the Olympic Games.

	ATHLETE[#]	SPORT	YEARS	GOLDS
1	Shaun White	Snowboarding	2003–12	12
2 =	Tanner Hall	Skiing	2001–08	7
=	Lindsey Jacobellis[†]	Snowboarding	2003–11	7
=	Nate Holland	Snowboarding	2006–12	7
5 =	Blair Morgan	Snowmobiling	2001–06	5
=	Shaun Palmer	Snowboarding, skiing, snow mountain-bike racing	1997–2000	5
=	Tara Dakides	Snowboarding	1999–2002	5
8 =	Aleisha Cline[†]	Skiing	1999–2003	4
=	Janna Meyen[†]	Snowboarding	2003–06	4
=	Tucker Hibbert	Snowmobiling Snowboarding	2000–11	4
=	Sarah Burke	Skiing	2007–11	4
=	Gretchen Bleiler	Snowboarding	2003–10	4
=	Levi Lavalle	Snowmobiling	2004–10	4

* Up to and including Winter X Games XVI in 2012
# All competitors from the USA except Morgan, Burke, and Cline, who are from Canada
† Female; all others male

▲ **Blair Morgan**
Canadian-born Morgan is the Winter X Games leading Snowmobile racer.

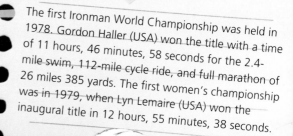

The first Ironman World Championship was held in 1978. Gordon Haller (USA) won the title with a time of 11 hours, 46 minutes, 58 seconds for the 2.4-mile swim, 112-mile cycle ride, and full marathon of 26 miles 385 yards. The first women's championship was in 1979, when Lyn Lemaire (USA) won the inaugural title in 12 hours, 55 minutes, 38 seconds.

TOP 10 **FASTEST WINNING TIMES OF THE IRONMAN WORLD CHAMPIONSHIP**

	ATHLETE / COUNTRY	YEAR	TIME HRS:MINS:SECS
1	Craig Alexander, Australia	2011	8:03:56
2	Luc Van Lierde, Belgium	1996	8:04:08
3	Mark Allen, USA	1993	8:07:45
4	Mark Allen, USA	1992	8:09:08
5	Mark Allen, USA	1989	8:09:15
6	Chris McCormack, Australia	2010	8:10:37
7	Normann Stadler, Germany	2006	8:11:56
8	Faris Al-Sultan, Germany	2005	8:14:17
9	Chris McCormack, Australia	2007	8:15:34
10	Luc Van Lierde, Belgium	1999	8:17:17

Source: Ironman World Championship

▶ **Craig Alexander**
Alexander's record time for the Ironman World Championship was at the age of 38.

MOST WINS IN THE IRONMAN WORLD CHAMPIONSHIP

Zimbabwe-born Paula Newby-Fraser won the Ironman World Championship a record eight times, two more than the leading male triathletes, Dave Scott and Mark Allen. Between 1985 and 1996 Newby-Fisher competed in 12 championships, adding one silver and two bronze medals to her eight golds. The lowest she finished was 4th in 1995.

TOP 10 **LEADING GOLD MEDALISTS AT THE SUMMER X GAMES***

	ATHLETE / COUNTRY / SPORT	YEARS	GOLDS
1	Dave Mirra, USA, BMX	1996–2005	13
2	Travis Pastrana, USA, Moto X/rally car racing	1999–2010	10
3	Tony Hawk, USA, Skateboarding	1995–2003	9
4	Andy Macdonald, USA, Skateboarding	1996–2002	8
5 =	Fabiola da Silva#, Brazil, Inline skating	1996–2007	7
=	Jamie Bestwick, England, BMX	2000–11	7
=	Pierre-Luc Gagnon, Canada, Skateboarding	2002–10	7
8 =	Bucky Lasek, USA, Skateboarding	1999–2006	6
=	Bob Burnquist, Brazil, Skateboarding	2001–11	6
10	Biker Sherlock, USA, Street luge	1996–98	5

* Up to and including X Games XVII in 2011
\# Female; all others male

▲ *Riding high*
X Games regular Travis Pastrana entered the world of NASCAR in 2011.

The first ESPN Extreme Games (now X Games) for "alternative" sports were held in June/July 1995. The Games are held every year, and since 1997 there has also been an annual Winter X Games. The sports contested at X Games XVII in 2011 were: BMX, Moto X, skateboarding, surfing, and rallying.

THE 10 **LATEST WINNERS OF THE WORLD'S STRONGEST MAN TITLE**

YEAR	CHAMPION / COUNTRY
2011	Brian Shaw, USA
2010	Zydrunas Savickas, Lithuania
2009	Zydrunas Savickas, Lithuania
2008	Mariusz Pudzianowski, Poland
2007	Mariusz Pudzianowski, Poland
2006	Phil Pfister, USA
2005	Mariusz Pudzianowski, Poland
2004	Vasyl Virastyuk, Ukraine
2003	Mariusz Pudzianowski, Poland
2002	Mariusz Pudzianowski, Poland

▶ *Pulling power*
Phil Pfister—the first US winner of the World's Strongest Man title in 24 years.

TOP 10 MOST VALUABLE SPORTS TEAMS

	TEAM*	SPORT	VALUE ($ BILLION)#
1	Manchester United, England	Soccer	1.86
2	Dallas Cowboys	Football	1.81
3	New York Yankees	Baseball	1.70
4	Washington Redskins	Football	1.55
5	Real Madrid, Spain	Soccer	1.45
6	New England Patriots	Football	1.37
7	Arsenal, England	Soccer	1.19
8	New York Giants	Football	1.18
9	Houston Texans	Football	1.17
10	New York Jets	Football	1.14

Source: Forbes Magazine

* All US unless otherwise stated
\# Based on valuation figures produced by Forbes Magazine in July 2011.

Top teams
Above: The Cowboys have an annual revenue of nearly $270 billion.
Left: Manchester United is now owned by the Glazer family.

TOP 10 MAJOR SPORTING LEAGUES WITH THE HIGHEST AVERAGE ATTENDANCES*

	LEAGUE / COUNTRY	SPORT	AVERAGE ATTENDANCE
1	National Football League USA	Football	66,953
2	Bundesliga Germany	Soccer	46,290
3	Australian Football League Australia	Australia rules football	36,428
4	Premier League England and Wales	Soccer	35,282
5	Major League Baseball USA	Baseball	30,352
6	Canadian Football League Canada	Canadian football	29,785
7	La Liga Spain	Soccer	29,128
8	Primera División de Mexico Mexico	Soccer	25,837
9	Nippon Professional Baseball League Japan	Baseball	25,626
10	Serie A Italy	Soccer	24,031

* As of the end of the last completed season

TOP 10 HIGHEST-EARNING SPORTSMEN

	SPORTSMAN / COUNTRY / SPORT	EARNINGS ($)
1	Tiger Woods USA, Golf	75,000,000
2	Kobe Bryant USA, Basketball	53,000,000
3	LeBron James Basketball	48,000,000
4	Roger Federer Switzerland, Tennis	47,000,000
5	Phil Mickelson USA, Golf	46,500,000
6	David Beckham UK, Soccer	40,000,000
7	Cristiano Ronaldo Portugal, Soccer	38,000,000
8	Alex Rodriguez USA, Baseball	35,000,000
9	Michael Schumacher Germany, Motor racing	34,000,000
10	Lionel Messi Argentina, Soccer	32,300,000

Source: Forbes Magazine

▲ Luke Donald
In 2011 Donald uniquely topped the money lists in the USA and Europe.

TOP 10 MONEY-WINNING MALE TENNIS PLAYERS AND GOLFERS, 2011*

	TENNIS PLAYER / COUNTRY	WINNINGS ($)	GOLFER / COUNTRY	WINNINGS ($)
1	Novak Djokovic, Serbia	12,619,803	Luke Donald, UK	8,905,258
2	Rafa Nadal, Spain	7,668,214	Webb Simpson, USA	6,335,434
3	Roger Federer, Switzerland	6,369,596	Nick Watney, USA	5,390,052
4	Andy Murray, UK	5,180,091	K. J. Choi, South Korea	4,632,647
5	Jo-Wilfried Tsonga, France	3,173,969	Rory McIlroy, UK	4,492,827
6	David Feffer, Spain	3,113,904	Dustin Johnson, USA	4,466,559
7	Tomas Berdych, Czech Republic	2,576,813	Matt Kuchar, USA	4,311,843
8	Mardy Fish, USA	1,882,091	Bill Haas, USA	4,133,535
9	Janko Tipsarevic, Serbia	1,692,919	Jason Day, Australia	4,038,699
10	Nicolas Almagro, Spain	1,571,007	Steve Stricker, USA	3,986,663

Source: ATP and PGA Tour

▲ Novak Djokovic
In 2011 Djokovic won three Grand Slam titles—Australian, US, and Wimbledon.

Tennis players earnings are based on worldwide winnings on the 2011 ATP Tour (men) and 2011 WTA Tour (women) in both singles and doubles. Golfers' earnings are based on the PGA (men) and LPGA (women) Worldwide Money Lists for 2011.

HIGHEST-EARNING SPORTSWOMAN MARIA SHARAPOVA'S CAREER EARNINGS ARE ONE THIRD OF TIGER WOODS'.

TOP 10 MONEY-WINNING FEMALE TENNIS PLAYERS AND GOLFERS, 2011*

	TENNIS PLAYER / COUNTRY	WINNINGS ($)	GOLFER / COUNTRY	WINNINGS ($)
1	Petra Kvitová, Czech Republic	5,145,943	Yani Tseng, Taiwan	2,921,713
2	Caroline Wozniacki, Denmark	4,065,581	Cristie Kerr, USA	1,470,979
3	Victoria Azarenka, Belarus	3,771,032	Na Yeon Choi, South Korea	1,357,382
4	Li Na, China	3,709,139	Stacy Lewis, USA	1,356,211
5	Samantha Stosur, Australia	3,476,153	Suzann Pettersen, Norway	1,322,770
6	Maria Sharapova, Russia	2,899,148	Brittany Lincicome, USA	1,154,234
7	Vera Zvonareva, Russia	2,673,018	Angela Stanford, USA	1,017,196
8	Agnieszka Radwanska, Poland	2,456,568	Ai Miyazato, Japan	1,007,633
9	Kim Clijsters, Belgium	2,325,741	Paula Creamer, USA	926,338
10	Serena Williams, USA	1,978,930	Amy Yang, South Korea	912,160

Sources: WTA and LPGA

◄ Petra Kvitová
Kvitová won the 2011 WTA Tour Championship at the first attempt.

FURTHER INFORMATION

THE UNIVERSE & THE EARTH

Caves
caverbob.com
Lists of long and deep caves

Disasters
emdat.be
Emergency Events Database covering major disasters since 1900

Encyclopedia Astronautica
astronautix.com
Spaceflight news and reference

Islands
worldislandinfo.com
Information on the world's islands

Mountains
peaklist.org
Lists of the world's tallest mountains

NASA
nasa.gov
The main website for the US space agency

Oceans
oceansatlas.org
The UN's resource on oceanographic issues

Planets
nineplanets.org
A multimedia tour of the Solar System

Rivers
rev.net/~aloe/river
The River Systems of the World website

Space exploration
spacefacts.de
Manned spaceflight data

LIFE ON EARTH

Animals
animaldiversity.ummz.umich.edu
A wealth of animal data

Birds
avibase.bsc-eoc.org
A database on the world's birds

Conservation
iucn.org
The leading nature conservation site

Endangered
cites.org
Lists of endangered species of flora and fauna

Extinct
nhm.ac.uk/nature-online/life/dinosaurs-other-extinct-creatures
Dinosaurs and other extinct animals

Fish
fishbase.org
Global information on fish

Food and Agriculture Organization
fao.org
Statistics from the UN's FAO website

Forests
fao.org/forestry
The FAO's forestry website

Insects
entnemdept.ufl.edu/walker/ufbir
The University of Florida Book of Insect Records

Sharks
flmnh.ufl.edu/fish/sharks
The Florida Museum of Natural History's shark attack files

THE HUMAN WORLD

FBI
fbi.gov
Information and links on crime in the USA

Health
cdc.gov/nchs
Information and links on health for US citizens

Leaders
terra.es/personal2/monolith
Facts about world leaders since 1945

Military
globalfirepower.com
World military statistics and rankings

Names
ssa.gov/OACT/babynames
Most common names since 1879 from the Social Security Administration

Nobel Prizes
nobelprize.org
The official website of the Nobel Foundation

Religion
worldchristiandatabase.org
World religions data (subscription required)

Rulers
rulers.org
A database of the world's rulers and political leaders

Supercentenarians
grg.org/calment.html
A world listing of those who have reached 110 or older

World Health Organization
who.int/en
World health information and advice

TOWN & COUNTRY

Bridges and tunnels
en.structurae.de
Facts and figures on the world's buildings, tunnels, and other structures

Bridges (highest)
highestbridges.com
Detailed facts and stats on the world's highest bridges

Buildings
emporis.com/en
The Emporis database of high-rise and other buildings

Country and city populations
citypopulation.de
A searchable guide to the world's countries and major cities

Country data
cia.gov/library/publications/the-world-factbook
The CIA's acclaimed *World Factbook*

Country populations
un.org/esa/population/unpop
The UN's worldwide data on population issues

Development
worldbank.org
Development and other statistics from around the world

Population
census.gov/ipc
International population statistics

Skyscrapers
skyscraperpage.com
Data and images of the world's skyscrapers

Tunnels
lotsberg.net
A database of the longest rail, road, and canal tunnels

CULTURE & LEARNING

Art
artnet.com
World art info, with price database available to subscribers

The Art Newspaper
theartnewspaper.com
News and views on the art world

Education
nces.ed.gov
The home of federal education data

Languages
ethnologue.com
Online reference work on the world's 6,909 living languages

Libraries
ala.org
US library information and book awards from the American Library Association

The Library of Congress
loc.gov
The gateway to one of the world's greatest collections of words and pictures

Newspapers
wan-press.org
The World Association of Newspapers' website

The New York Public Library
nypl.org
One of the country's foremost libraries, with an online catalog

The Pulitzer Prize
pulitzer.org
A searchable guide to the prestigious US literary prize

UNESCO
unesco.org
Comparative international statistics on education and culture

MUSIC

All Music Guide
allmusic.com
A comprehensive guide to all genres of music

American Society of Composers, Authors, and Publishers
ascap.com
ASCAP songwriter and other awards

Billboard
billboard.com
US music news and charts data

Classical music
classicalusa.com
An online guide to classical music in the USA

Country Music Hall of Fame
countrymusichalloffame.com
The history of and information about country music

Grammy Awards
naras.org
The official site for the famous US music awards

MTV
mtv.com
The online site for the TV music channel

Recording Industry of America
riaa.org
Searchable data on gold and platinum disk award winners

Rock and Roll Hall of Fame
www.rockhall.com
The museum of the history of rock

Rolling Stone
rollingstone.com
Features on popular music since 1967

ENTERTAINMENT

Academy Awards
oscars.org
The official "Oscars" website

E! Online
eonline.com
Celebrity and entertainment news and gossip

Emmy Awards
emmyonline.org
Emmy TV awards from the National Television Academy site

Hollywood
hollywood.com
A US cinema site with details on all the new releases

Internet Broadway Database
ibdb.com
Broadway theater information

Internet Movie Database
The best of the publicly accessible movie websites; IMDbPro is available to subscribers

Internet Theatre Database
theatredb.com
A Broadway-focused searchable stage site

Tony Awards
tonyawards.com
Official website of the American Theatre Wing's Tonys

Variety
variety.com
Extensive entertainment information (extra features available to subscribers)

Yahoo! Movies
movies.yahoo.com
Charts plus features and links to the latest movie releases

THE COMMERCIAL WORLD

The Economist
economist.com
Global economic and political news

Energy
eia.doe.gov
Official US energy statistics

Environment
epi.yale.edu
The latest Environmental Performance Index rankings

Internet
internetworldstats.com
Internet World Stats

Organization for Economic Co-operation and Development
oecd.org
World economic and social statistics

Rich lists
forbes.com
Forbes magazine's celebrated lists of the world's wealthiest people

Telecommunications
itu.int
Worldwide telecommunications statistics

Travel industry
ustravel.org
Information on US travel

The World Bank
worldbank.org
World development, trade and labor statistics, now freely accessible

World Tourism Organization
world-tourism.org
The world's principal travel and tourism organization

ON THE MOVE

Aircraft crashes
baaa-acro.com
The Aircraft Crashes Record Office database

Airlines
airfleets.net
Statistics on the world's airlines and aircraft

Airports
airports.org
Airports Council International statistics on the world's airports

Air safety
aviation-safety.net
Data on air safety and accidents

Air speed records
fai.org/records
The website of the official air speed record governing body

Car manufacture
oica.net
The International Organization of Motor Vehicle Manufacturers' website

Metros
metrobits.org
An exploration of the world's subway systems

Rail
uic.org
World rail statistics

Railways
railwaygazette.com
The world's railway business in depth from *Railway Gazette International*

Shipwrecks
shipwreckregistry.com
A huge database of the world's wrecked and lost ships

SPORT

Baseball
mlb.com
The official website of Major League Baseball

Basketball
nba.com
The official website of the NBA

Football
nfl.com
The official website of the NFL

Golf
pgatour.com
The Professional Golfers' Association Tour

Hockey
nhl.com
The official website of the NHL

Olympics
olympic.org
The official Olympics website

Skiing
fis-ski.com
Fédèration Internationale de Ski, the world governing body of skiing and snowboarding

Sports Illustrated
sportsillustrated.cnn.com
Sports Illustrated's comprehensive coverage of all major sports

Tennis
lta.org.uk
The official site of the British Lawn Tennis Association

Track and field
iaaf.org
The world governing body of athletics

INDEX

PICTURE CREDITS

t top b bottom l left c centre r right bg background

© **Activision:** 162tl Activision Blizzard.

akg-images: 73br Album/Tribeca Productions; 105br North Wind Picture Archives; 153b Album/ Summit Entertainment; 157tl Album/MGM.

Alamy: 47b Stefan Sollfors; 155bl & 163tr AF Archive; 164br Oleksiy Maksymenko Photography; 165cl Moviestore Collection; 191br John Warburton-Lee.

© **AlpTransit Gotthard Ltd:** 94b.

© **Apple:** 164tl & r.

© **Automobili Lamborghini:** 186–187 main.

© **Blizzard Entertainment:** 163tl.

The Bridgeman Art Library: 74tl Imperial War Museum/George Horace Davis; 97 inset Christie's/ Private Collection/© C.S. Lewis 1950. Illustrations by Pauline Baynes © C S Lewis Ptd Ltd. Illustrations reprinted by permission of C S Lewis & HarperCollins Publishers Ltd; 110tl Christie's Images/Private Collection; 111tl Christie's Images/Private Collection; 195t Guildhall Library, City of London.

Corbis: 8 inset epa/Matiullah Achakzai; 10tl Underwood & Underwood; 10bc Transtock/Bruce Benedict; 11t Science Faction/Louie Psihoyos; 14t Ocean; 15bl Bettmann; 16cl National Geographic Society; 18tl Sakis Papadopoulos; 18b Jean-Baptiste Rabouan; 19c Photolibrary; 20b Science Faction/ Fred Hirschmann; 21b amanaimages/Walter Bibikow; 22t Alison Wright; 23t Atlantide Phototravel/Guido Cozzi; 23b Robert Harding World Imagery/Gavin Hellier; 24tl Kazuyoshi Nomachi; 25tr Image Plan; 26t Science Faction/Ed Darack; 26b zrimages/Anne Ryan; 27t Richard T Nowtiz; 27b Muench; 28–29 main Paul Souders; 28tr Ted Horowitz; 29ct Dean Conger; 29b Imaginechina; 30 Xinhua Press/Gong Zhihong; 31b epa/Andrew Brownbill; 37t Science Faction/ Steven Kazlowski; 38bl Paul Souders; 39tr Winfried Wisniewski; 40–41c Specialist Stock/Masa Ushioda; 42tl Robert Harding World Imagery/James Hager; 42tr All Canada Photos/Glenn Bartley; 43t Momatiuk – Eastcott; 45br Visuals Unlimited/Dave Watts; 48r Joe McDonald; 48b, 49br & 52tl Paul Souders; 53tr Altaf Qadri; 54–55bg Thomas Kitchin & Victoria Hurst; 55t Loop Images/Jon Bower; 56 inset Bettmann/Walt Sisco; 57 inset Bettmann; 58tr Visuals Unlimited; 59tl Science Photo Library/Photo Quest; 59tc Science Photo Library/Roger Harris; 60b epa; 61tr National Geographic Society/Ira Block; 61c George Steinmetz; 62tl Ruggero Vanni; 62c epa/Murty Colin; 63c epa/ STR; 63b epa/Narong Sangnak; 64b Paul Souders; 65t epa/Dai Kurokawa; 65b Reuters/Juan Carlos Ulate; 66tl The Gallery Collection; 66br Hulton-Deutsch; 67tl Aurora/Stefan Chow; 67tr Reuters/HO; 68t epa/ Stephane Pilick; 68b Reuters/Thomas Peter; 69br Reuters/Bryan Snyder; 70t Reuters/China Daily; 72br epa/Mike Nelson; 73tl Sygma/Mike Stewart; 73 bl & bc Bettmann; 74b Hulton-Deutsch; 75t Stocktrek; 75c Bettmann; 75b Corbis/Hulton-Deutsch; 76–77bg Corbis; 76 top left Corbis/Xinhua Press/Liu Yinghua; 76tr CNP/US Navy; 76b Sygma/Jason Bleibtreu; 77t; 78t Demotix/Bernard A; 78t inset Amit Bhargava;

79t Brooks Kraft; 80cl Eurasia/Steven Vidler; 81t Rudy Sulgan; 81bl MG1408; 81br Demotix/Scott Larson; 82 inset Jon Hicks; 84br SOPA/Maurizio Rellini; 84–85tc Kazuyoshi Nomachi; 85tr Dennis Degnan; 85b Charlie Munsey; 86t Bettmann; 86b B.S.P.I; 87t Gavriel Jecan; 87b Xinhua Press/photomall; 89t JAI/ Alan Copson; 90–91bg Micha Pawlitzki; 90b Jon Hicks; 90t Imaginechina; 90b Ted Soqui; 92t Blaine Harrington III; 93t George Tiedmann; 93br Tibor Bognar; 94t Xinhua Press/Liu Jiling; 94c Tim McGuire; 95t amanaimages/GYRO Photography; 95t Khaled Elfiqi; 98br Patrick Ward; 99tc Monalyn Gracia; 99b Imagine China; 100b Earl & Nazima Kowall; 101t Xinhua Press/Ren Zhenglai; 101b Jane Hahn; 102t Blue Lantern Studio; 103t Jean-Pierre Lescourret; 103c Philippe Renault; 104tr Rune Hellestad; 104bl Bettman; 104br jirkacafa; 105tr Blue Lantern Studio; 107t Sygma/Bernard Annebicque; 108t; 108b Simard; 109t epa/Peter Kneffel; 113t Seth Joel; 113cl Reuters/ Peter Morgan; 114 inset David Lefranc; 116l Retna/ Brian Dowling; 116b Rune Hellestad; 117br People Avenue/Stephane Cardinale; 118t epa/Hans Klaus Techt; 118br Wally McNamee; 119t Chad Batka; 119b John A. Angelillo; 120tr In Pictures/Andy Aitchison; 121tl epa/Lea Meilandt Mathiesen; 121tr Retna/Gerry Maceda; 122tr Neal Preston; 122bl Reuters/Christian Charisius; 123tl Splash News; 123br Reuters/Mario Anzuoni; 124t Rune Hellestad; 124b Reuters/Lucas Jackson; 125t Rune Hellestad; 126tl Retna/Scott D. Smith; 126br Retna/Rob Grabowski; 127t Reuters/ Mike Blake; 127b Amy Harris; 128bl ZUMA Press/K C Alfred; 129b Reuters/Kieran Doherty; 131t Retna/ Rob Grabowski; 132br Rune Hellestad; 132t Retna/ Samantha Shrader; 132c Reuters/Mike Blake; 135c Minneapolis Star Tribune/Tom Wallace; 136bl Reuters/ CHINA NEWSPHOTO; 136br & 137tr Robbie Jack; 158tr Sunset Boulevard; 158bc Mike Blake; 160tl Radius Images; 166–167 main Reuters/Phil McCarten; 167 inset top Monique Jaques; 167 inset bottom Lynn Goldsmith; 168t Jay Fram; 170tl Xinhua Press/ Qi Heng; 171t epa/Peter Foley; 172tl Bettmann; 173tl epa/Sergei Ilnitsky; 173tr Retna/David Atlas; 175t epa/Stringer; 176tl Robert van der Hilst; 177b epa/Andreas Gebert; 178b dpa; 180t Ocean; 180cl Atlantide Phototravel; 180cr dpa/euroluftbild.de; 180b Fernando Alda; 182tl epa/Tugela Ridley; 183cb Douglas Peebles; 185tl Rune Hellestad; 185c People Avenue/Stephane Cardinale; 185br CNP/Ron Sachs; 186 inset Kim Sayer; 188cl Car Culture; 188–189t Neil Rabinowitz; 189b Imagine China; 190tl George Steinmetz; 191t & 193b ImagineChina; 194tr epa/ Divyakant Solanki; 194b Richard T Nowitz; 195b Paul Souders; 196tl Gideon Mendel; 197t Yang Liu; 198br Heritage Images/Ann Ronan Picture Library; 199tc; 199tr Bettmann; 199bl Science Faction/digital ve; 199bc Museum of Flight; 202–203 main Tony Roberts; 203 inset left Reuters/Mike Blake; 204t Reuters/© London 2012; 205b NewSport/Troy Wayrynen; 206tl Dave & Les Jacobs; 207tr Sampics; 207bl Leo Mason Photos; 207br Paul Panayiotou; 208cr Bettmann; 209tr Bettmann; 211t George Tiedemann; 214tl Bettmann; 214b Icon Sports Media Inc.; 215t Reuters/ Nicky Loh; 216tr epa/John G. Mabanglo; 217t Icon Sports Media Inc.; 218b; 220b Reuters/Shaun Best; 221cl Bettmann; 222tl AMA/Matthew Ashton; 223t dpa/Federica Gambarini; 223b Neil Marchand; 224b Icon SMI/Cliff Welch; 225t apa/Paul Buck; 226t Offside Sports Photography/David Wilkinson; 228t epa/Everett Kennedy Brown; 229bl Icon SMI/Cynthia

Lum; 214tl Bettmann; 214b Icon Sports Media Inc.; 215t Reuters/Nicky Loh; 216tr epa/John G Mabanglo; 217t Icon Sports Media Inc.; 218b; 220b Reuters/ Shaun Best; 221cl Bettmann; 222tl AMA/Matthew Ashton; 223t dpa/Federica Gambarini; 223b Neil Marchand; 224b Icon SMI/Cliff Welch; 225t apa/ Paul Buck; 226t Offside Sports Photography/David Wilkinson; 228t epa/Everett Kennedy Brown; 229bl Icon SMI/Cynthia Lum; 230 Reuters/Tim Shaffer; 235t epa/Mikael Fritzon; 236tl Reuters/Jeff Mitchell; 239t Tim Clayton; 239c Xinhua Press/Fan Jun; 240tl Duomo/Chris Trotman; 240tr Reuters/Lee Jae-Won; 241tl epa/Franco Debernardi; 241b epa/Fehim Demir; 242b epa/Bruce Omori;244t Icon SMI/Cliff Welch; 244c epa/Kerim Okten; 245tl epa/Ali Haider; 245tr epa/Joe Castro; 245bl Martin Philbey.

Dreamstime: 22b Owasia; 52tr Sutprattana; 134–135bg Drx; 142br Sashkinw; 144t & 145r Somakram; 148–149bg kroty; 150–151bg Philcold; 152–153bg giantkiwi; 152–153 insets Leonardo25; 156–157bg Beawolf78; 164bl Jbk_photography; 180br Cyclops53; 212–213bg Cameo; 227br Leighleo.

© **DreamWorks II Distribution Co., LLC. All Rights Reserved:** 142bl.

© **Electronic Arts Inc.:**162tr © Lucas Arts/BioWare/ Electronic Arts Inc. Star Wars™: The Old Republic™; 163bl & br.

ESA:15t Halley's Multicolor Camera Telescope/Giotto Project; 17t.

FBI: 72tcr; 72tr; 72bl; 73cl.

FLPA: 41tl Steve Trewhella.

Fotolia: 10bg Kasia Biel; 10t EtiAmmos; 11b Roman Krochuk; 12c Nicemonkey; 15br ricknoll; 18bg vrihu; 18l lunamarina; 18c Vanessa; 20tr Kristina Afanasyeva; 21bg chasingmoments; 22–23bg Dhoxax; 23l Styleuneed; 24–25bg Jean-Jacques Cordier; 24–25b ReinhardT; 26–27bg Cosmity; 28tbg Yuriy Kulik; 34–35bg Les Cunliffe; 34–35b Fotolia/Decom; 36cl Richard Carey; 36c nito; 36cr Eric Isselée; 36bl Ioannis Pantzi; 36br Poles; 37cl Neo Edmund; 37c Al Mueller; 37r Eric Isselée; 37bl felinda; 38–39bg forcdan; 38br Duncan Noakes; 39tc Alex Kalmbach; 42–43bg galam; 43b outdoorsman; 43br Eric Isselée; 44–45bg Wong Sze Fei; 44tr chwalitpix; 44b Eric Isselée; 46bg Carlos Caetano; 46tr Viktoriya Sukhanova; 46l Ionescu Bogdan; 46c pozsgaig; 46cl Darren Whittingham; 46b pozsgaig; 47bg Zakharov Vitaly; 47l Sharpshot; 49bl Kletr; 50 tl Eric Isselée; 50tr hsfelix; 50 r Purece Daniel; 50b rgbspace; 51tl Eric Isselée; 51tr AlienCat; 51cr Irochka; 51bl & br Eric Isselée; 52–53bg Eleanathewise; 52bl soleg; 52bcl & 52br Eric Isselée; 53tl Maksim Shebeko; 53bl Anatolii; 53bc far left Eric Isselée; 53bcl Irina Khomenko; 53bcr chas53; 53bc far right anankkml; 53br DuncanNoakes; 54tl Skyline; 54tc Ramona Heim; 54tr James Thew; 54cr john lee; 54b Ramona Heim; 55c Rada; 58l dimdimich; 59tr Irochka; 59br Benko Zsolt; 60–61bg morrbyte; 61tl Ruth Black; 62–63bg epic; 62b adimas; 64t Africa Studio; 66–67bg Luftbildfotograf; 66bl air; 66bl inset left ilolab; 66bl inset right Anterovium; 68–69bg pressmaster; 69t inset Piumadaquila; 69t Cameraman; 71tcr Sean Gladwell; 72–73bg Nicolai Sorokin; 73tr

Andy Dean; 74–75bg Tomáš Hašlar; 74tr Vibe Images; 78–79bg Elnur; 80bg Fotolia/maigi; 80tl James Leynse; 80tr Mirabella; 80 cr Andreas Karelias; 80br Anton Balazh; 84bg winyasuk_arm; 84t jeremyculpdesign; 88–89bg Charles Taylor; 88t dja65; 88t inset Kristina Afanasyeva; 88br Arto; 89bl Alex; 89br Palabra; 93bg galam; 93bl SeanPavonePhoto; 94–95bg Jan Kranendonk; 95b Sverrir Valgeirsson; 98–99bg Tony Schönherr; 99tl iadams; 99tr Tombaky; 100–101bg EtiAmmos; 100tl Glenda Powers; 100c patpitchaya; 101cr raven; 102–103bg FreeSoulProduction; 102cl Stephen Sweet; 102cr Andrzej Tokarski; 102bl & r Marcel Mooij; 104tl milosluz; 105bl DenisNata; 106–107bg verte; 106bl Sandra Kemppainen; 106br babimu; 108–109bg javarman; 108cl Accent; 109c bittedankeschön; 110–111bg nito; 111b nito; 112–113bg klikk; 112t Yuriy Panyukov; 112cl rrrob; 117tr AGcuesta; 118–119bg JAY; 122–123bg DWP; 123tr DeshaCAM; 123bl James Steidl; 124–125bg TMLP; 128–129bg Itestro; 128tl Jason Stitt; 130–131bg carmela45; 131bc OlgaYakovenko; 131bc inset Igor Kolos; 131br log88off; 132–133bg nikkytok; 132bl & I DWP; 136–137bg filipw; 137tl Dani Simmonds; 141c Elnur; 142tr James Steidl; 146c Alexirius; 156tr Texelart; 158br laxmi; 160–161bg nuttakit; 160tc Mazim_Kazmin; 160b inset kmit; 164–165bg nikkytok; 164tl & r insets, bc bloomua; 165cr Jackin; 168–169bg S; 168–169b Kurhan; 168br Maksym Yemelyanov; 169b klikk; 170–171 Christian42; 170tc Rich Wolf; 170tl koya79; 170ctl Cobalt; 170ct Aleksejs Pivnenkko; 170ctr Michael Shake; 170cbc 3desc; 170cbr Alex; 170bl Kit Wai Chan; 170bc karam miri; 170br remik44992; 172–173 klikk; 173c cardiae; 173tc ErickN; 174–175bg lily; 174tl Elena Schweitzer; 174bl Olga Nayashkova; 174bcr & br idar akhmerov; 175c Tein; 175cr scol22; 175b far left Olga Nayashkova; 175bl David Smith; 175bcl Alexander Raths; 175bcr Beboy; 175br Sharpshot; 175b far right Norman Chan; 176–177bg Dario Sabljak; 176tr gunterkremer; 176b Gino Santa Maria; 177tl Karandaev; 178–179bg Shariff Che'Lah; 178tr Lack-O'Keen; 179tl TebNad; 179b Henry Bonn; 180–181bg Lulu Berlu; 180t galam; 180t top inset AKS; 180bl itestro; 182–183bg majeczka; 183tl borzaya; 183l puckillustrations; 183c Jean-Jacques Cordier; 184–185bg anson tsui; 184tl FotolEdhar; 188–189bg high_resolution; 188–189 insets piai; 189tr lunamarina; 190–191bg iofoto; 190cl innocent; 191c csdesign999; 193t Lagui; 193cl Binski; 194bg Agnyeshka; 195bg kalafoto; 196–197bg adisa; 196bl Milissenta; 197bl Arto; 197bc philhol; 198tl Brian Weed; 198tr rook76; 199br Irochka; 200–201bg Alexander Marushin; 200–201bg evron.info; 200–201bg Irina Belousa; 204bg Gino Santa Maria; 205bg R. Roulet; 206tr Veneratio; 208cl Mark Matysiak; 210–211bg Miroslav Beneda; 210tc OneO2; 212br Woodsy; 214–215bg Melinda Nagy; 216–217bg Georghe Roman; 216tl lilufoto; 220–221 svetlyachok; 222–223bg Karl O'Sullivan; 222bl creativedoxfoto; 224–225bg lawcain; 226–227bg lilufofo; 228–229bg Burtsc; 230–231bg Vojtech Vlk; 231br Richard Sweeney; 232–233bg Sportlibrary; 236bl pizuttipics; 236br Irochka; 238–239bg Schiller Renato; 238bl StarJumper; 238br Malena und Philipp K; 239br delkro; 240–241 sobanr; 241tr Philippe Devanne; 242–243bg Vo; 246–247bg Victoria; 246t strixcode; 247t k-artz.

Getty Images: 16r Science & Society Picture Library; 19b Minden Pictures II/Norbert Wu; 21tl Ken Fisher;

24tl Aurora/Mario Colonel; 25tl Time Life Pictures/Walter Daran; 29t Olivier Grunewald; 30–31 AFP/Sadatsugu Tomizawa; 30t AFP/Toshifumi Kitamura; 32–33 Allan Baxter/Photodisc; 35c Dorling Kindersley; 36tl AFP/Adek Berry; 36tr & 38tl Minden Pictures/Thomas Marent; 39b Digital Vision/Natphotos; 40tl Alexander Safonov; 44tl Minden Pictures/Claus Meyer; 45tr Peter Arnold/Compost–Visage; 46tl Dorling Kindersley/Colin Keates; 46tr inset Dorling Kindersley/Frank Greenaway; 47tr Brand X Pictures/PHOTO 24; 48l Flickr/suebg1 photography; 49tr Minden Pictures/Mike Parry; 55b Photolibrary/Peter Harrison; 60tl The Asahi Shimbun; 63t Hulton Archive/Imagno; 67b National Geographic/Ira Block; 69bl AFP/Stan Honda; 71tcl Greater Manchester Police; 71tr Hulton Archive/Apic; 88bl Richard Funke; 89c AFP/Christophe Simon; 92b AFP/Fayez Nureldine; 106tl AFP/Karen Bleier; 107b Robert Harding World Imagery; 110br AFP/Stephan Agostini; 111tr Hulton Archive; 112cr AFP/Fabrice Coffrini; 112 b; 114–115 main RedfermsRobert Knight Archive; 120–121bg NY Daily News Archive/Paul DeMaria; 120 tl Redferns/Gary Wolstenholme; 121c Chris Batten; 121br Blank Archives; 128br Gallo Images/Foto24; 129t Frazer Harrison; 130b Michael Ochs Archives; 132t Redferns/Ron Howard; 134t Mario Tama; 134b Michael Ochs Archives; 135t WireImage/Kevin Mazur; 151cl Science & Society Picture Library; 151br; 161c NBC Universal Inc.; 162b James Meritt; 164tc Blomberg/David Paul Morris; 169t AFP/STR; 172tc AFP/Frederic J Brown; 172bl Blomberg/Chris Goodney; 177tr isifa/Radim Beznoska; 178tl Jeff Fusco; 179tr AFP/Mikhail Mordasov; 183tr hemis.fr/Patrick Escudero; 183b Franck Guiziou; 184b AFP/Karen Bleier; 198–199bg Science and Society Picture Library; 198bl Science and Society Picture Library; 200bl AFP/George Bendrihem; 204b Allsport/IOC; 205t Bongarts/Lars Baron; 208b Popperfoto; 209tl Hulton Archive; 209bl Allsport/IOC Olympic Museum; 209br Popperfoto; 210bl Andy Lyons; 211b Mike Powell; 212t AFP/Lakrunwan Wanniarachchi; 212bl Matthew Lewis; 213cl; 213r Matthew Lewis; 215b Jed Jacobshon; 216bl Stephen Dunn; 218t Jonathan Daniel; 219tr WireImage; 219b AFP/Pierre-Philippe Marcou; 220t Dave Sandford; 221t Sports Illustrated/Richard Mackson; 222br AFP/Daniel Garcia; 224t Matthew Stockman; 226b Matthew Lewis; 227t Hannah Johnston; 227bl Cameron Spencer; 229cr & 230b Hulton Archive; 231t David Cannon; 231b AFP/Timothy Clary; 232t Allsport/Grazia Neri; 232b Jamie Squire; 233b Sports Illustrated/Neil Leifer; 234t Gallo Images/Steve Haag; 234b Bryn Lennon; 235b GP/Mirco Lazzari; 237b Mike Hewitt; 238t AFP/Javier Soriano; 242t Riccardo S. Savi; 243t WireImage/Allen Kee; 243b NY Daily News Archive/Ron Antonelli.

Sam Higton: 49bc.

iStockphoto.com: 41tr melhi; 52bcr GlobalP; 98bl Bennewitz; 104–105bg Cimmerian.

The Kobal Collection: 96–97 main Waltz Disney Pictures/Walden Media; 139 inset MGM; 142tl Red Chillies Entertainment/Eros International/Winford Productions; 143t Blumhouse Productions; 143b Castle Rock/Bruce McBroom; 144cl Walt Disney Pictures; 145c Danjaq/EON/UA; 146t Silver Pictures; 147t Warner Bros/DC Comics; 147br Paramount; 148br LUCASFILM/20th Century Fox; 149bl

LUCASFILM/Paramount; 149br New Line Cinema; 150c Twentieth Century-Fox Film Corporation; 150b Paramount Pictures; 151t Dreamworks Animation; 152b Universal Pictures; 153t Stephan Vaughn/SMPSP TM and © 2005 by Regency Entertainment (USA), Inc. and Monarchy Enterprises S.a.r.l.; 154tl Warner Bros; 154b Dreamworks Annimation; 155t Relativity/Spyglass/Universal; 156tl Universal; 156bl Imagine Entertainment/Melinda Sue Gordon; 157b Walt Disney Pictures; 158tl Film 4; 159t La Classe Americane/Ufilm/France 3; 159b MGM.

© London 2012: 206–207bg.

Mary Evans Picture Library: 105tl; 190cr; 198cr; 206br; 208t.

NASA: 8–9 main; 11bg; 12b; 13; 14cr; 16–17bg; 16tl; 17b; 20tl; 20cl.

Panos Pictures: 168c Robin Hammond.

Photofest: 141br.

Photolibrary: 42b; 45tl Santiago Fdez Fuentes.

Press Association Images: 71tl; 113b Tass/Photas; 200br AP; 201tl Topham Picturepoint; 210b Abaca USA; 228b Darron Cummings; 233t DPA/David Ebener; 236tr AP/James Crisp.

Rex Features: 56–57 main Everett/c.CSU Archv; 108cr Sipa Press; 130t ITV; 138–139 main Everett/Buena Vista; 140t Kevin Foy; 140b Alastair Muir; 141bl Donald Cooper; 144br Everett/Walt Disney Pictures; 145t Everett/20th Century Fox; 145br Everett/MGM; 146b Everett/Buena Vista; 148t Everett/20th Century Fox; 148bl Everett Collection; 149t Everett/Touchstone; 150t Everett/Buena Vista; 151cr & bl Everett; 152t Everett/Paramount/Marvel; 155br Everett/20th Century Fox; 161t Everett/CBS; 165t Everett/ABC Inc.; 174cl; 190b ZUMA/Keystone USA; 184t SIPA/Chine Nouvelle; 193t main Michael Friedel.

The Ronald Grant Archive: 156c Warner Bros/J K Rowling.

Royal Caribbean International:192t.

Science Photo Library: 12t Henning Dalhoff; 14cl Chris Butler; 15bg Detlev van Ravenswaay; 16c Mark Williamson; 34–35t Richard Harris; 35t Jaime Chirinos; 41b Adam Jones.

TopFoto: 16tr, 109b & 196cr Ria Novosti; 203 inset right; 188t HIP/National Motor Museum.

USGS: 20bg EROS.

Additional photographs were kindly supplied by Fotolia and iStockphoto.com for the chapter banners and title pages.

Packager's Acknowledgements
Palazzo Editions would like to thank
Richard Constable for his design contribution

Cover Concept and Design: www.gradedesign.com

ACKNOWLEDGMENTS

Special research
Ian Morrison (sport); Dafydd Rees (music)

Academy of Motion Picture Arts and Sciences
  – Oscar statuette is the registered trademark
  and copyrighted property of the Academy of
  Motion Picture Arts and Sciences
Air Crashes Record Office
Airports Council International
Alexa
Apple
Applied Animal Behaviour Science
Artnet
Art Newspaper
Association of Leading Visitor Attractions
Association of Tennis Professionals
Audit Bureau of Circulations Ltd
BARB
Barclaycard Mercury Prize
BBC
Roland Bert
Billboard
Boeing
Peter Bond
Box Office Mojo
BP Statistical Review of World Energy
Richard Braddish
Breeders' Cup
Thomas Brinkhoff
BRIT Awards
British Academy of Songwriters, Composers
  and Authors (Ivor Novello Awards)
British Association of Aesthetic Plastic Surgeons
British Film Institute
British Library
British Phonographic Industry
Cameron Mackintosh Ltd
Carbon Dioxide Information Analysis Center
Charities Direct
Checkout
Christie's
Duggan Collingwood
Computer Industry Almanac
ComScore.com
Stanley Coren
Crime in England and Wales (Home Office)
Department for Culture, Media and Sport
Department for Environment, Food and
  Rural Affairs
Department for Transport
Department of Trade and Industry
Earth Policy Institute
The Economist
Philip Eden
Emporis
Environmental Performance Index
Ethnologue
Euromonitor International
FA Premier League
Federal Bureau of Investigation
Fédération Internationale de Football
  Association
Fédération Internationale de Motorcyclisme
Fédération Internationale de Ski
FIFA
Film Database
Financial Times
Food and Agriculture Organization of the
  United Nations
Christopher Forbes

Forbes magazine
Forbes Traveler
Forestry Commission
Fortune
FourFourTwo
General Register Office for Scotland
Global Education Digest (UNESCO)
Global Forest Resources Assessment (FAO)
Gold Survey (Gold Fields Mineral Services Ltd)
Russell E. Gough
Governing Council of the Cat Fancy
Robert Grant
Bob Gulden
Highestbridges.com
Home Office
Barney Hooper
The Iditarod
Imperial War Museum
Indianapolis Motor Speedway
Interbrand
International Air Transport Association
International Association of Athletics
  Federations
International Association of Volcanology and
  Chemistry of the Earth's Interior
International Centre for Prison Studies
International Energy Association
International Federation of Audit Bureaux of
  Circulations
International Game Fish Association
International Labour Organization
International Obesity Task Force
International Olympic Committee
International Organization of Motor Vehicle
  Manufacturers
International Paralympic Committee
International Rugby Board
International Shark Attack File, Florida Museum
  of Natural History
International Telecommunication Union
International Union for Conservation of Nature
  and Natural Resources
Internet Movie Database
Internet World Stats
Inter-Parliamentary Union
Claire Judd
Kennel Club
Ladies Professional Golf Association
Major League Baseball
Man Booker Prize
Chris Mead
The Military Balance (International Institute for
  Strategic Studies)
MTV
Music Information Database
National Academy of Recording Arts and
  Sciences (Grammy Awards)
National Aeronautics and Space Administration
National Basketball Association
National Football League
National Gallery, London
National Hockey League
National Snow & Ice Data Centre
National Statistics
Natural History Museum, London
AC Nielsen
Nielsen Media Research
Nobel Foundation
Northern Ireland Statistics Research Agency
NSS GEO2 Committee on Long and Deep Caves

Office for National Statistics
Official Charts Company
Organisation for Economic Co-operation and
  Development
Organisation Internationale des Constructeurs
  d'Automobiles
Roberto Ortiz de Zarate
Oxford English Corpus
Julian Page
Power & Motoryacht
Professional Bowlers Association
Professional Golfers' Association
Population Reference Bureau
PRS for Music
Railway Gazette International
River Systems of the World
Royal Aeronautical Society
Royal Astronomical Society
Royal Opera House, Covent Garden
Royal Society for the Protection of Birds
Peter Sabol
Eric Sakowski
Screen Digest
Screen International
Robert Senior
Sotheby's
State of the World's Forests (FAO)
Stockholm International Peace Research
  Institute
Stores
Sustainable Cities Index (Forum for the Future)
Tate Modern, London
Trades Union Congress
The Tree Register of the British Isles
twitterholic.com
United Nations
United Nations Educational, Scientific and
  Cultural Organization
United Nations Environment Programme
United Nations Population Division
United Nations Statistics Division
Universal Postal Union
US Census Bureau
US Census Bureau International Data Base
US Geological Survey
Lucy T. Verma
Ward's Motor Vehicle Facts & Figures
World Association of Girl Guides and Girl
  Scouts
World Association of Newspapers
World Bank
World Broadband Statistics (Point Topic)
World Christian Database
World Development Indicators (World Bank)
World Factbook (Central Intelligence Agency)
World Health Organization
World Metro Database
World Organization of the Scout Movement
World Population Data Sheet (Population
  Reference Bureau)
World Silver Survey (The Silver Institute/Gold
  Fields Mineral Services Ltd)
World Resources Institute
World Sailing Speed Record Council
World Tennis Association
World Tourism Organization
World Trade Organization

60 Years of the
Official Singles Chart